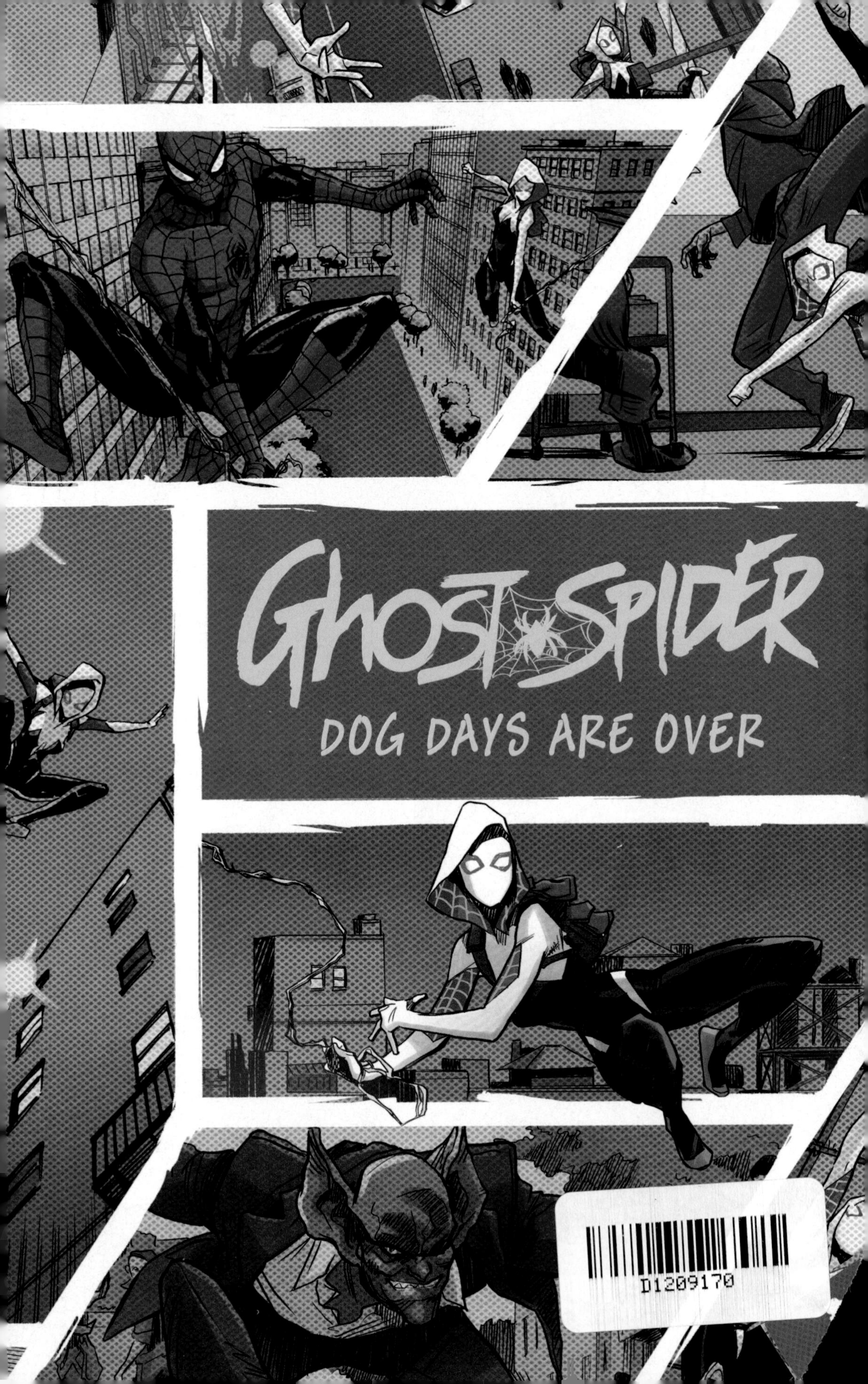
GHOST-SPIDER
DOG DAYS ARE OVER

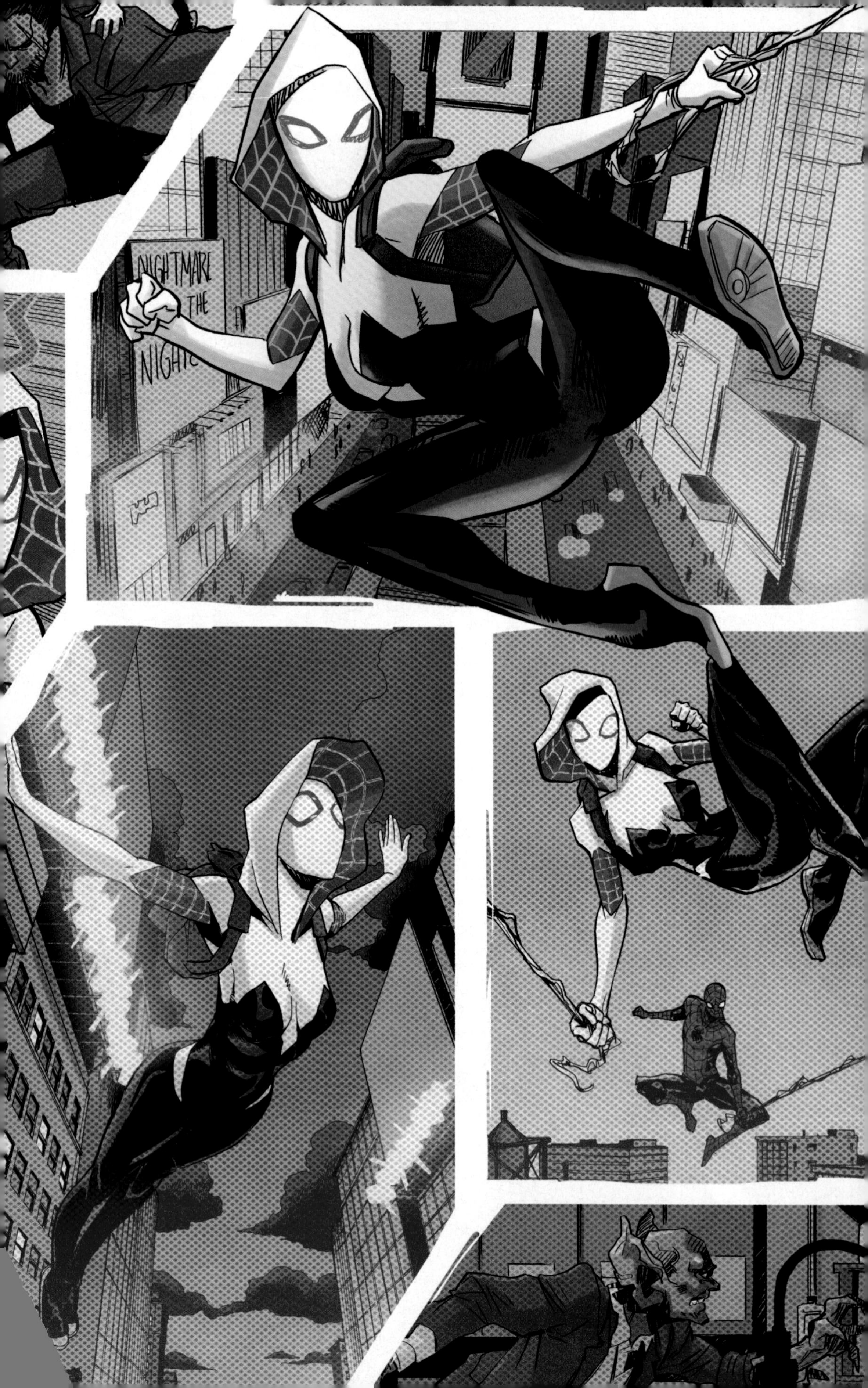
NIGHTMARE
THE

Gwen Stacy (A.K.A. Ghost-Spider) no longer has a secret identity on her
universe of Earth-65 – but that celebrity status has come at a price.

Gwen can now travel between universes with the use of a pendant and is coming to Earth-616 in an
attempt to regain some semblance of a normal life...by getting herself a college education!

GHOST-SPIDER
DOG DAYS ARE OVER

Seanan McGuire
WRITER

Takeshi Miyazawa
with **Ig Guara** (#5)
PENCILERS

Takeshi Miyazawa (#1-3) & Rosi Kämpe (#2-5)
with **Ig Guara** (#5)
INKERS

Ian Herring
COLOR ARTIST

VC's Clayton Cowles
LETTERER

Jorge Molina
COVER ART

Danny Khazem
ASSISTANT EDITOR

Devin Lewis
EDITOR

COLLECTION EDITOR **JENNIFER GRÜNWALD** • ASSISTANT MANAGING EDITOR **MAIA LOY** • ASSISTANT EDITOR **CAITLIN O'CONNELL**
EDITOR, SPECIAL PROJECTS **MARK D. BEAZLEY** • VP PRODUCTION & SPECIAL PROJECTS **JEFF YOUNGQUIST** • BOOK DESIGNER **STACIE ZUCKER**
SVP PRINT, SALES & MARKETING **DAVID GABRIEL** • EDITOR IN CHIEF **C.B. CEBULSKI**

GHOST-SPIDER VOL. 1: DOG DAYS ARE OVER. Contains material origina... ...012-8. Published by MARVEL WORLDWIDE,
INC., a subsidiary of MARVEL ENTERTAINMENT, LLC. OFFICE OF PUBLICAT... ...mes, characters, persons, and/or institutions
in this magazine with those of any living or dead person or institution is ... ...EIGE, Chief Creative Officer; DAN BUCKLEY,
President, Marvel Entertainment; JOHN NEE, Publisher; JOE QUESADA, E... ...of Talent Affairs; Publishing & Partnership;
DAVID GABRIEL, VP of Print & Digital Publishing; JEFF YOUNGQUIST, VP o... ...LES, Director of Publishing Operations; DAN
EDINGTON, Managing Editor; SUSAN CRESPI, Production Manager; STAN L... ...ase contact Vit DeBellis, Custom Solutions &
Integrated Advertising Manager, at vdebellis@marvel.com. For Marvel subs... ...SOLISCO PRINTERS, SCOTT, QC, CANADA.

10 9 8 7 6 5 4 3 2 1

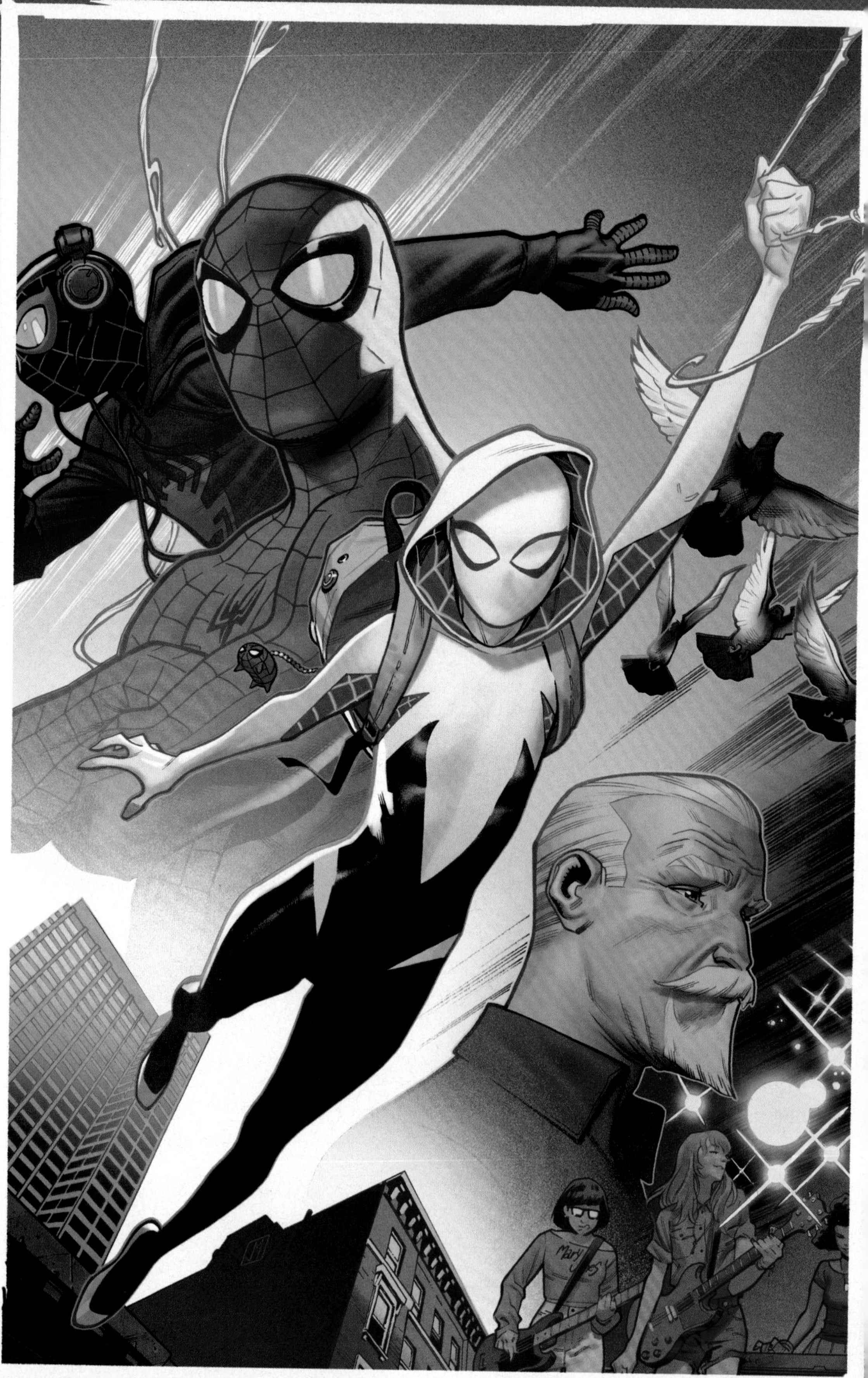

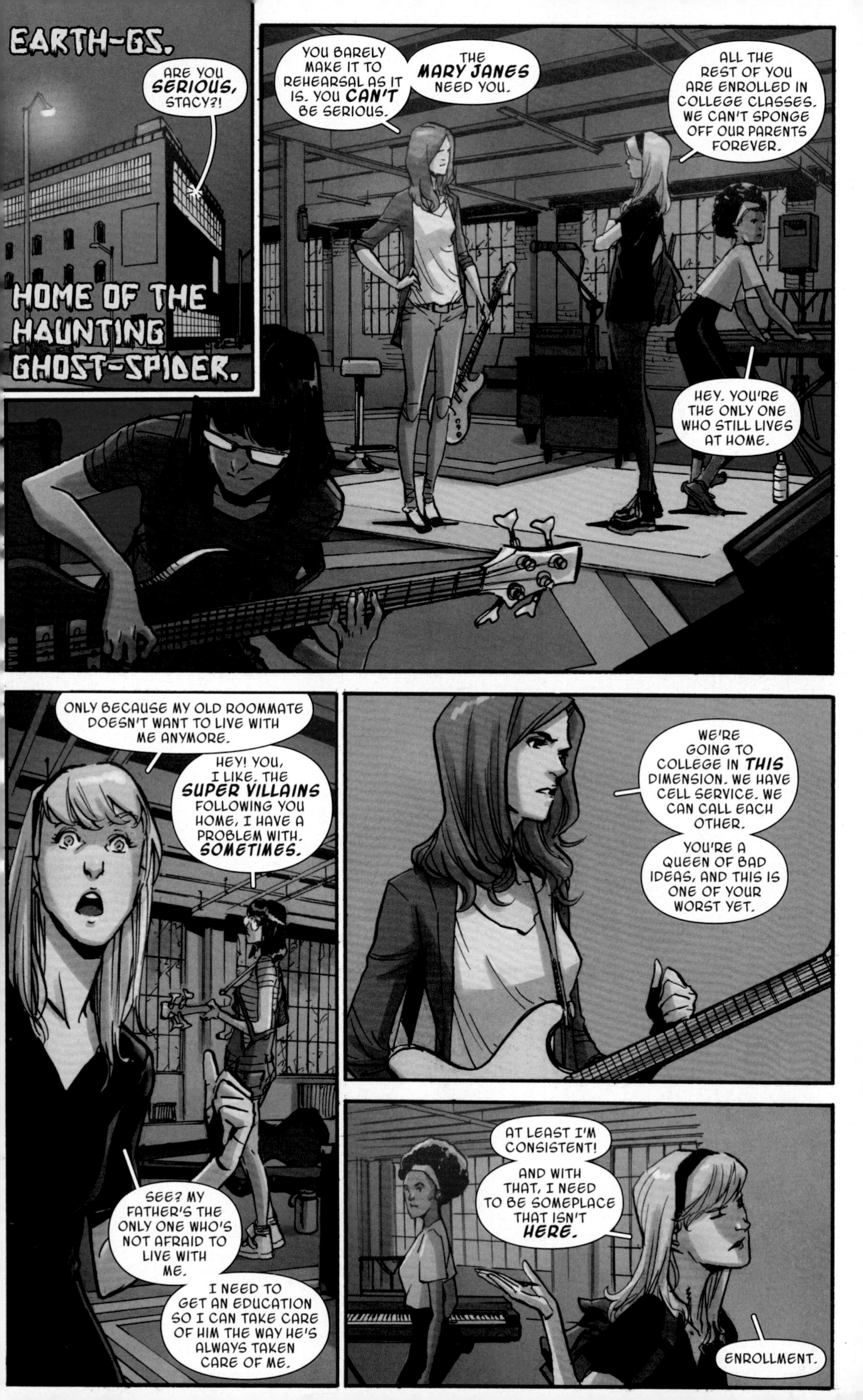
EARTH-65.
ARE YOU SERIOUS, STACY?!
HOME OF THE HAUNTING GHOST-SPIDER.
YOU BARELY MAKE IT TO REHEARSAL AS IT IS. YOU CAN'T BE SERIOUS.
THE MARY JANES NEED YOU.
ALL THE REST OF YOU ARE ENROLLED IN COLLEGE CLASSES. WE CAN'T SPONGE OFF OUR PARENTS FOREVER.
HEY. YOU'RE THE ONLY ONE WHO STILL LIVES AT HOME.
ONLY BECAUSE MY OLD ROOMMATE DOESN'T WANT TO LIVE WITH ME ANYMORE.
HEY! YOU, I LIKE. THE SUPER VILLAINS FOLLOWING YOU HOME, I HAVE A PROBLEM WITH. SOMETIMES.
SEE? MY FATHER'S THE ONLY ONE WHO'S NOT AFRAID TO LIVE WITH ME.
I NEED TO GET AN EDUCATION SO I CAN TAKE CARE OF HIM THE WAY HE'S ALWAYS TAKEN CARE OF ME.
WE'RE GOING TO COLLEGE IN THIS DIMENSION. WE HAVE CELL SERVICE. WE CAN CALL EACH OTHER.
YOU'RE A QUEEN OF BAD IDEAS, AND THIS IS ONE OF YOUR WORST YET.
AT LEAST I'M CONSISTENT!
AND WITH THAT, I NEED TO BE SOMEPLACE THAT ISN'T HERE.
ENROLLMENT.

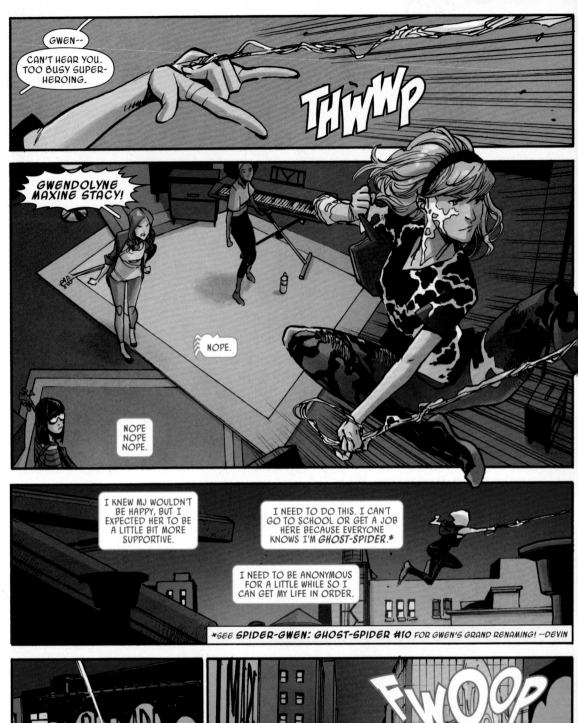

GWEN-- CAN'T HEAR YOU. TOO BUSY SUPER-HEROING.

THWWP

GWENDOLYNE MAXINE STACY!

NOPE.

NOPE NOPE NOPE.

I KNEW MJ WOULDN'T BE HAPPY, BUT I EXPECTED HER TO BE A LITTLE BIT MORE SUPPORTIVE.

I NEED TO DO THIS. I CAN'T GO TO SCHOOL OR GET A JOB HERE BECAUSE EVERYONE KNOWS I'M *GHOST-SPIDER.**

I NEED TO BE ANONYMOUS FOR A LITTLE WHILE SO I CAN GET MY LIFE IN ORDER.

*SEE **SPIDER-GWEN: GHOST-SPIDER #10** FOR GWEN'S GRAND RENAMING! --DEVIN

NIGHTMARE AT THE NIGHTCLUB

I NEED TO GO *BACK* TO SCHOOL.

FWOOP

IF THAT MEANS BECOMING AN EXCHANGE STUDENT, THAT'S HOW IT HAS TO BE.

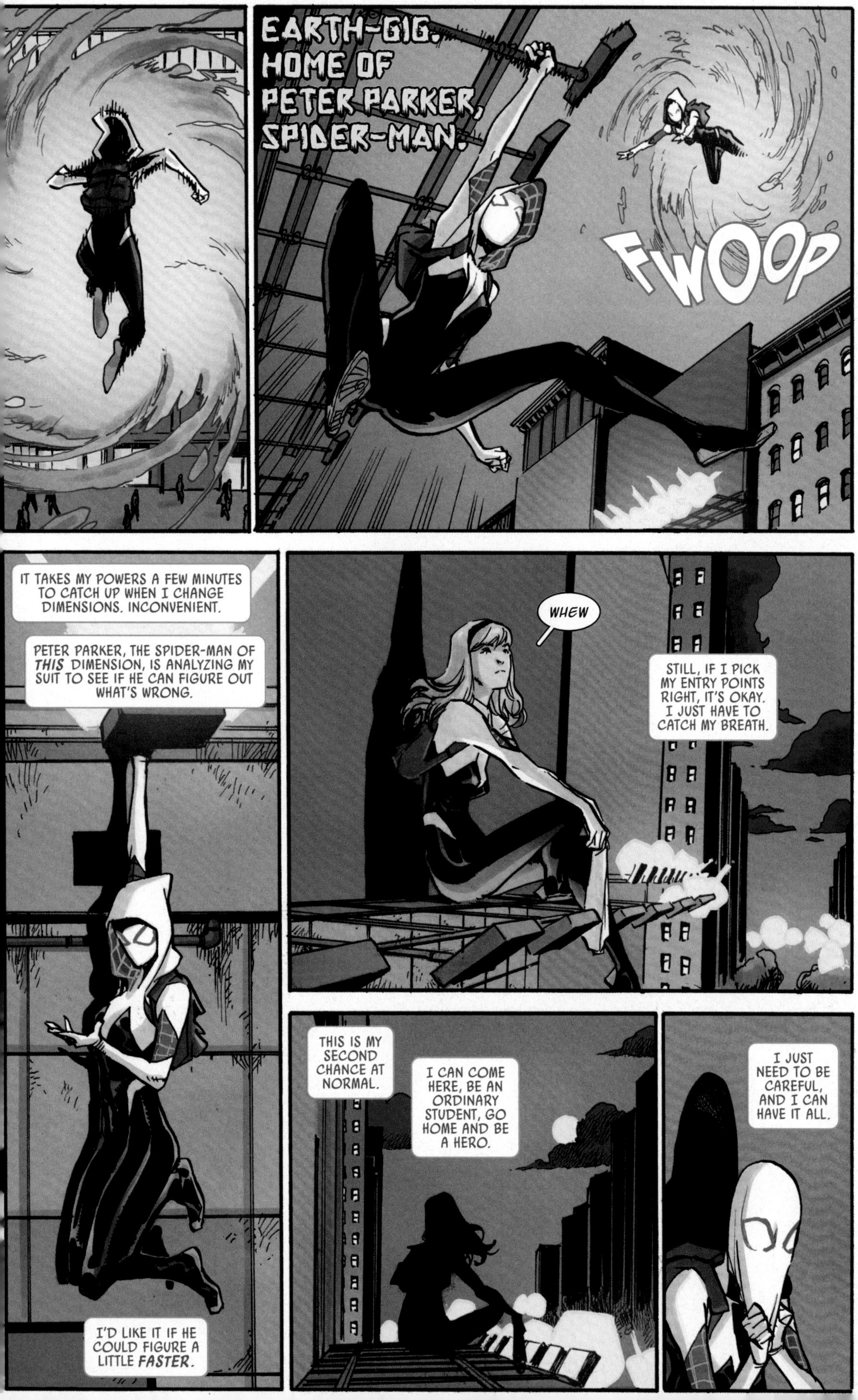
EARTH-616. HOME OF PETER PARKER, SPIDER-MAN.
FWOOP
IT TAKES MY POWERS A FEW MINUTES TO CATCH UP WHEN I CHANGE DIMENSIONS. INCONVENIENT.
PETER PARKER, THE SPIDER-MAN OF THIS DIMENSION, IS ANALYZING MY SUIT TO SEE IF HE CAN FIGURE OUT WHAT'S WRONG.
I'D LIKE IT IF HE COULD FIGURE A LITTLE FASTER.
WHEW
STILL, IF I PICK MY ENTRY POINTS RIGHT, IT'S OKAY. I JUST HAVE TO CATCH MY BREATH.
THIS IS MY SECOND CHANCE AT NORMAL.
I CAN COME HERE, BE AN ORDINARY STUDENT, GO HOME AND BE A HERO.
I JUST NEED TO BE CAREFUL, AND I CAN HAVE IT ALL.

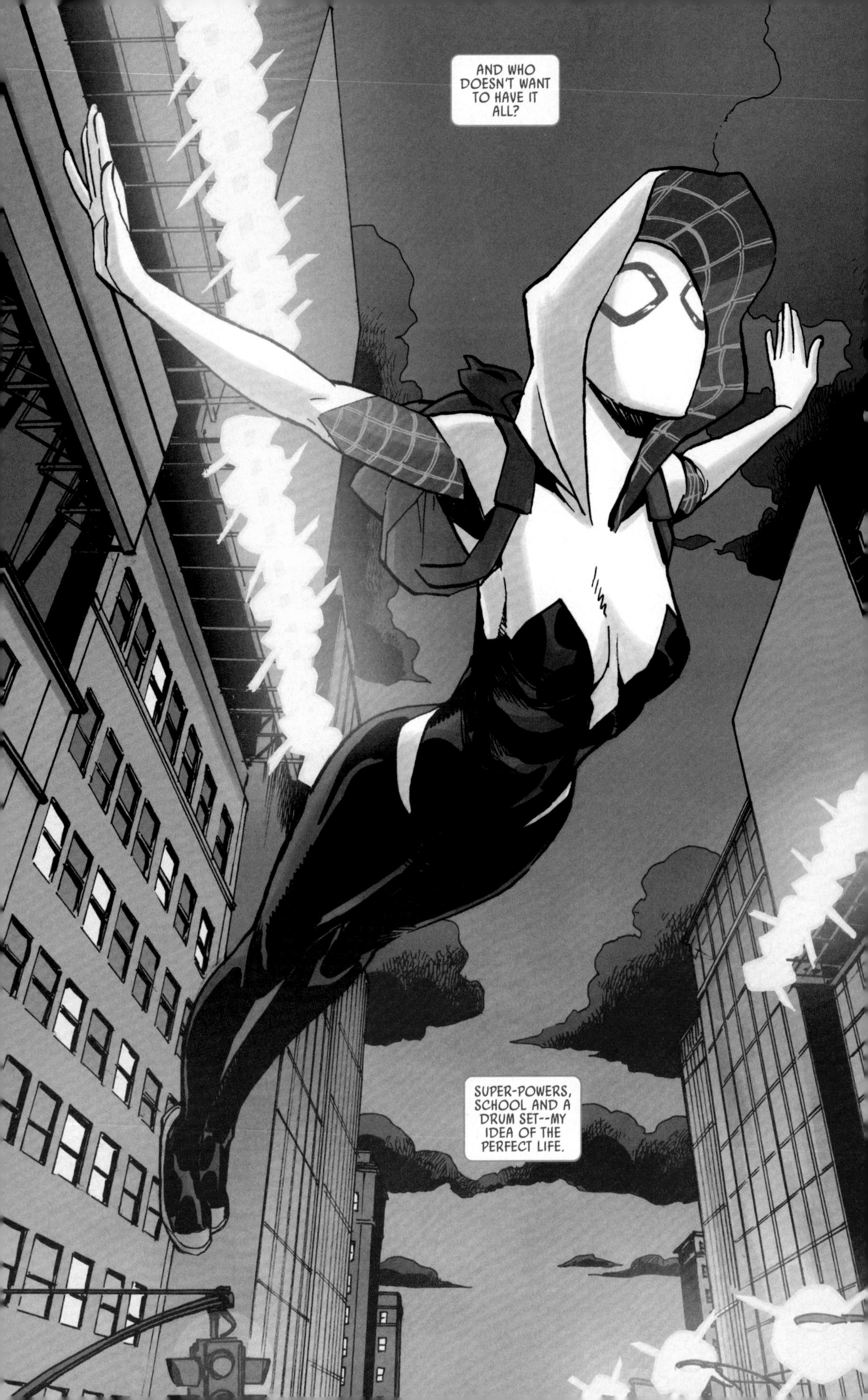
AND WHO DOESN'T WANT TO HAVE IT ALL?
SUPER-POWERS, SCHOOL AND A DRUM SET--MY IDEA OF THE PERFECT LIFE.

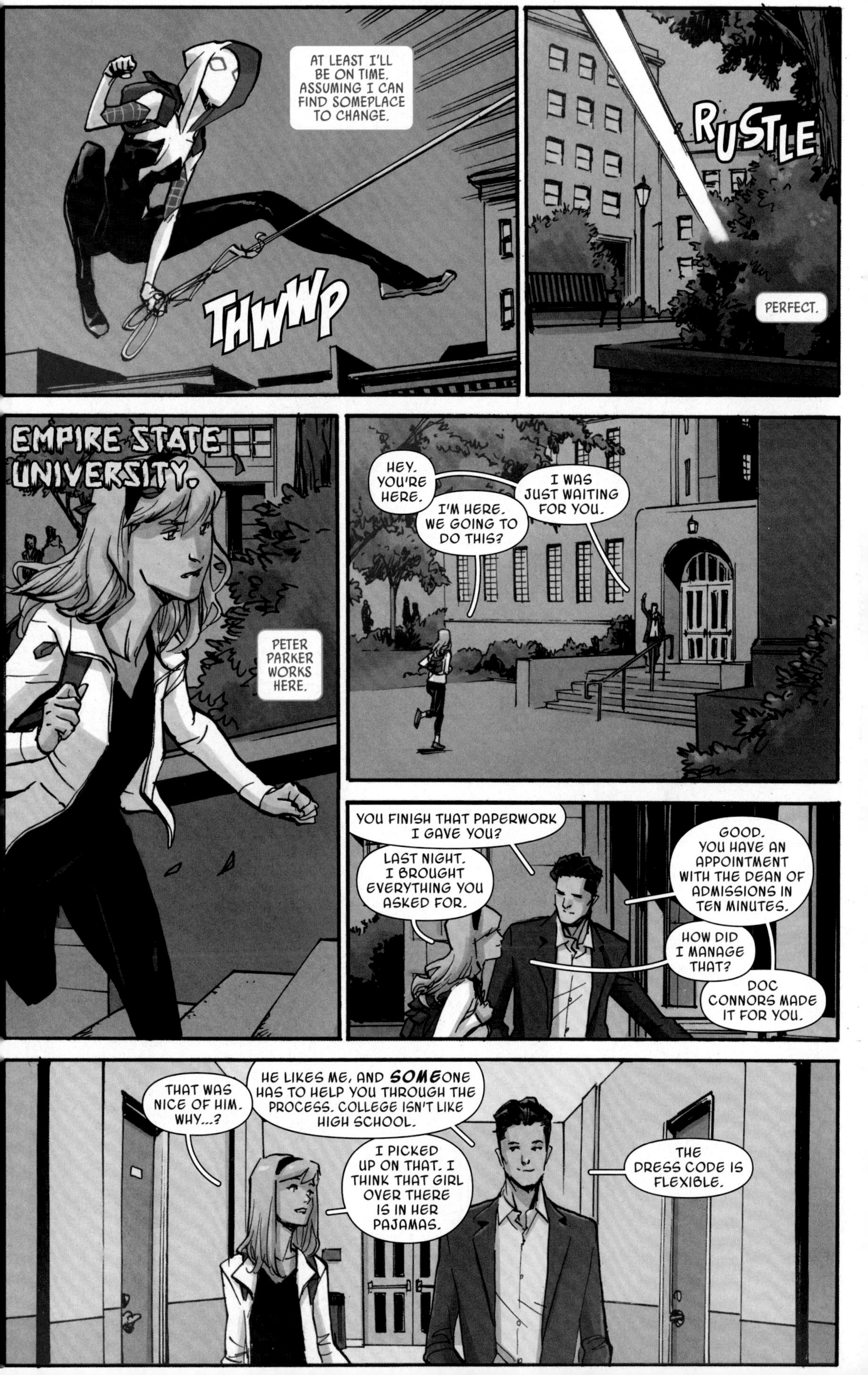
AT LEAST I'LL BE ON TIME. ASSUMING I CAN FIND SOMEPLACE TO CHANGE.
THWWP
RUSTLE
PERFECT.
EMPIRE STATE UNIVERSITY.
PETER PARKER WORKS HERE.
HEY. YOU'RE HERE.
I'M HERE. WE GOING TO DO THIS?
I WAS JUST WAITING FOR YOU.
YOU FINISH THAT PAPERWORK I GAVE YOU?
LAST NIGHT. I BROUGHT EVERYTHING YOU ASKED FOR.
GOOD. YOU HAVE AN APPOINTMENT WITH THE DEAN OF ADMISSIONS IN TEN MINUTES.
HOW DID I MANAGE THAT?
DOC CONNORS MADE IT FOR YOU.
THAT WAS NICE OF HIM. WHY...?
HE LIKES ME, AND SOMEONE HAS TO HELP YOU THROUGH THE PROCESS. COLLEGE ISN'T LIKE HIGH SCHOOL.
I PICKED UP ON THAT. I THINK THAT GIRL OVER THERE IS IN HER PAJAMAS.
THE DRESS CODE IS FLEXIBLE.

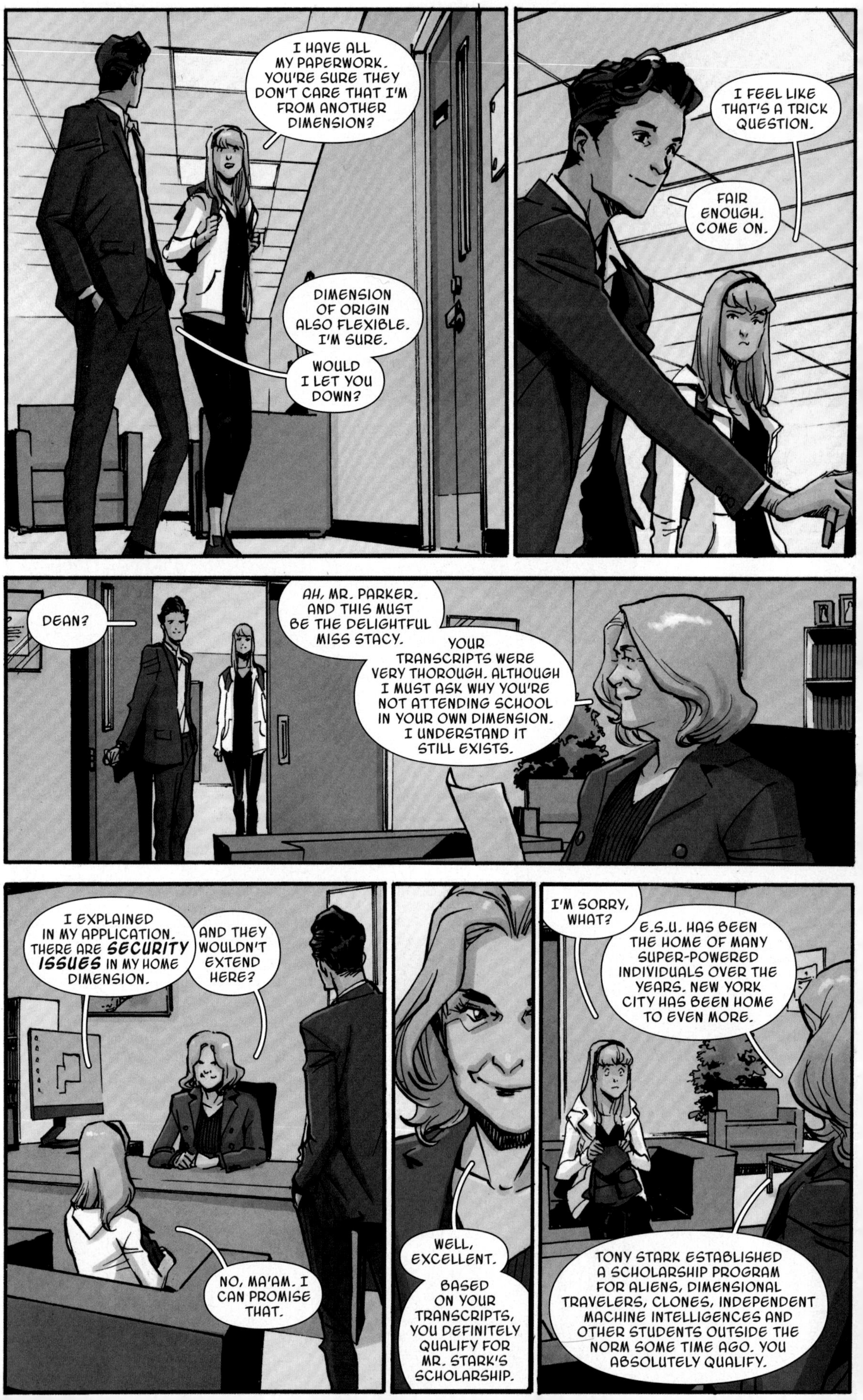
I HAVE ALL MY PAPERWORK. YOU'RE SURE THEY DON'T CARE THAT I'M FROM ANOTHER DIMENSION?
DIMENSION OF ORIGIN ALSO FLEXIBLE. I'M SURE.
WOULD I LET YOU DOWN?
I FEEL LIKE THAT'S A TRICK QUESTION.
FAIR ENOUGH. COME ON.
DEAN?
AH, MR. PARKER. AND THIS MUST BE THE DELIGHTFUL MISS STACY.
YOUR TRANSCRIPTS WERE VERY THOROUGH. ALTHOUGH I MUST ASK WHY YOU'RE NOT ATTENDING SCHOOL IN YOUR OWN DIMENSION. I UNDERSTAND IT STILL EXISTS.
I EXPLAINED IN MY APPLICATION. THERE ARE SECURITY ISSUES IN MY HOME DIMENSION.
AND THEY WOULDN'T EXTEND HERE?
NO, MA'AM. I CAN PROMISE THAT.
WELL, EXCELLENT.
BASED ON YOUR TRANSCRIPTS, YOU DEFINITELY QUALIFY FOR MR. STARK'S SCHOLARSHIP.
I'M SORRY, WHAT?
E.S.U. HAS BEEN THE HOME OF MANY SUPER-POWERED INDIVIDUALS OVER THE YEARS. NEW YORK CITY HAS BEEN HOME TO EVEN MORE.
TONY STARK ESTABLISHED A SCHOLARSHIP PROGRAM FOR ALIENS, DIMENSIONAL TRAVELERS, CLONES, INDEPENDENT MACHINE INTELLIGENCES AND OTHER STUDENTS OUTSIDE THE NORM SOME TIME AGO. YOU ABSOLUTELY QUALIFY.

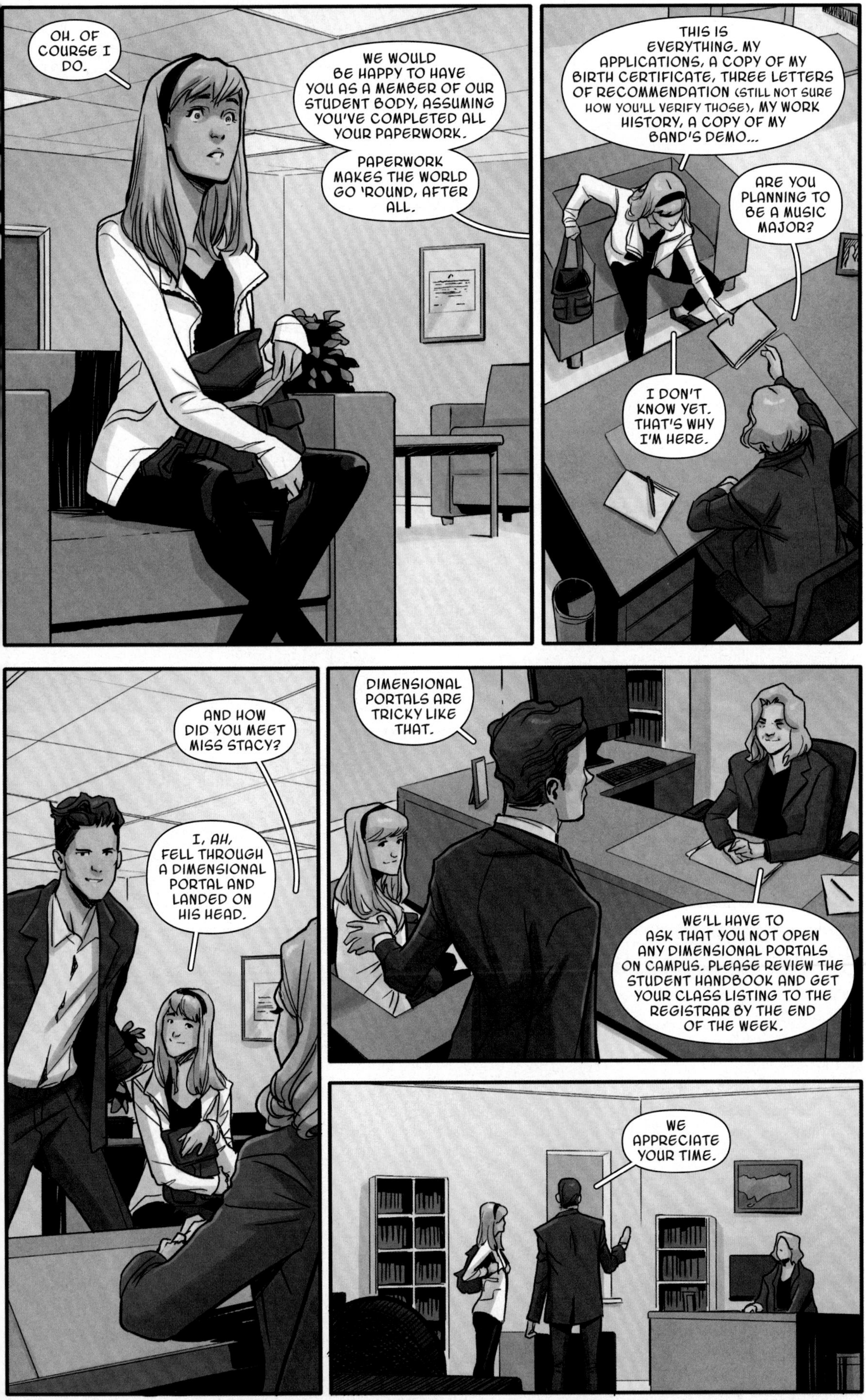
OH. OF COURSE I DO.
WE WOULD BE HAPPY TO HAVE YOU AS A MEMBER OF OUR STUDENT BODY, ASSUMING YOU'VE COMPLETED ALL YOUR PAPERWORK.
PAPERWORK MAKES THE WORLD GO 'ROUND, AFTER ALL.
THIS IS EVERYTHING. MY APPLICATIONS, A COPY OF MY BIRTH CERTIFICATE, THREE LETTERS OF RECOMMENDATION (STILL NOT SURE HOW YOU'LL VERIFY THOSE), MY WORK HISTORY, A COPY OF MY BAND'S DEMO...
ARE YOU PLANNING TO BE A MUSIC MAJOR?
I DON'T KNOW YET. THAT'S WHY I'M HERE.
AND HOW DID YOU MEET MISS STACY?
I, AH, FELL THROUGH A DIMENSIONAL PORTAL AND LANDED ON HIS HEAD.
DIMENSIONAL PORTALS ARE TRICKY LIKE THAT.
WE'LL HAVE TO ASK THAT YOU NOT OPEN ANY DIMENSIONAL PORTALS ON CAMPUS. PLEASE REVIEW THE STUDENT HANDBOOK AND GET YOUR CLASS LISTING TO THE REGISTRAR BY THE END OF THE WEEK.
WE APPRECIATE YOUR TIME.

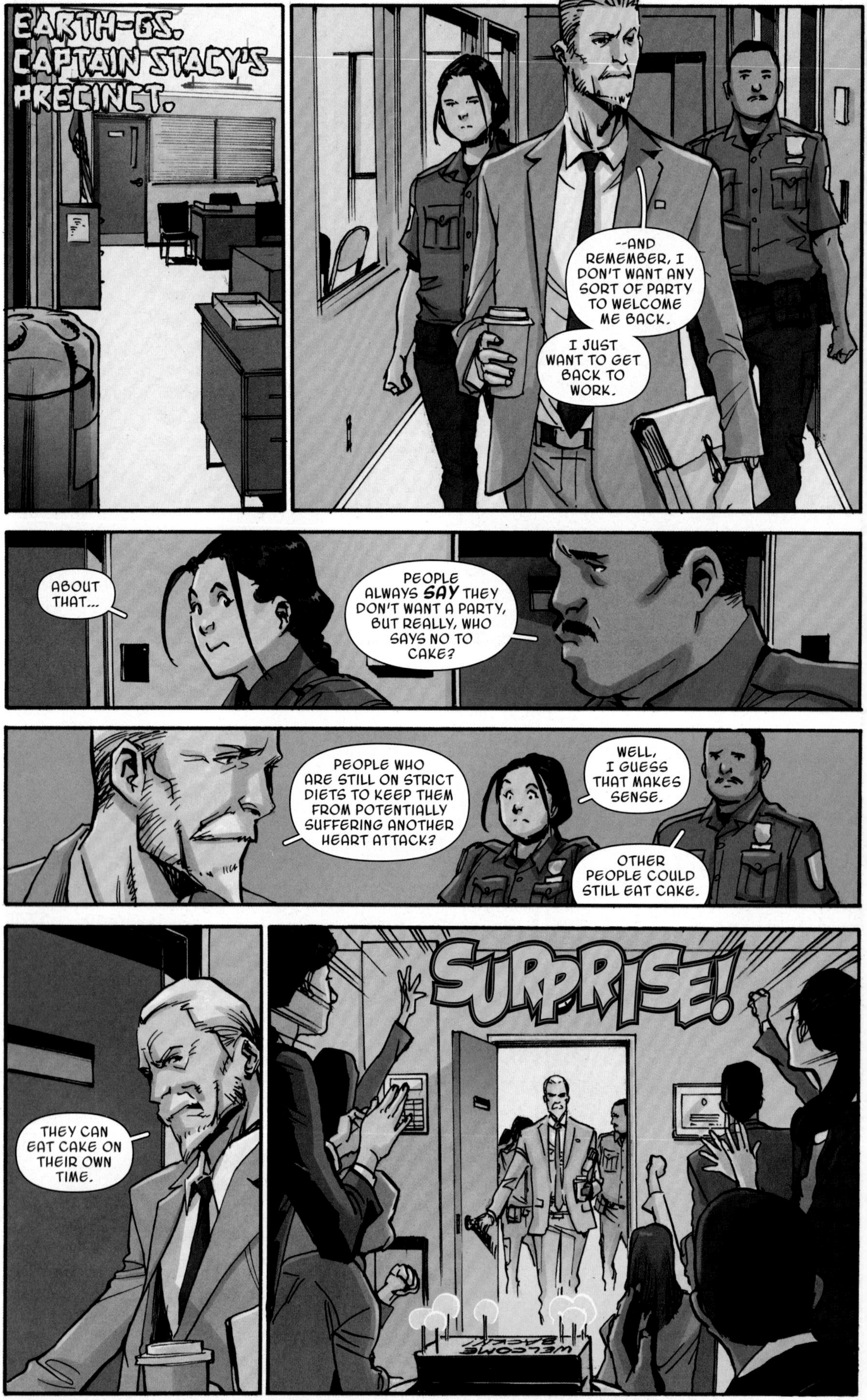
EARTH-65. CAPTAIN STACY'S PRECINCT.
--AND REMEMBER, I DON'T WANT ANY SORT OF PARTY TO WELCOME ME BACK.
I JUST WANT TO GET BACK TO WORK.
ABOUT THAT...
PEOPLE ALWAYS SAY THEY DON'T WANT A PARTY, BUT REALLY, WHO SAYS NO TO CAKE?
PEOPLE WHO ARE STILL ON STRICT DIETS TO KEEP THEM FROM POTENTIALLY SUFFERING ANOTHER HEART ATTACK?
WELL, I GUESS THAT MAKES SENSE.
OTHER PEOPLE COULD STILL EAT CAKE.
THEY CAN EAT CAKE ON THEIR OWN TIME.
SURPRISE!
WELCOME BACK!!

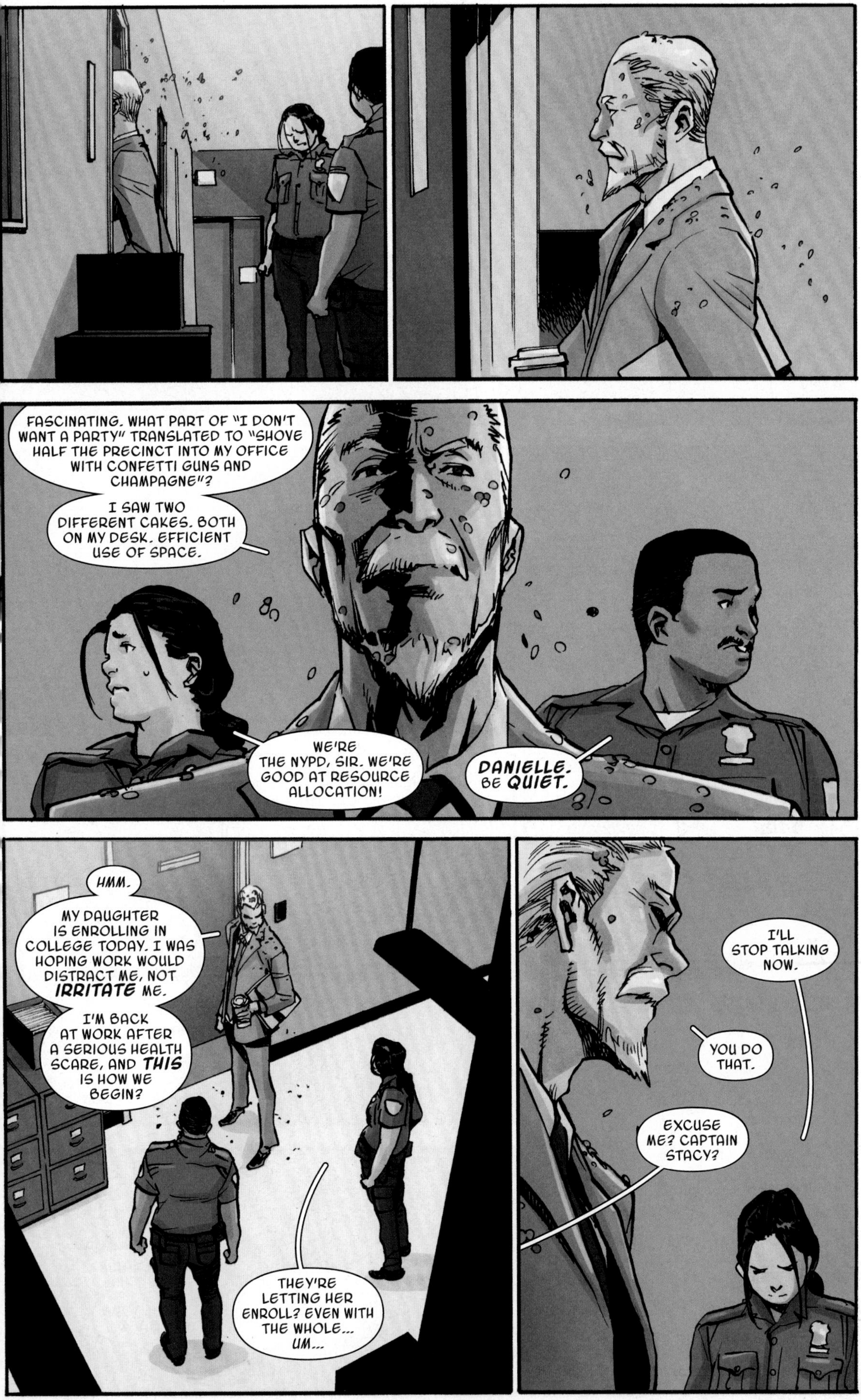
FASCINATING. WHAT PART OF "I DON'T WANT A PARTY" TRANSLATED TO "SHOVE HALF THE PRECINCT INTO MY OFFICE WITH CONFETTI GUNS AND CHAMPAGNE"?
I SAW TWO DIFFERENT CAKES. BOTH ON MY DESK. EFFICIENT USE OF SPACE.
WE'RE THE NYPD, SIR. WE'RE GOOD AT RESOURCE ALLOCATION!
DANIELLE. BE QUIET.
HMM.
MY DAUGHTER IS ENROLLING IN COLLEGE TODAY. I WAS HOPING WORK WOULD DISTRACT ME, NOT IRRITATE ME.
I'M BACK AT WORK AFTER A SERIOUS HEALTH SCARE, AND THIS IS HOW WE BEGIN?
THEY'RE LETTING HER ENROLL? EVEN WITH THE WHOLE... UM...
EXCUSE ME? CAPTAIN STACY?
YOU DO THAT.
I'LL STOP TALKING NOW.

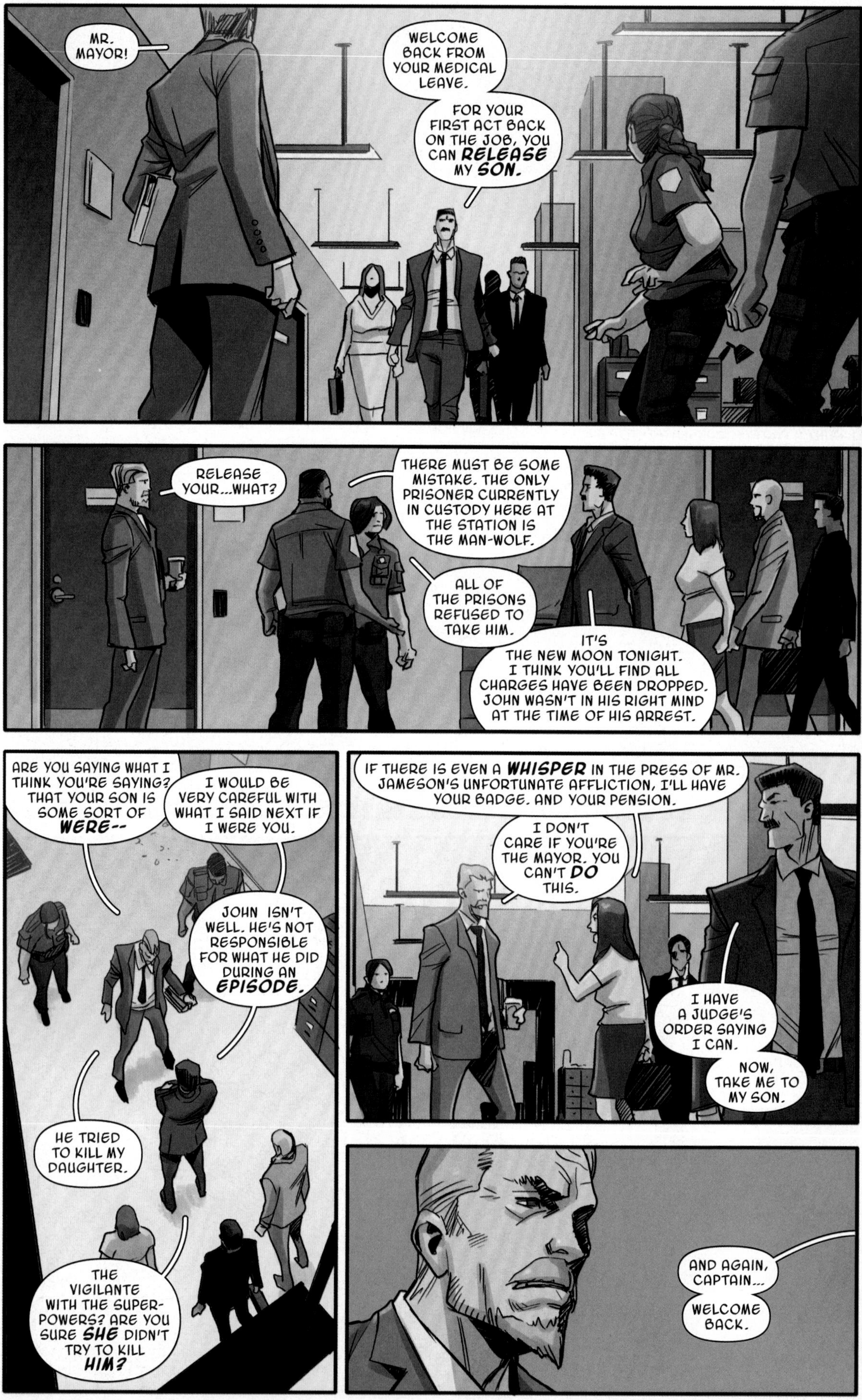
MR. MAYOR!
WELCOME BACK FROM YOUR MEDICAL LEAVE.
FOR YOUR FIRST ACT BACK ON THE JOB, YOU CAN RELEASE MY SON.
RELEASE YOUR...WHAT?
THERE MUST BE SOME MISTAKE. THE ONLY PRISONER CURRENTLY IN CUSTODY HERE AT THE STATION IS THE MAN-WOLF.
ALL OF THE PRISONS REFUSED TO TAKE HIM.
IT'S THE NEW MOON TONIGHT. I THINK YOU'LL FIND ALL CHARGES HAVE BEEN DROPPED. JOHN WASN'T IN HIS RIGHT MIND AT THE TIME OF HIS ARREST.
ARE YOU SAYING WHAT I THINK YOU'RE SAYING? THAT YOUR SON IS SOME SORT OF WERE--
I WOULD BE VERY CAREFUL WITH WHAT I SAID NEXT IF I WERE YOU.
JOHN ISN'T WELL. HE'S NOT RESPONSIBLE FOR WHAT HE DID DURING AN EPISODE.
HE TRIED TO KILL MY DAUGHTER.
THE VIGILANTE WITH THE SUPER-POWERS? ARE YOU SURE SHE DIDN'T TRY TO KILL HIM?
IF THERE IS EVEN A WHISPER IN THE PRESS OF MR. JAMESON'S UNFORTUNATE AFFLICTION, I'LL HAVE YOUR BADGE. AND YOUR PENSION.
I DON'T CARE IF YOU'RE THE MAYOR. YOU CAN'T DO THIS.
I HAVE A JUDGE'S ORDER SAYING I CAN.
NOW, TAKE ME TO MY SON.
AND AGAIN, CAPTAIN...
WELCOME BACK.

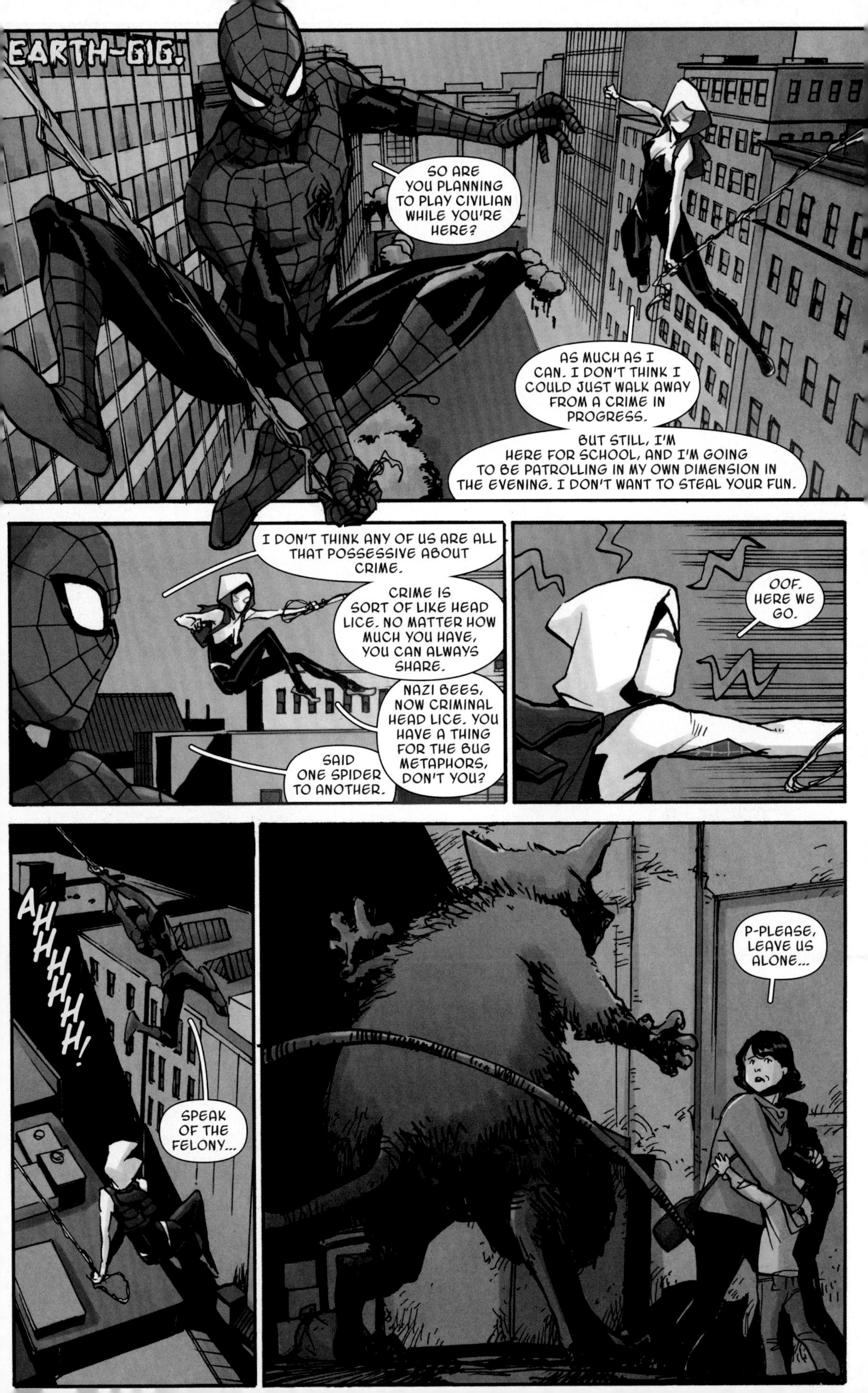
EARTH-616.
SO ARE YOU PLANNING TO PLAY CIVILIAN WHILE YOU'RE HERE?
AS MUCH AS I CAN. I DON'T THINK I COULD JUST WALK AWAY FROM A CRIME IN PROGRESS.
BUT STILL, I'M HERE FOR SCHOOL, AND I'M GOING TO BE PATROLLING IN MY OWN DIMENSION IN THE EVENING. I DON'T WANT TO STEAL YOUR FUN.
I DON'T THINK ANY OF US ARE ALL THAT POSSESSIVE ABOUT CRIME.
CRIME IS SORT OF LIKE HEAD LICE. NO MATTER HOW MUCH YOU HAVE, YOU CAN ALWAYS SHARE.
NAZI BEES, NOW CRIMINAL HEAD LICE. YOU HAVE A THING FOR THE BUG METAPHORS, DON'T YOU?
SAID ONE SPIDER TO ANOTHER.
OOF. HERE WE GO.
AHHHHHH!
SPEAK OF THE FELONY...
P-PLEASE, LEAVE US ALONE...

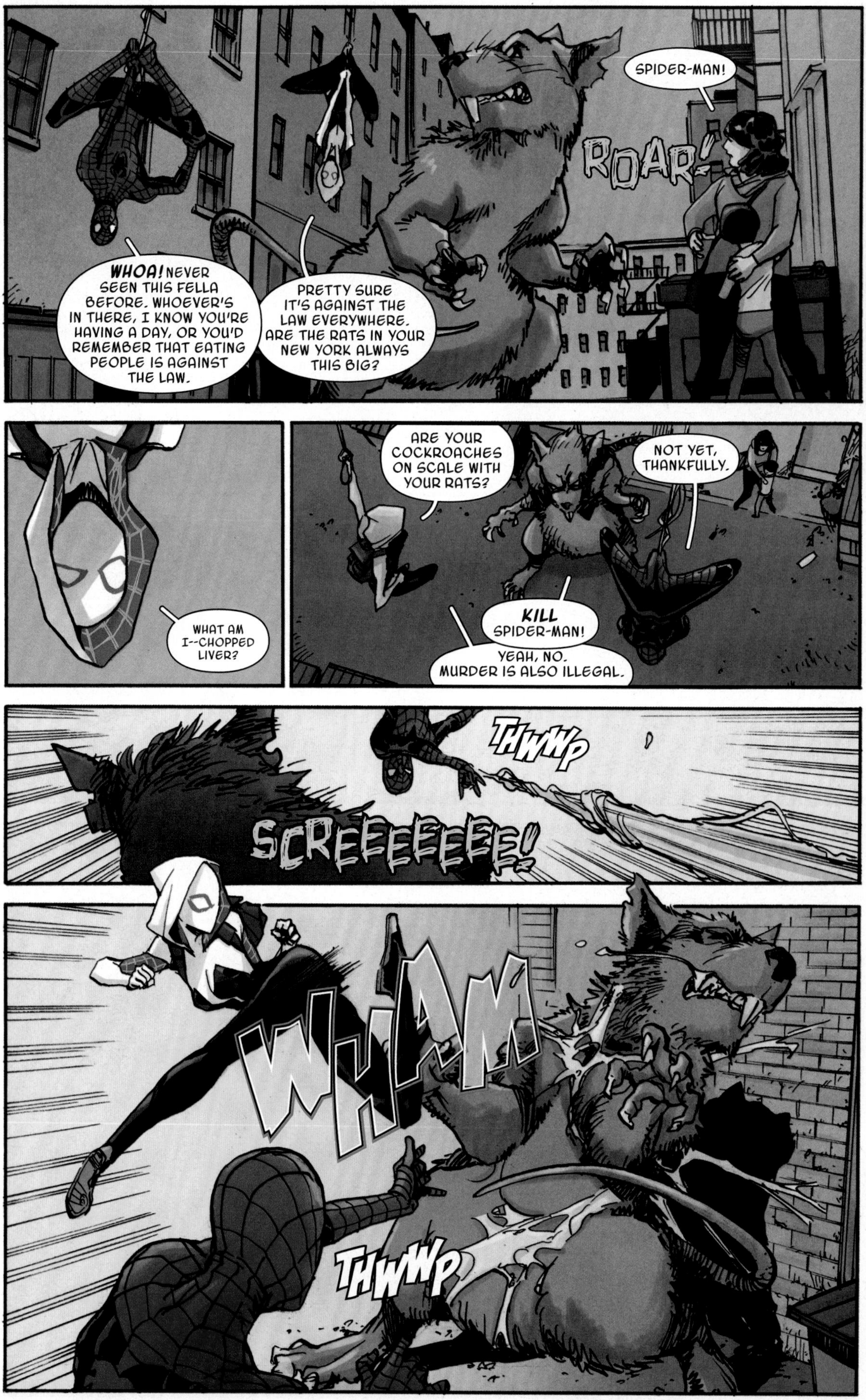
SPIDER-MAN!
ROAR!
WHOA! NEVER SEEN THIS FELLA BEFORE. WHOEVER'S IN THERE, I KNOW YOU'RE HAVING A DAY, OR YOU'D REMEMBER THAT EATING PEOPLE IS AGAINST THE LAW.
PRETTY SURE IT'S AGAINST THE LAW EVERYWHERE. ARE THE RATS IN YOUR NEW YORK ALWAYS THIS BIG?
WHAT AM I--CHOPPED LIVER?
ARE YOUR COCKROACHES ON SCALE WITH YOUR RATS?
NOT YET, THANKFULLY.
KILL SPIDER-MAN!
YEAH, NO. MURDER IS ALSO ILLEGAL.
THWWP
SCREEEEEEEE!
WHAM
THWWP

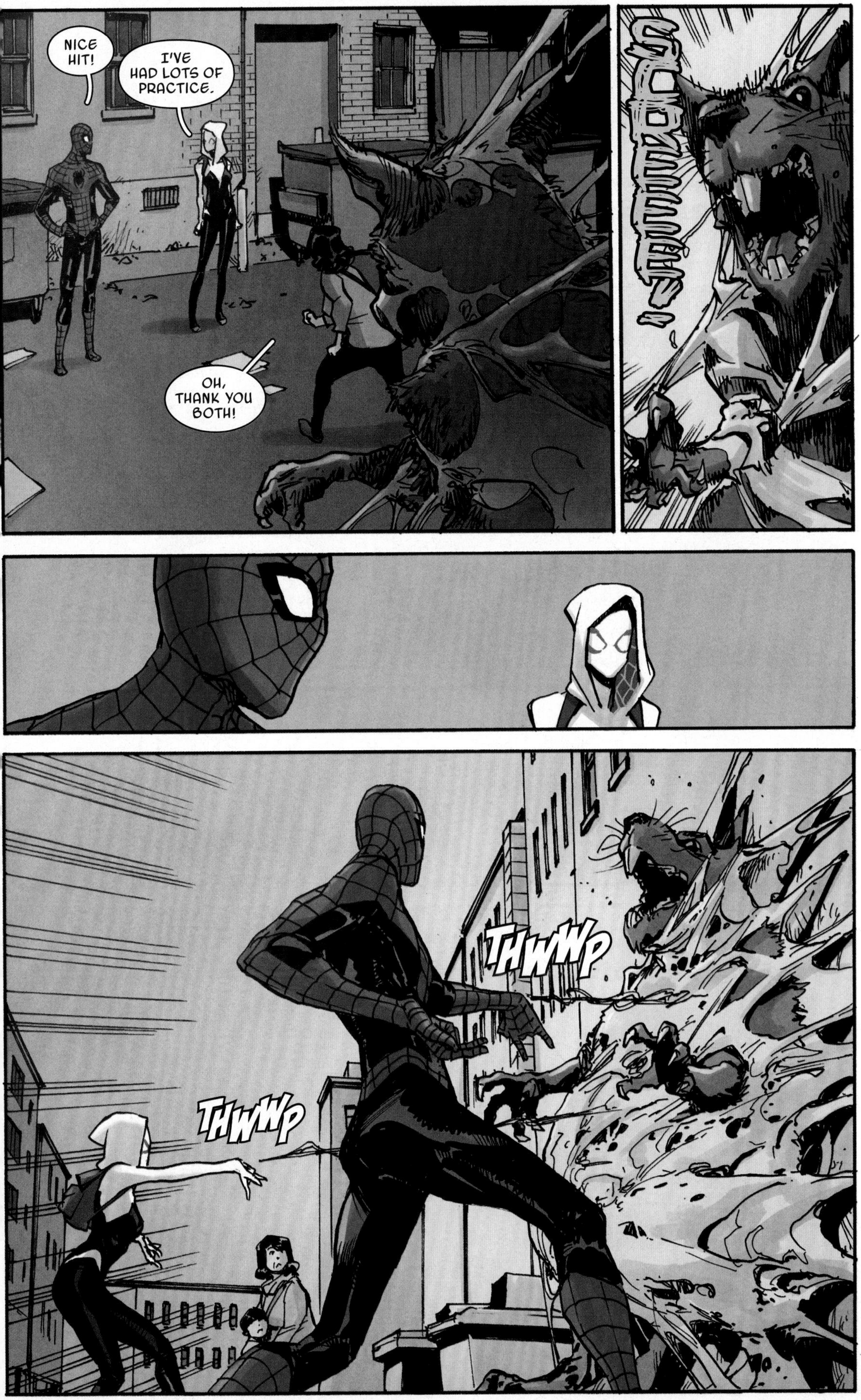
NICE HIT!
I'VE HAD LOTS OF PRACTICE.
OH, THANK YOU BOTH!
SCREEEEEE!!
THWWP
THWWP

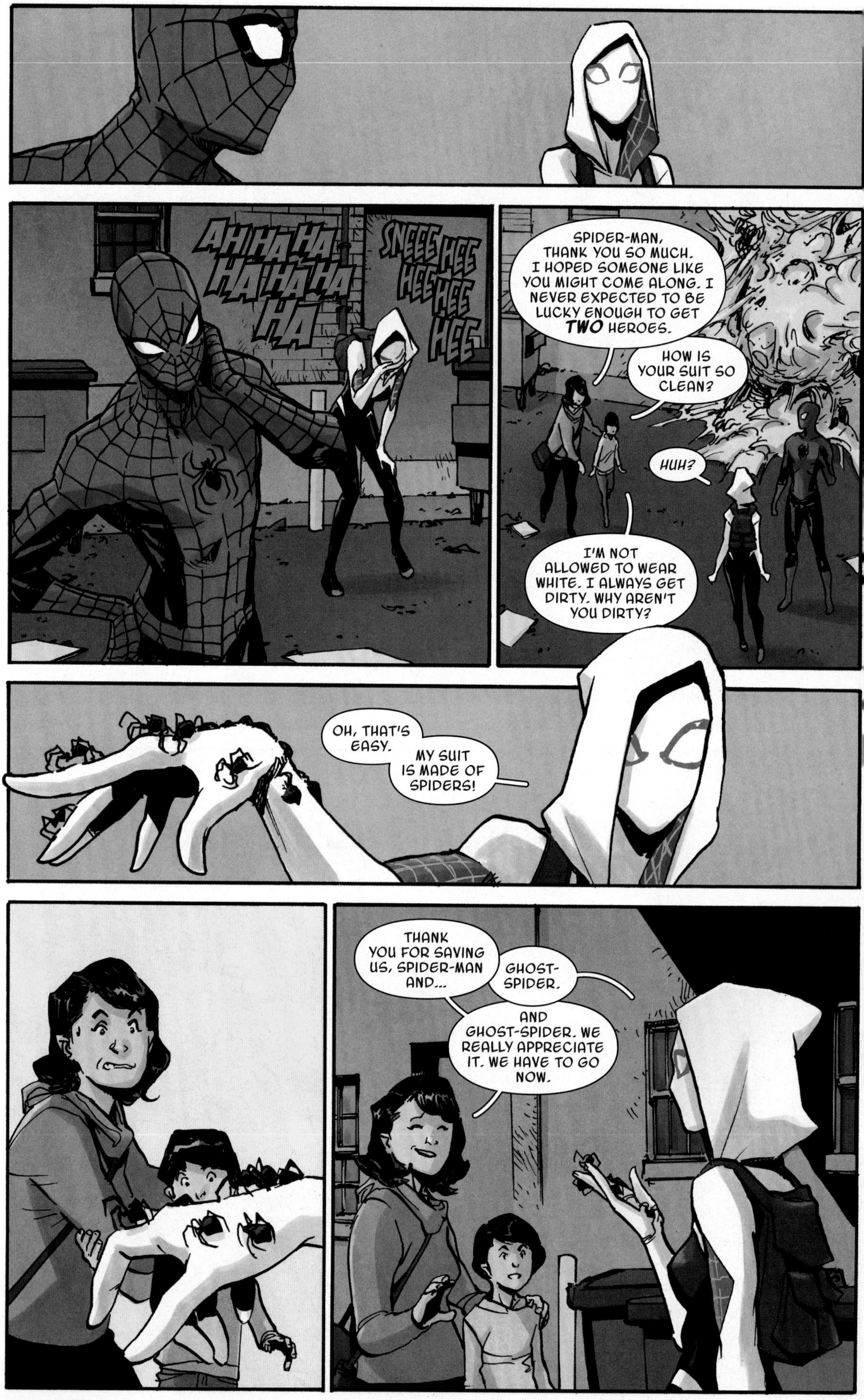
AH HA HA HA HA HA HA
SNEEE HEE HEE HEE HEE HEE
SPIDER-MAN, THANK YOU SO MUCH. I HOPED SOMEONE LIKE YOU MIGHT COME ALONG. I NEVER EXPECTED TO BE LUCKY ENOUGH TO GET TWO HEROES.
HOW IS YOUR SUIT SO CLEAN?
HUH?
I'M NOT ALLOWED TO WEAR WHITE. I ALWAYS GET DIRTY. WHY AREN'T YOU DIRTY?
OH, THAT'S EASY.
MY SUIT IS MADE OF SPIDERS!
THANK YOU FOR SAVING US, SPIDER-MAN AND...
GHOST-SPIDER.
AND GHOST-SPIDER. WE REALLY APPRECIATE IT. WE HAVE TO GO NOW.

OKAY, MAYBE THE SPIDERS MAKE SOME PEOPLE UNCOMFORTABLE...

I STILL HAVE THE ONES YOU GAVE ME.

YOU'VE BEEN ABLE TO KEEP THEM ALIVE?

OH YEAH! HUNGRY TOO. I HAVE A THEORY ABOUT YOUR POWER ISSUES. I THINK YOUR SUIT IS UNDERFED.

SAY WHAT?

I'VE SEEN THE WAY YOU EAT--

IF THIS IS ABOUT TO BECOME A JOKE ABOUT MY WEIGHT, I WARN YOU, I KICK LIKE A MULE.

ALL SPIDERS DO. I'M NOT MAKING A JOKE. YOUR SUIT GETS NUTRIENTS FROM WHAT YOU EAT.

SYMBIOTE, CHECK.

MOST SUPER HEROES HAVE A BIG APPETITE. WEB-SLINGING BURNS A LOT OF CALORIES. BUT YOU'RE LITERALLY EATING FOR TWO. AND YOU DON'T EAT ENOUGH.

SO MY SUIT IS STARVING.

PRETTY MUCH.

I COULD BUY IT A PIZZA, I GUESS.

IT MIGHT PREFER A BIG PILE OF CELERY. IT NEEDS THE CELLULOSE.

CELLULOSE? LIKE IN WOOD?

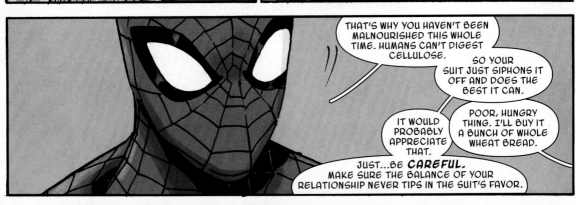

THAT'S WHY YOU HAVEN'T BEEN MALNOURISHED THIS WHOLE TIME. HUMANS CAN'T DIGEST CELLULOSE.

SO YOUR SUIT JUST SIPHONS IT OFF AND DOES THE BEST IT CAN.

IT WOULD PROBABLY APPRECIATE THAT.

POOR, HUNGRY THING. I'LL BUY IT A BUNCH OF WHOLE WHEAT BREAD.

JUST...BE CAREFUL. MAKE SURE THE BALANCE OF YOUR RELATIONSHIP NEVER TIPS IN THE SUIT'S FAVOR.

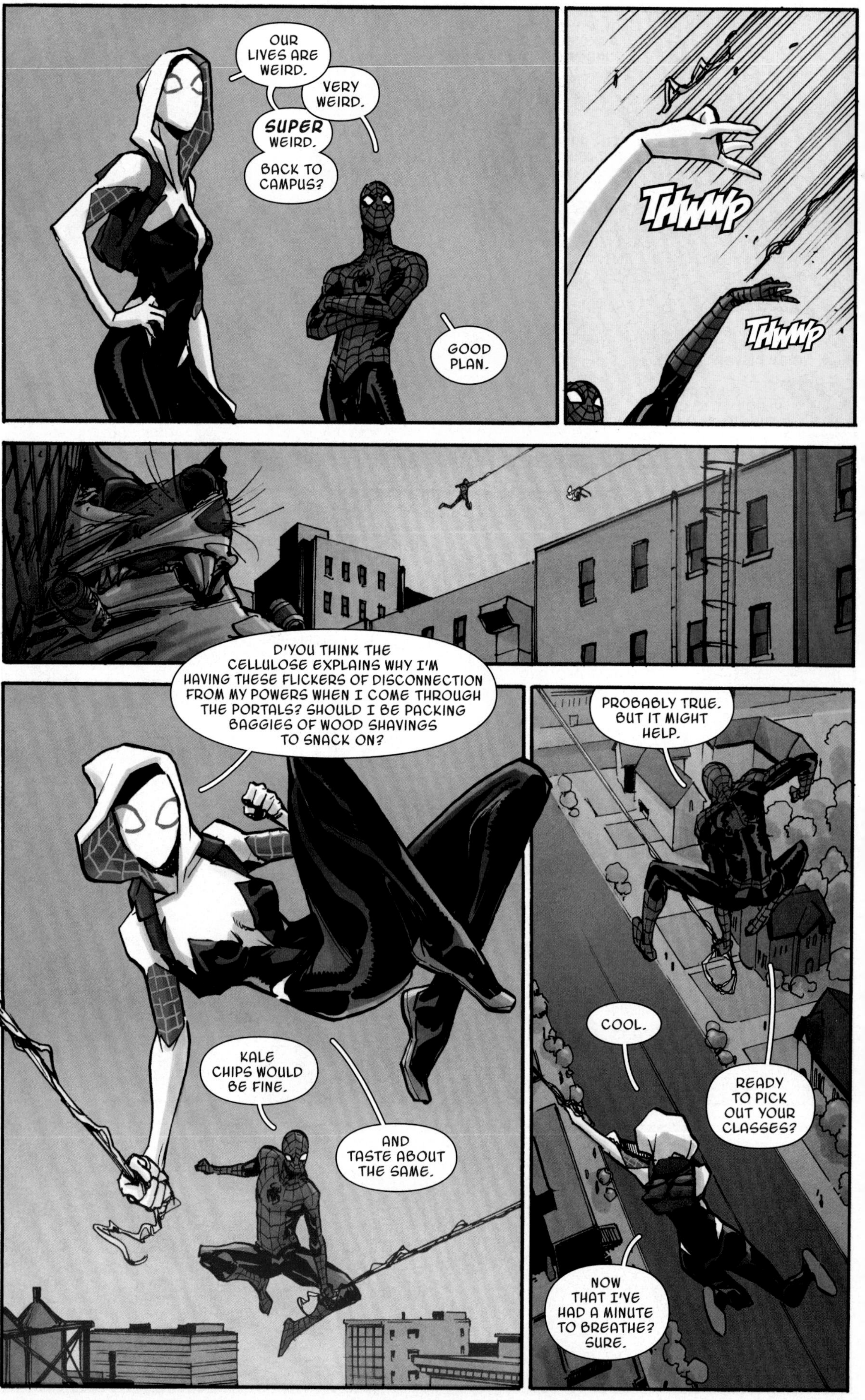

OUR LIVES ARE WEIRD.
VERY WEIRD.
SUPER WEIRD.
BACK TO CAMPUS?
GOOD PLAN.
THWWP
THWWP
D'YOU THINK THE CELLULOSE EXPLAINS WHY I'M HAVING THESE FLICKERS OF DISCONNECTION FROM MY POWERS WHEN I COME THROUGH THE PORTALS? SHOULD I BE PACKING BAGGIES OF WOOD SHAVINGS TO SNACK ON?
KALE CHIPS WOULD BE FINE.
AND TASTE ABOUT THE SAME.
PROBABLY TRUE. BUT IT MIGHT HELP.
COOL.
READY TO PICK OUT YOUR CLASSES?
NOW THAT I'VE HAD A MINUTE TO BREATHE? SURE.

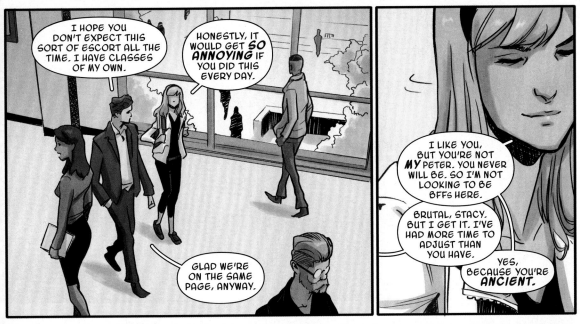

I HOPE YOU DON'T EXPECT THIS SORT OF ESCORT ALL THE TIME. I HAVE CLASSES OF MY OWN.

HONESTLY, IT WOULD GET **SO ANNOYING** IF YOU DID THIS EVERY DAY.

GLAD WE'RE ON THE SAME PAGE, ANYWAY.

I LIKE YOU, BUT YOU'RE NOT **MY** PETER. YOU NEVER WILL BE. SO I'M NOT LOOKING TO BE BFFS HERE.

BRUTAL, STACY. BUT I GET IT. I'VE HAD MORE TIME TO ADJUST THAN YOU HAVE.

YES, BECAUSE YOU'RE **ANCIENT.**

YES, YES, I'M LIKE THE CRYPT KEEPER.

THE WHO?

YOU REMEMBER--IT WAS THIS HORROR SHOW ON CABLE TV.

YOU MEAN THE GRAVEDIGGER?

DO ME A FAVOR. TAKE A MEDIA STUDIES CLASS.

ARE THERE ANY LAWS AGAINST TRANSPORTING DVDs BETWEEN REALITIES?

ONLY MORAL ONES.

SEE, I'M CONSIDERING PRELAW. I THINK THAT MEANS MORAL OBJECTIONS ARE CANCELED.

KNOCK KNOCK

COME IN!

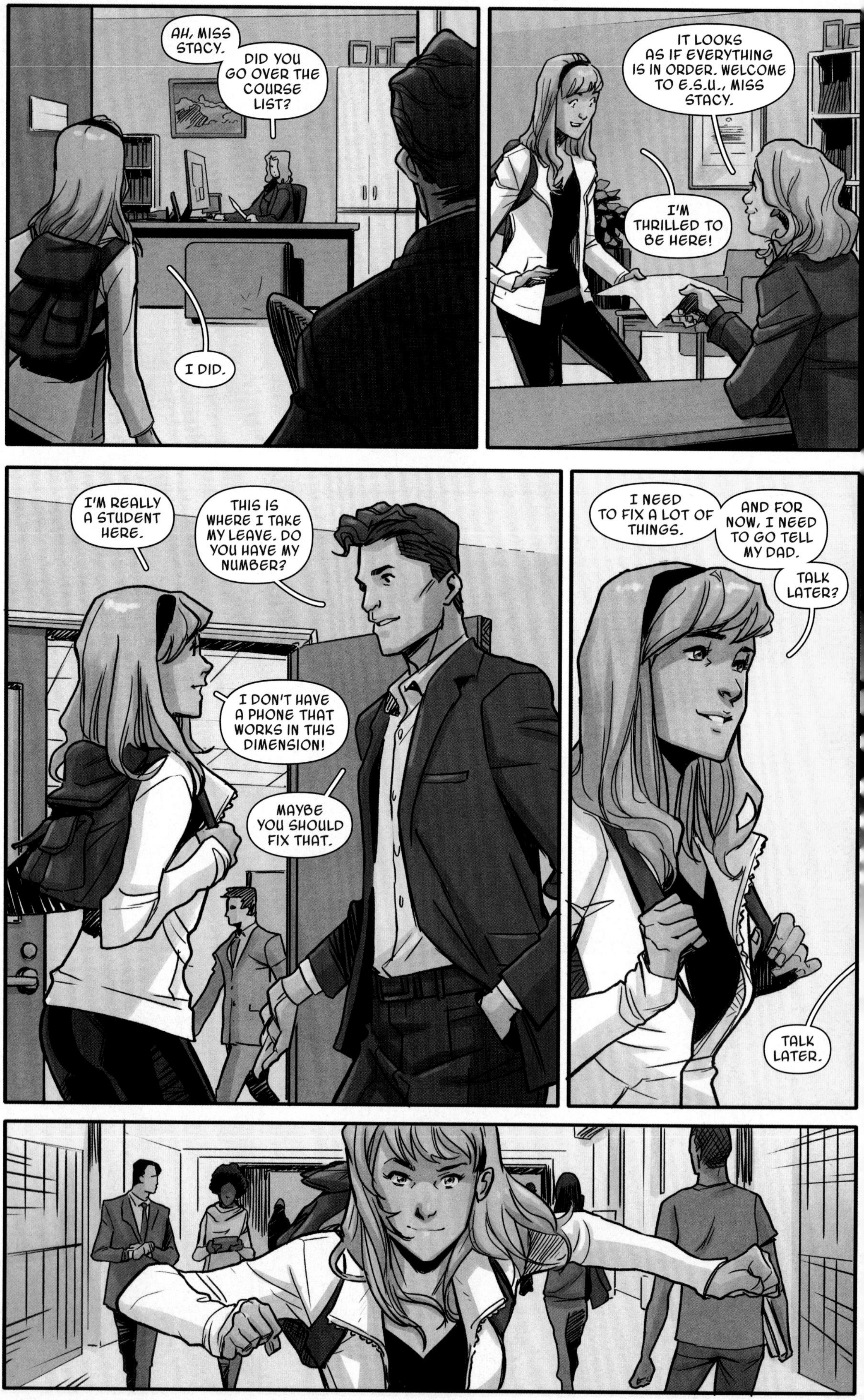
AH, MISS STACY.
DID YOU GO OVER THE COURSE LIST?
I DID.
IT LOOKS AS IF EVERYTHING IS IN ORDER. WELCOME TO E.S.U., MISS STACY.
I'M THRILLED TO BE HERE!
I'M REALLY A STUDENT HERE.
THIS IS WHERE I TAKE MY LEAVE. DO YOU HAVE MY NUMBER?
I DON'T HAVE A PHONE THAT WORKS IN THIS DIMENSION!
MAYBE YOU SHOULD FIX THAT.
I NEED TO FIX A LOT OF THINGS.
AND FOR NOW, I NEED TO GO TELL MY DAD.
TALK LATER?
TALK LATER.

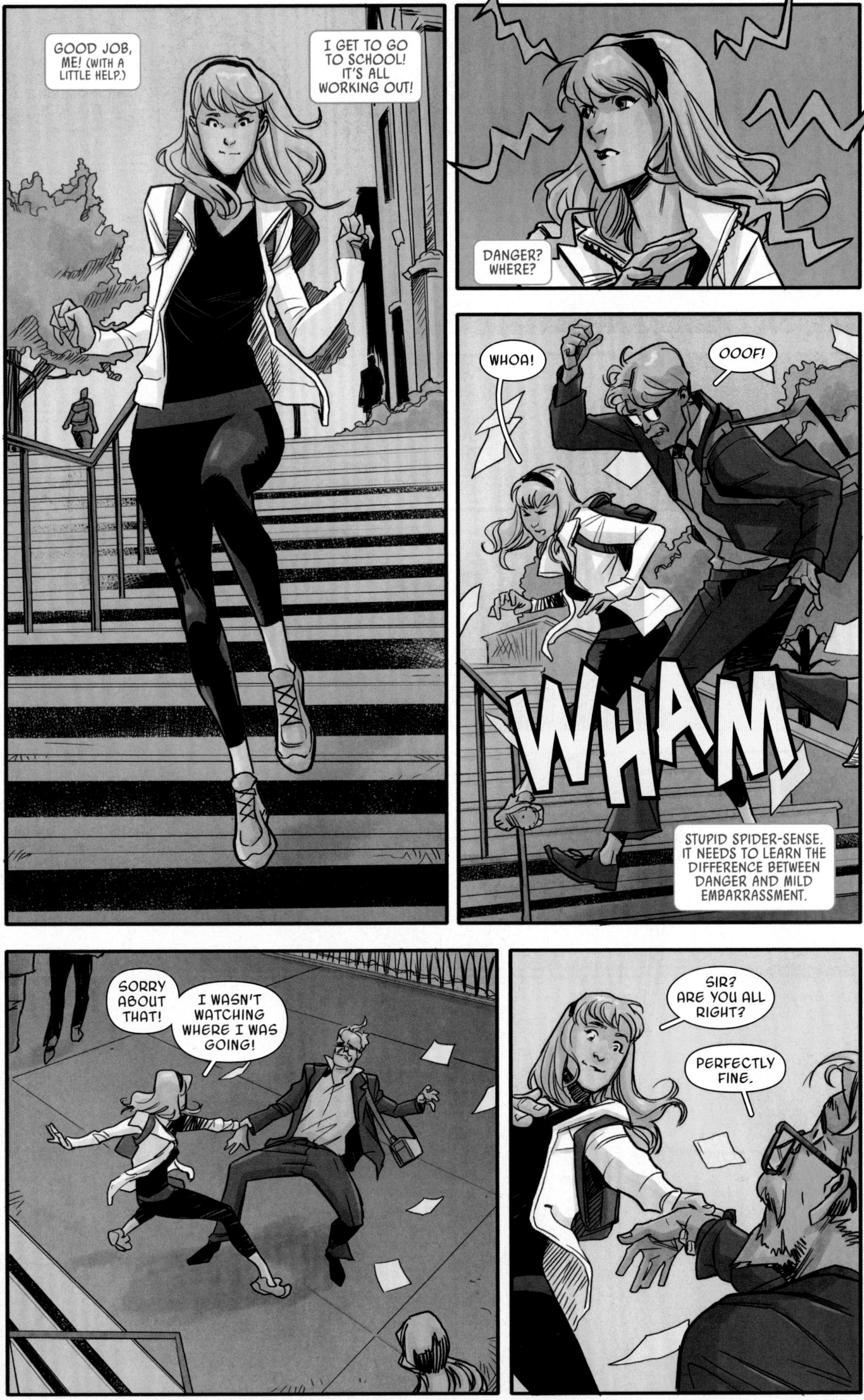
GOOD JOB, ME! (WITH A LITTLE HELP.)
I GET TO GO TO SCHOOL! IT'S ALL WORKING OUT!
DANGER? WHERE?
WHOA!
OOOF!
WHAM
STUPID SPIDER-SENSE. IT NEEDS TO LEARN THE DIFFERENCE BETWEEN DANGER AND MILD EMBARRASSMENT.
SORRY ABOUT THAT!
I WASN'T WATCHING WHERE I WAS GOING!
SIR? ARE YOU ALL RIGHT?
PERFECTLY FINE.

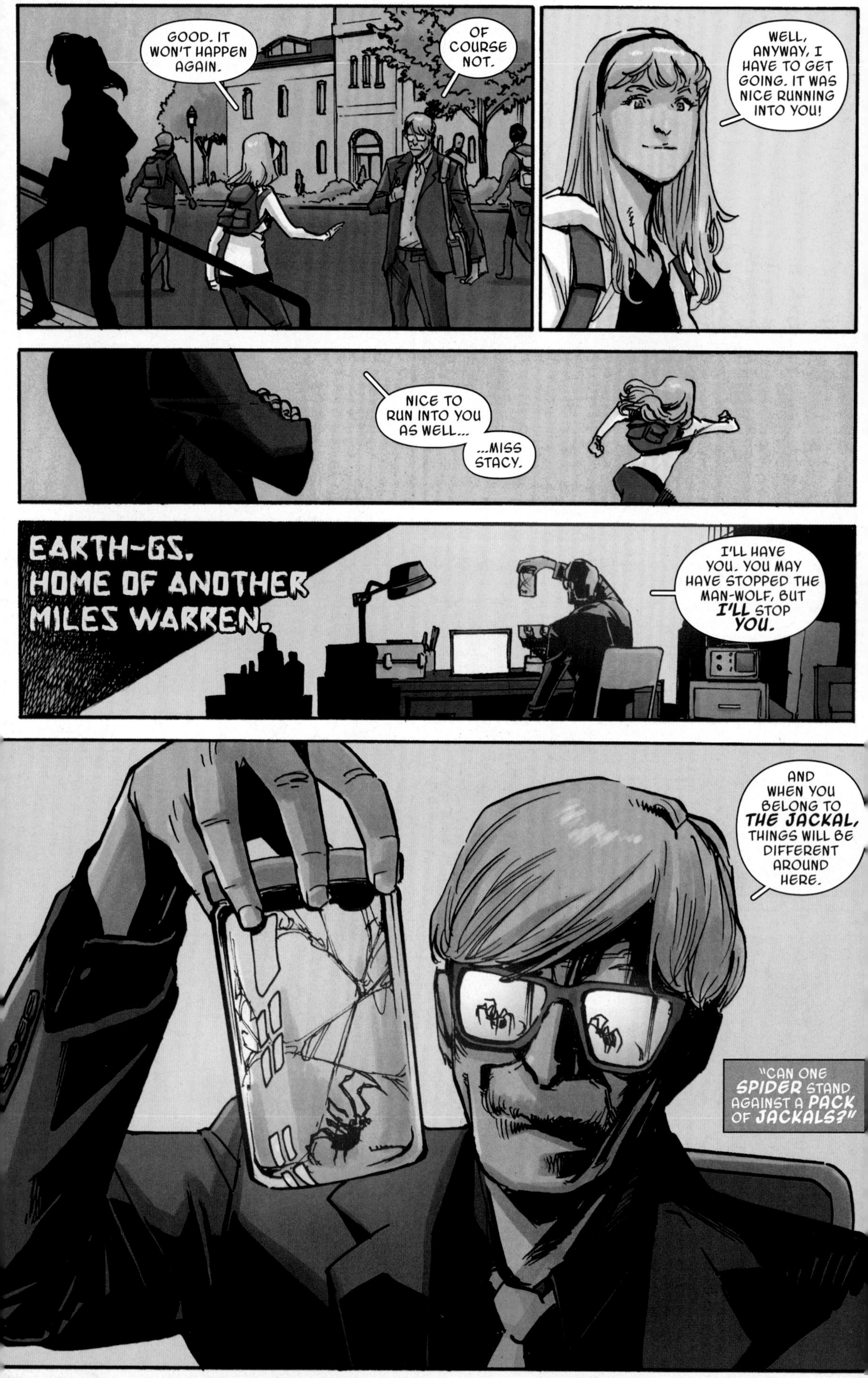
GOOD. IT WON'T HAPPEN AGAIN.
OF COURSE NOT.
WELL, ANYWAY, I HAVE TO GET GOING. IT WAS NICE RUNNING INTO YOU!
NICE TO RUN INTO YOU AS WELL...
...MISS STACY.
EARTH-GS. HOME OF ANOTHER MILES WARREN.
I'LL HAVE YOU. YOU MAY HAVE STOPPED THE MAN-WOLF, BUT I'LL STOP YOU.
AND WHEN YOU BELONG TO THE JACKAL, THINGS WILL BE DIFFERENT AROUND HERE.
"CAN ONE SPIDER STAND AGAINST A PACK OF JACKALS?"

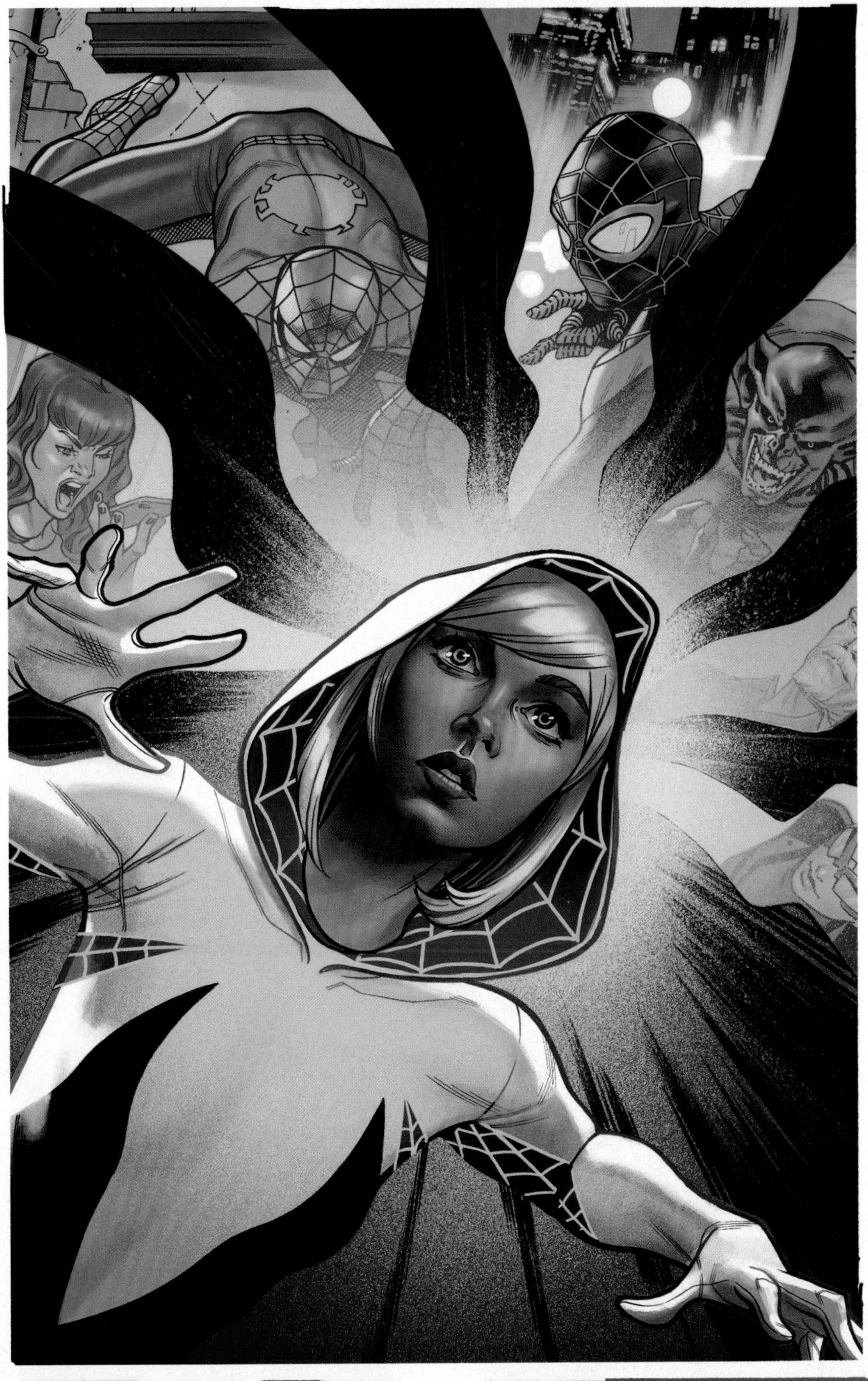

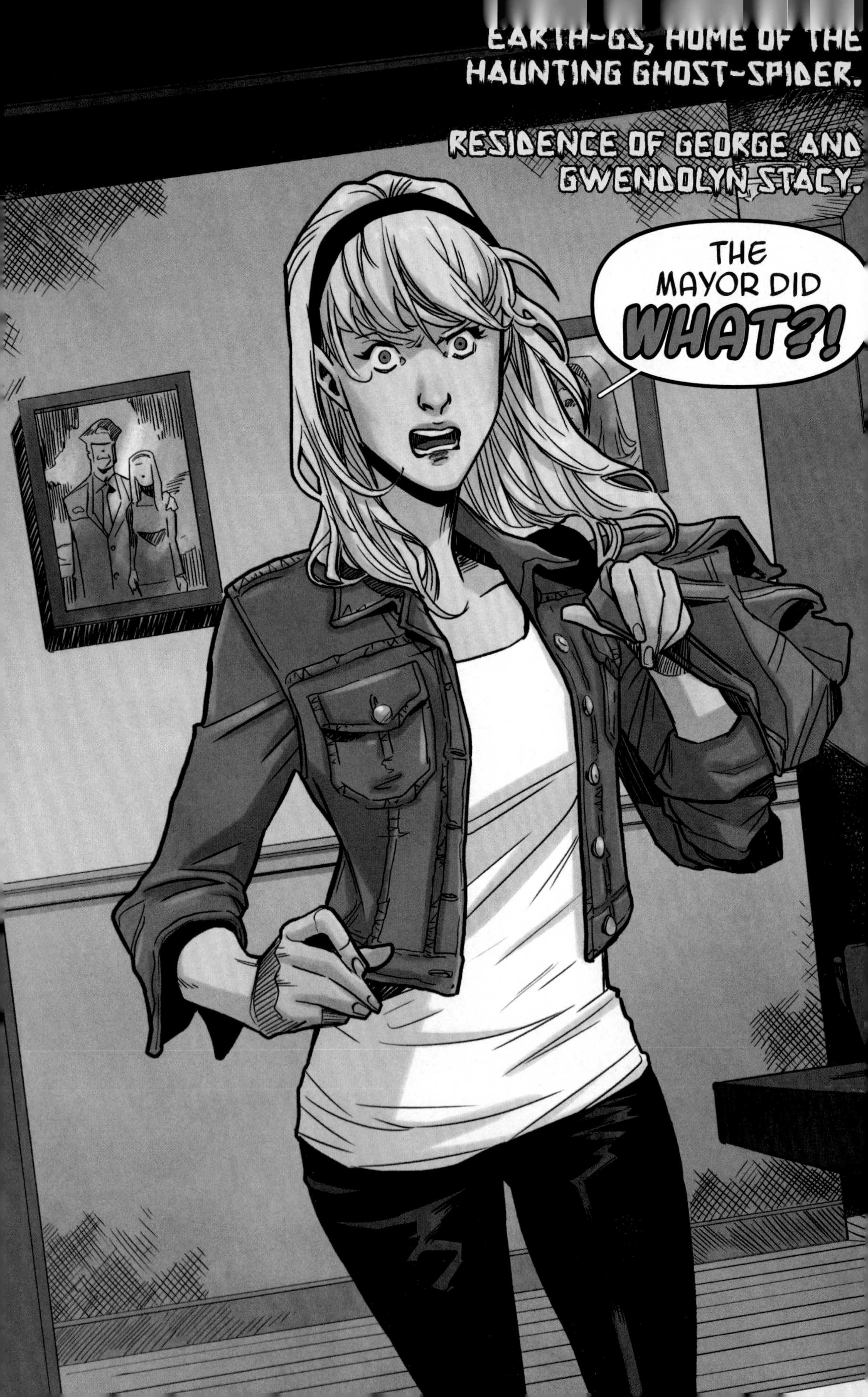
EARTH-65, HOME OF THE HAUNTING GHOST-SPIDER.
RESIDENCE OF GEORGE AND GWENDOLYN STACY.
THE MAYOR DID WHAT?!

HE RELEASED THE MAN-WOLF FROM CUSTODY.

APPARENTLY YOUR NEW NEMESIS IS THE MAYOR'S MISSING *SON.*

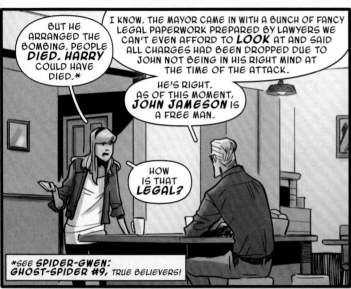

BUT HE ARRANGED THE BOMBING. PEOPLE *DIED. HARRY* COULD HAVE DIED.*

I KNOW. THE MAYOR CAME IN WITH A BUNCH OF FANCY LEGAL PAPERWORK PREPARED BY LAWYERS WE CAN'T EVEN AFFORD TO *LOOK* AT AND SAID ALL CHARGES HAD BEEN DROPPED DUE TO JOHN NOT BEING IN HIS RIGHT MIND AT THE TIME OF THE ATTACK.

HE'S RIGHT. AS OF THIS MOMENT, *JOHN JAMESON* IS A FREE MAN.

HOW IS THAT *LEGAL?*

*SEE SPIDER-GWEN: GHOST-SPIDER #9, TRUE BELIEVERS!

IT SHOULDN'T BE. BUT WITH THE POWER OF JAMESON'S OFFICE AND THE MONEY HE HAS TO THROW AROUND...

I'M SORRY, SWEETHEART. THIS IS OUT OF MY HANDS.

THIS IS ALL JUST SO-- *AARGH!*

IT'S NOT *FAIR!*

CRACK

OOPS. DAD, I'M SORRY, I DIDN'T MEAN--

IT'S FINE. IF I COULD PUNCH HOLES IN GRANITE, I'D BE THE NEW POTHOLE KING OF BROOKLYN.

IT'S JUST NOT FAIR.

NO, IT'S NOT.

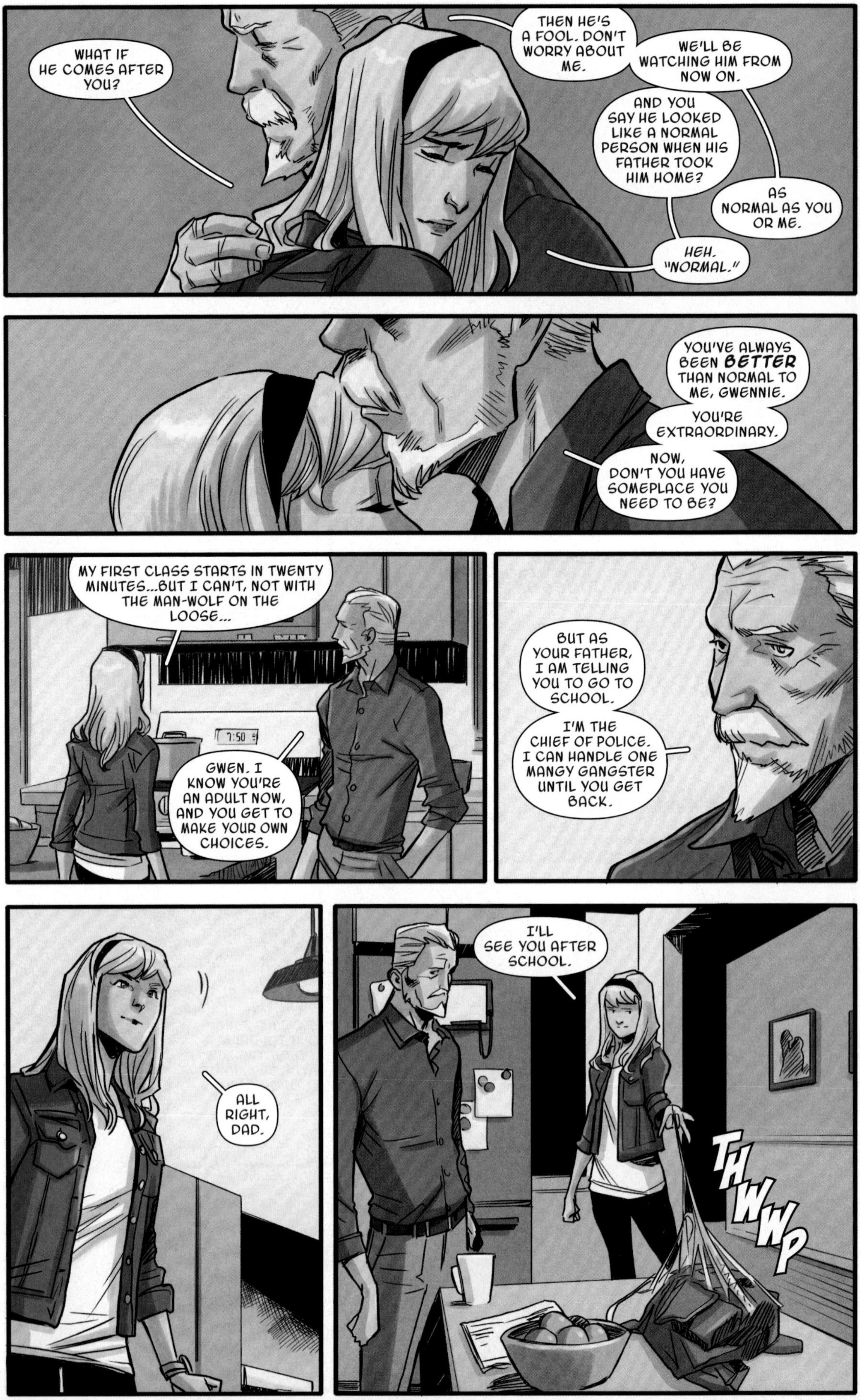
WHAT IF HE COMES AFTER YOU?
THEN HE'S A FOOL. DON'T WORRY ABOUT ME.
WE'LL BE WATCHING HIM FROM NOW ON.
AND YOU SAY HE LOOKED LIKE A NORMAL PERSON WHEN HIS FATHER TOOK HIM HOME?
AS NORMAL AS YOU OR ME.
HEH. "NORMAL."
YOU'VE ALWAYS BEEN BETTER THAN NORMAL TO ME, GWENNIE.
YOU'RE EXTRAORDINARY.
NOW, DON'T YOU HAVE SOMEPLACE YOU NEED TO BE?
MY FIRST CLASS STARTS IN TWENTY MINUTES...BUT I CAN'T, NOT WITH THE MAN-WOLF ON THE LOOSE...
7:50
GWEN. I KNOW YOU'RE AN ADULT NOW, AND YOU GET TO MAKE YOUR OWN CHOICES.
BUT AS YOUR FATHER, I AM TELLING YOU TO GO TO SCHOOL.
I'M THE CHIEF OF POLICE. I CAN HANDLE ONE MANGY GANGSTER UNTIL YOU GET BACK.
ALL RIGHT, DAD.
I'LL SEE YOU AFTER SCHOOL.
THWWP

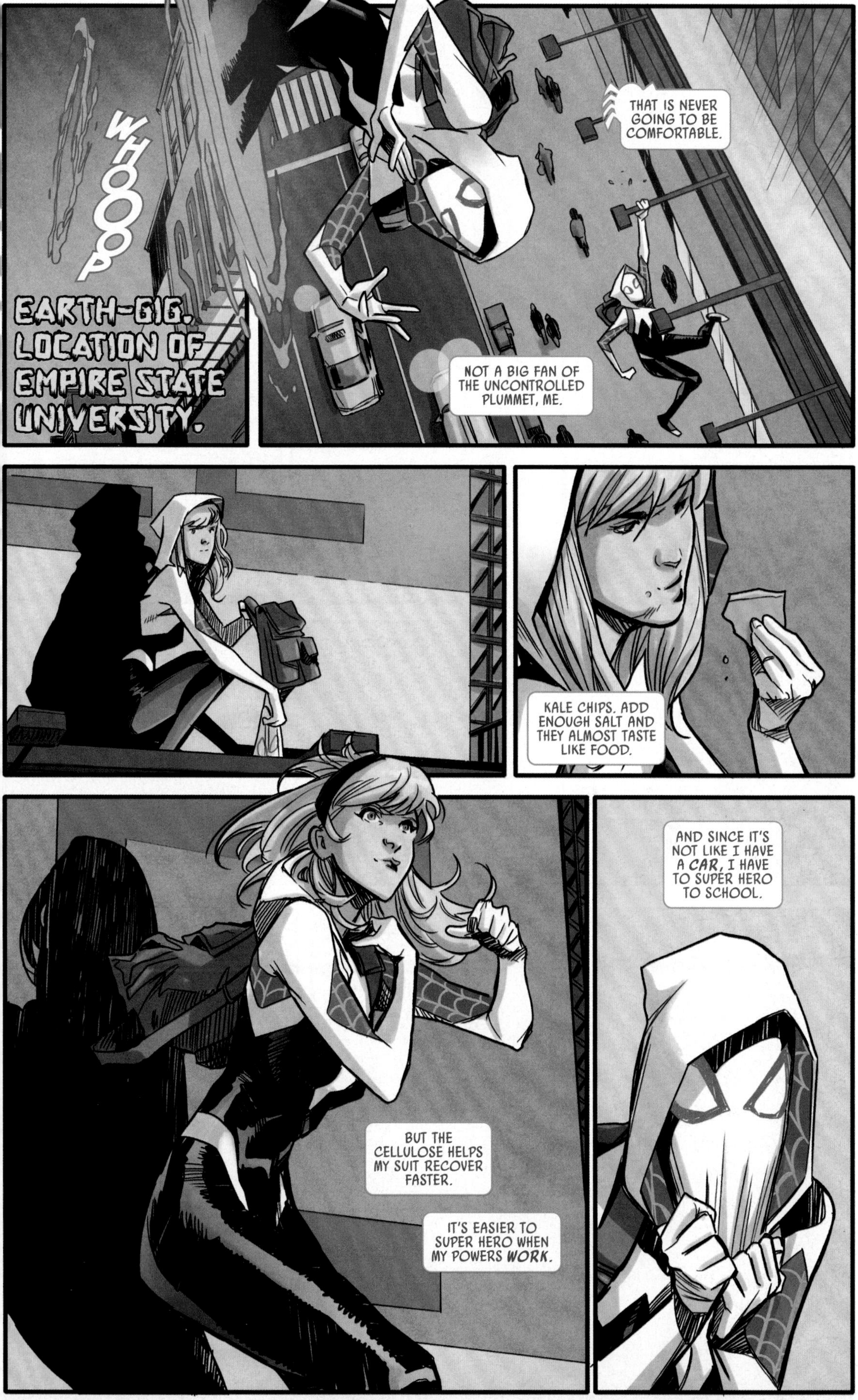
WHOOOOP
EARTH-65. LOCATION OF EMPIRE STATE UNIVERSITY.
THAT IS NEVER GOING TO BE COMFORTABLE.
NOT A BIG FAN OF THE UNCONTROLLED PLUMMET, ME.
KALE CHIPS. ADD ENOUGH SALT AND THEY ALMOST TASTE LIKE FOOD.
BUT THE CELLULOSE HELPS MY SUIT RECOVER FASTER.
IT'S EASIER TO SUPER HERO WHEN MY POWERS WORK.
AND SINCE IT'S NOT LIKE I HAVE A CAR, I HAVE TO SUPER HERO TO SCHOOL.

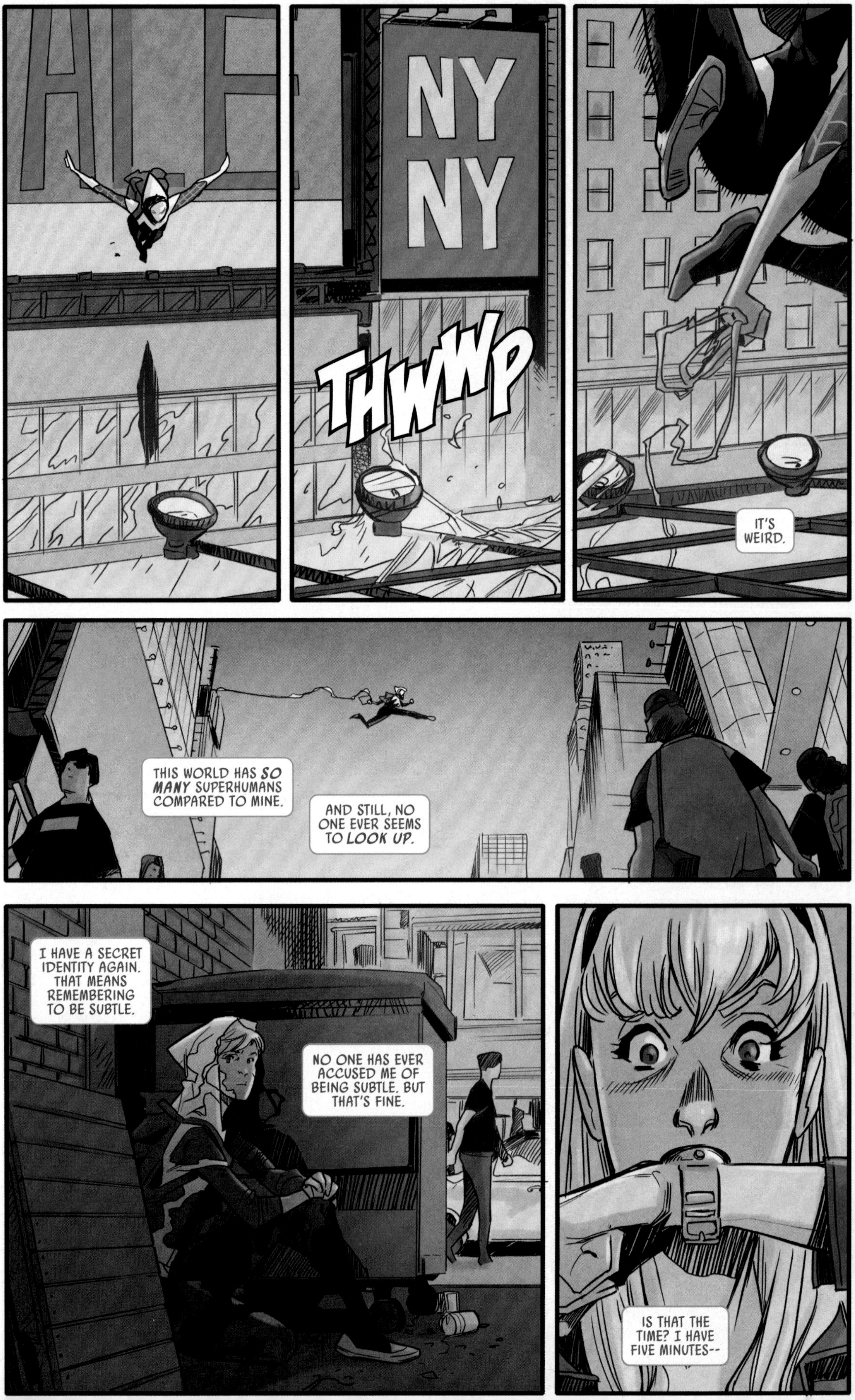
NY
NY
THWWP
IT'S WEIRD.
THIS WORLD HAS SO MANY SUPERHUMANS COMPARED TO MINE.
AND STILL, NO ONE EVER SEEMS TO LOOK UP.
I HAVE A SECRET IDENTITY AGAIN. THAT MEANS REMEMBERING TO BE SUBTLE.
NO ONE HAS EVER ACCUSED ME OF BEING SUBTLE. BUT THAT'S FINE.
IS THAT THE TIME? I HAVE FIVE MINUTES--

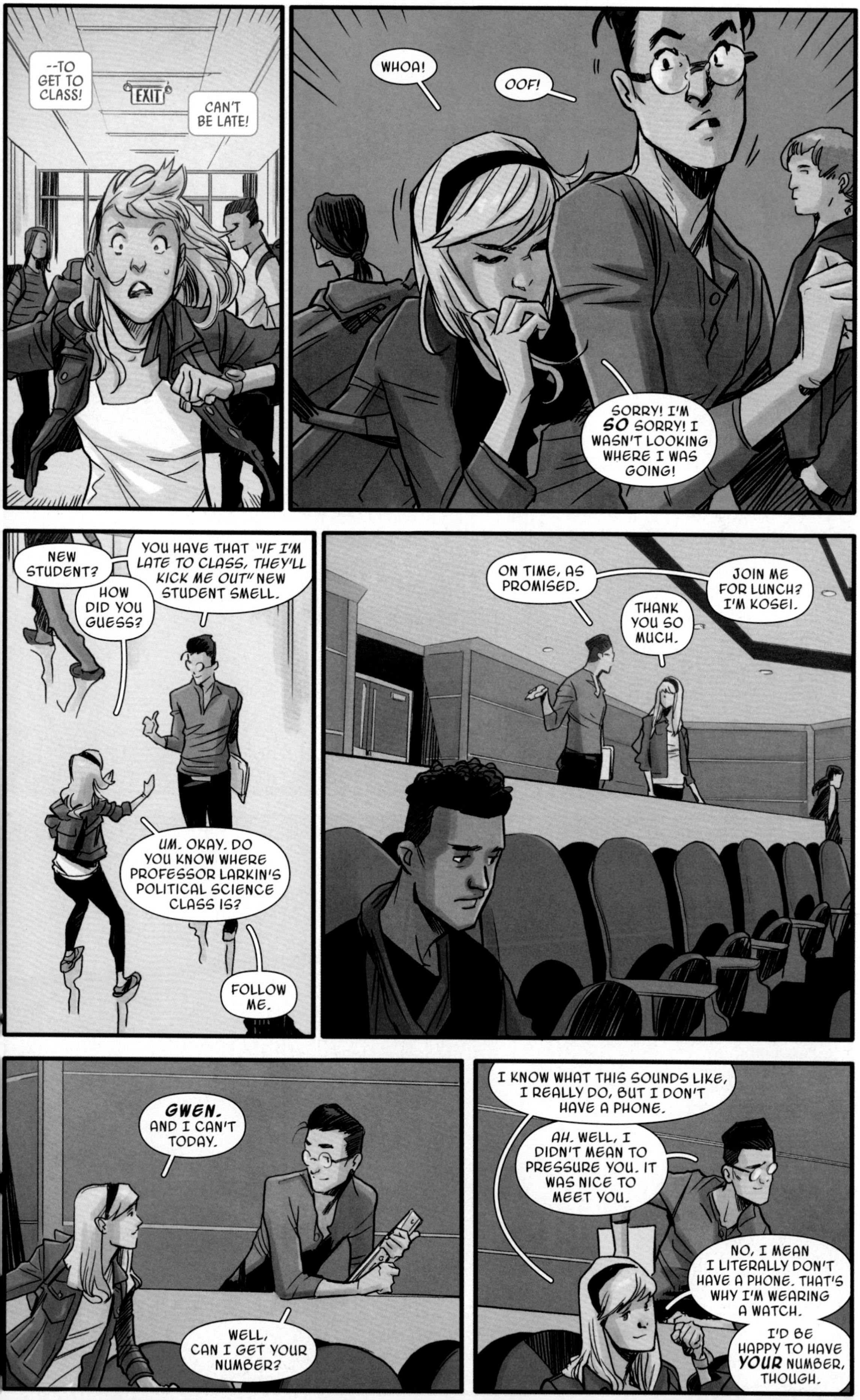
--TO GET TO CLASS!
CAN'T BE LATE!
EXIT
WHOA!
OOF!
SORRY! I'M SO SORRY! I WASN'T LOOKING WHERE I WAS GOING!
NEW STUDENT?
YOU HAVE THAT "IF I'M LATE TO CLASS, THEY'LL KICK ME OUT" NEW STUDENT SMELL.
HOW DID YOU GUESS?
UM. OKAY. DO YOU KNOW WHERE PROFESSOR LARKIN'S POLITICAL SCIENCE CLASS IS?
FOLLOW ME.
ON TIME, AS PROMISED.
JOIN ME FOR LUNCH? I'M KOSEI.
THANK YOU SO MUCH.
GWEN. AND I CAN'T TODAY.
WELL, CAN I GET YOUR NUMBER?
I KNOW WHAT THIS SOUNDS LIKE, I REALLY DO, BUT I DON'T HAVE A PHONE.
AH. WELL, I DIDN'T MEAN TO PRESSURE YOU. IT WAS NICE TO MEET YOU.
NO, I MEAN I LITERALLY DON'T HAVE A PHONE. THAT'S WHY I'M WEARING A WATCH.
I'D BE HAPPY TO HAVE YOUR NUMBER, THOUGH.

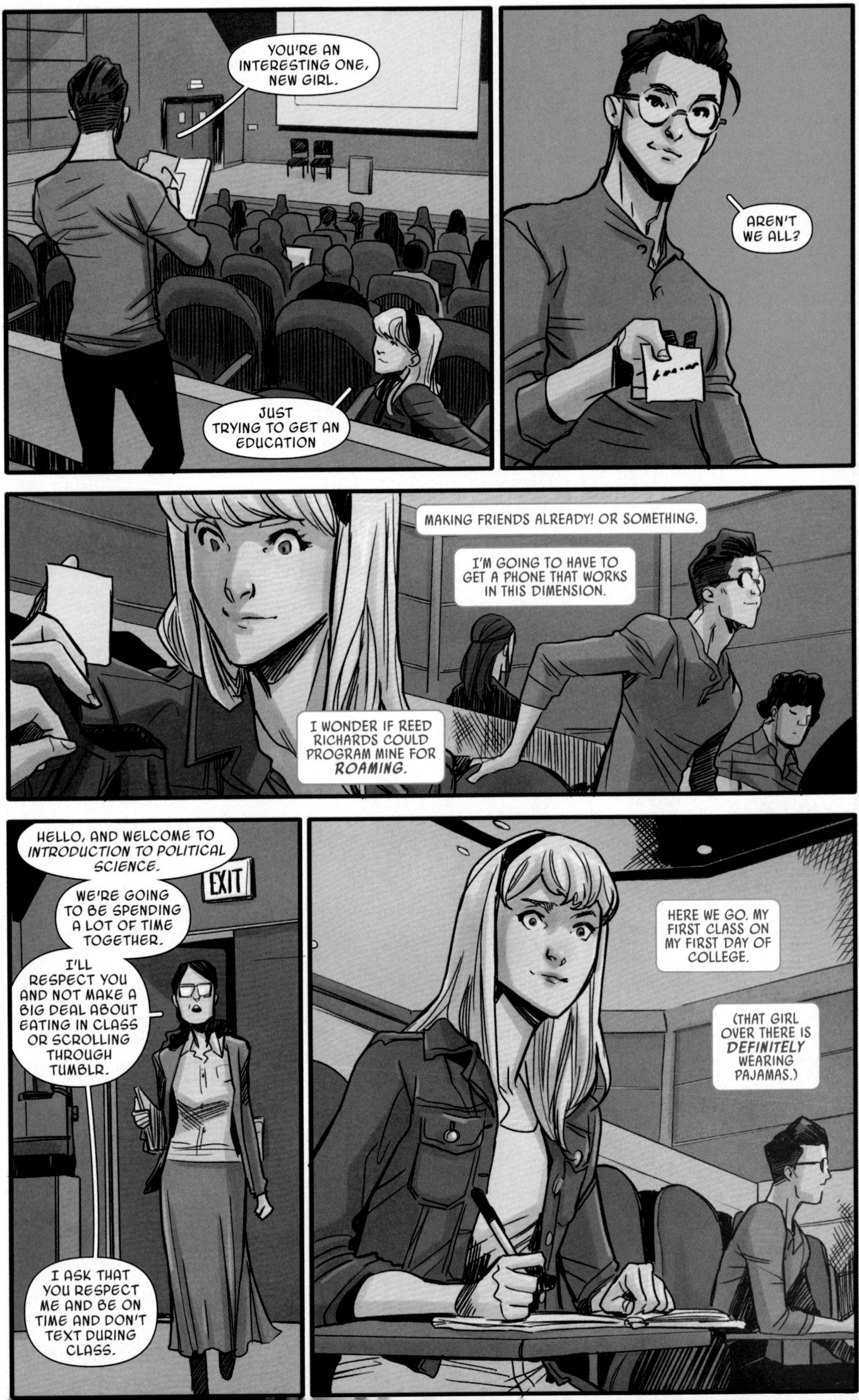

YOU'RE AN INTERESTING ONE, NEW GIRL.
JUST TRYING TO GET AN EDUCATION
AREN'T WE ALL?
MAKING FRIENDS ALREADY! OR SOMETHING.
I'M GOING TO HAVE TO GET A PHONE THAT WORKS IN THIS DIMENSION.
I WONDER IF REED RICHARDS COULD PROGRAM MINE FOR *ROAMING.*
HELLO, AND WELCOME TO *INTRODUCTION TO POLITICAL SCIENCE.*
EXIT
WE'RE GOING TO BE SPENDING A LOT OF TIME TOGETHER.
I'LL RESPECT YOU AND NOT MAKE A BIG DEAL ABOUT EATING IN CLASS OR SCROLLING THROUGH TUMBLR.
I ASK THAT YOU RESPECT ME AND BE ON TIME AND DON'T TEXT DURING CLASS.
HERE WE GO. MY FIRST CLASS ON MY FIRST DAY OF COLLEGE.
(THAT GIRL OVER THERE IS *DEFINITELY* WEARING PAJAMAS.)

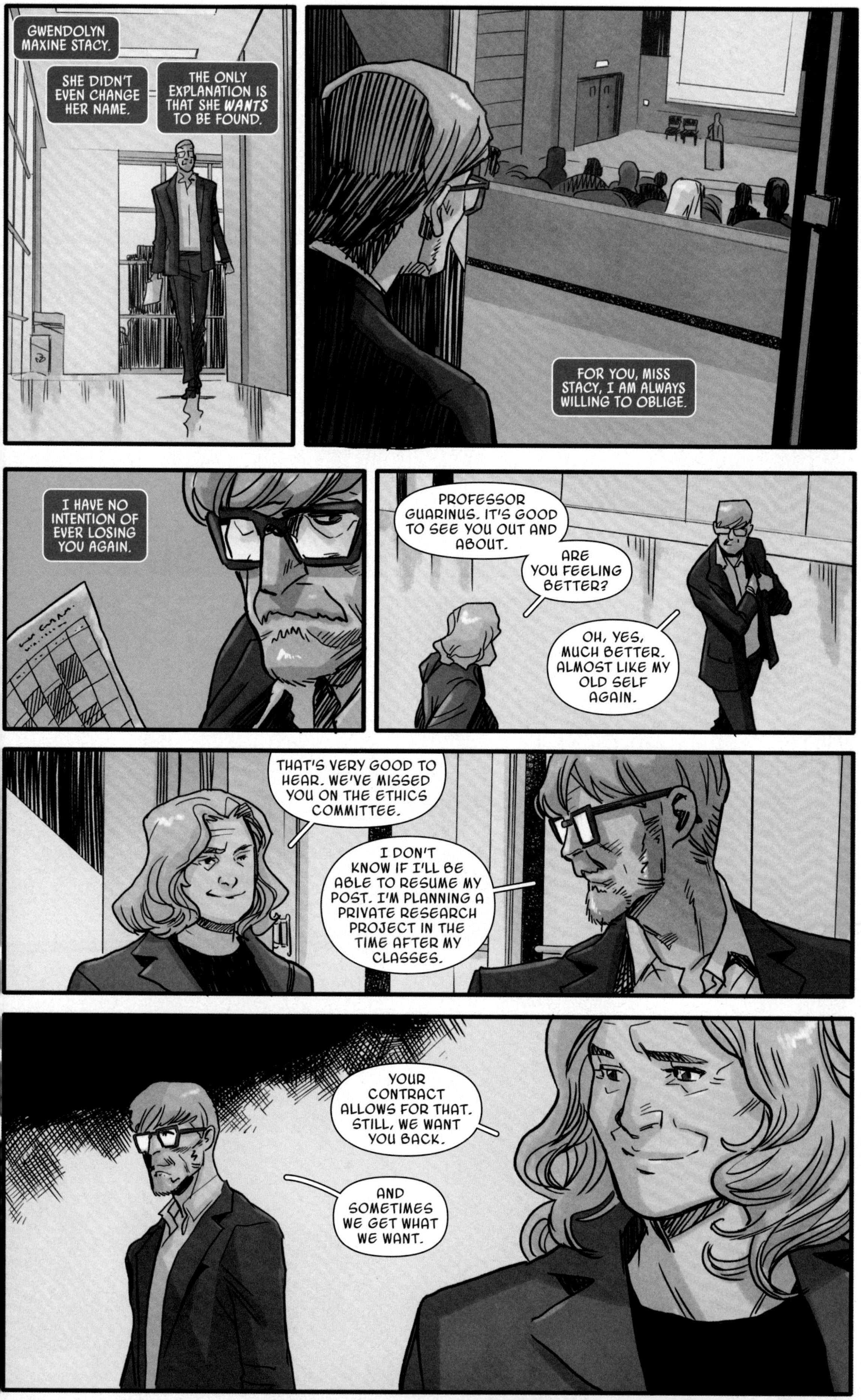
GWENDOLYN MAXINE STACY.
SHE DIDN'T EVEN CHANGE HER NAME.
THE ONLY EXPLANATION IS THAT SHE *WANTS* TO BE FOUND.
FOR YOU, MISS STACY, I AM ALWAYS WILLING TO OBLIGE.
I HAVE NO INTENTION OF EVER LOSING YOU AGAIN.
PROFESSOR GUARINUS. IT'S GOOD TO SEE YOU OUT AND ABOUT.
ARE YOU FEELING BETTER?
OH, YES, MUCH BETTER. ALMOST LIKE MY OLD SELF AGAIN.
THAT'S VERY GOOD TO HEAR. WE'VE MISSED YOU ON THE ETHICS COMMITTEE.
I DON'T KNOW IF I'LL BE ABLE TO RESUME MY POST. I'M PLANNING A PRIVATE RESEARCH PROJECT IN THE TIME AFTER MY CLASSES.
YOUR CONTRACT ALLOWS FOR THAT. STILL, WE WANT YOU BACK.
AND SOMETIMES WE GET WHAT WE WANT.

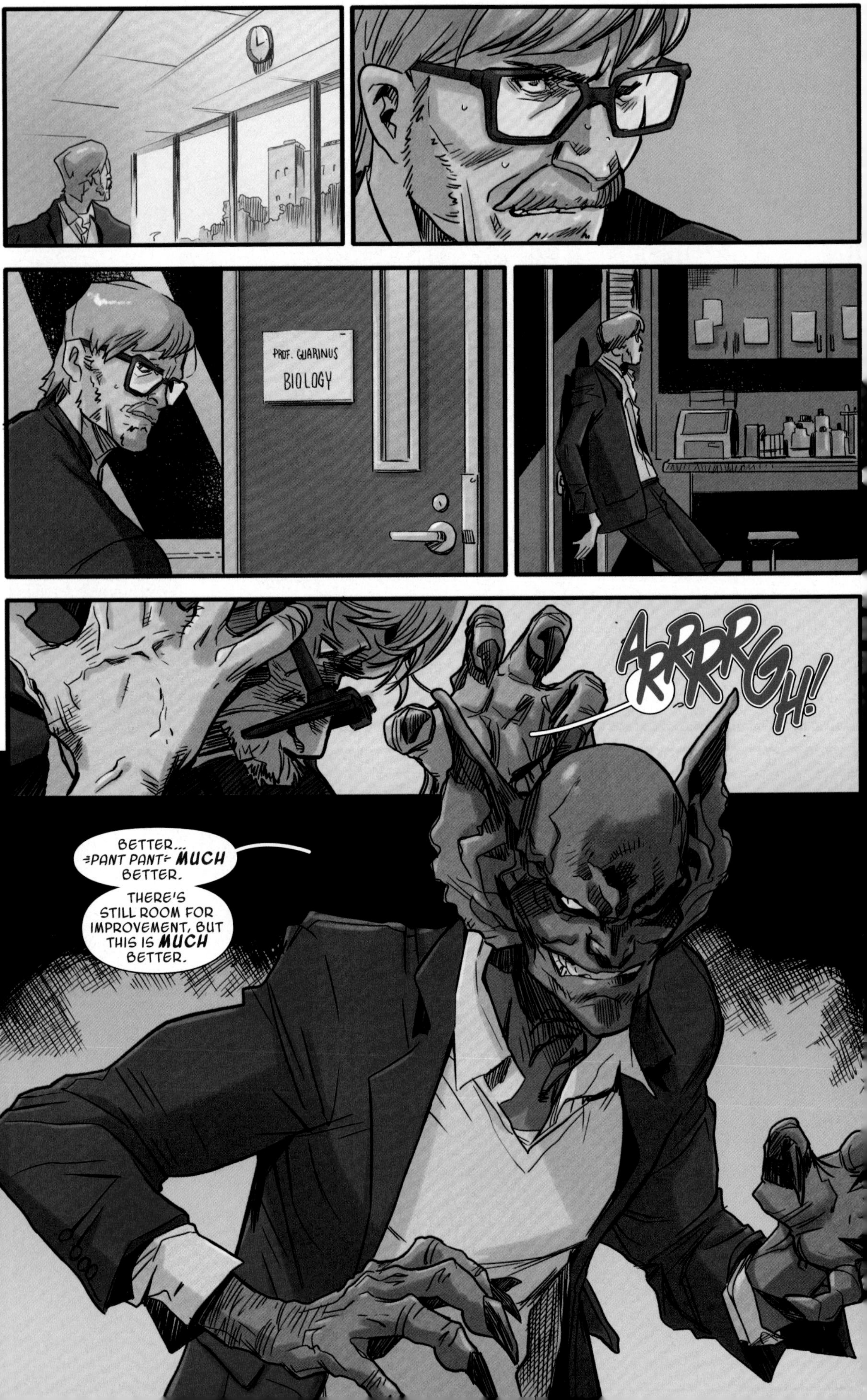
PROF. GUARINUS
BIOLOGY
ARRRRGH!
BETTER... =PANT PANT= MUCH BETTER.
THERE'S STILL ROOM FOR IMPROVEMENT, BUT THIS IS MUCH BETTER.

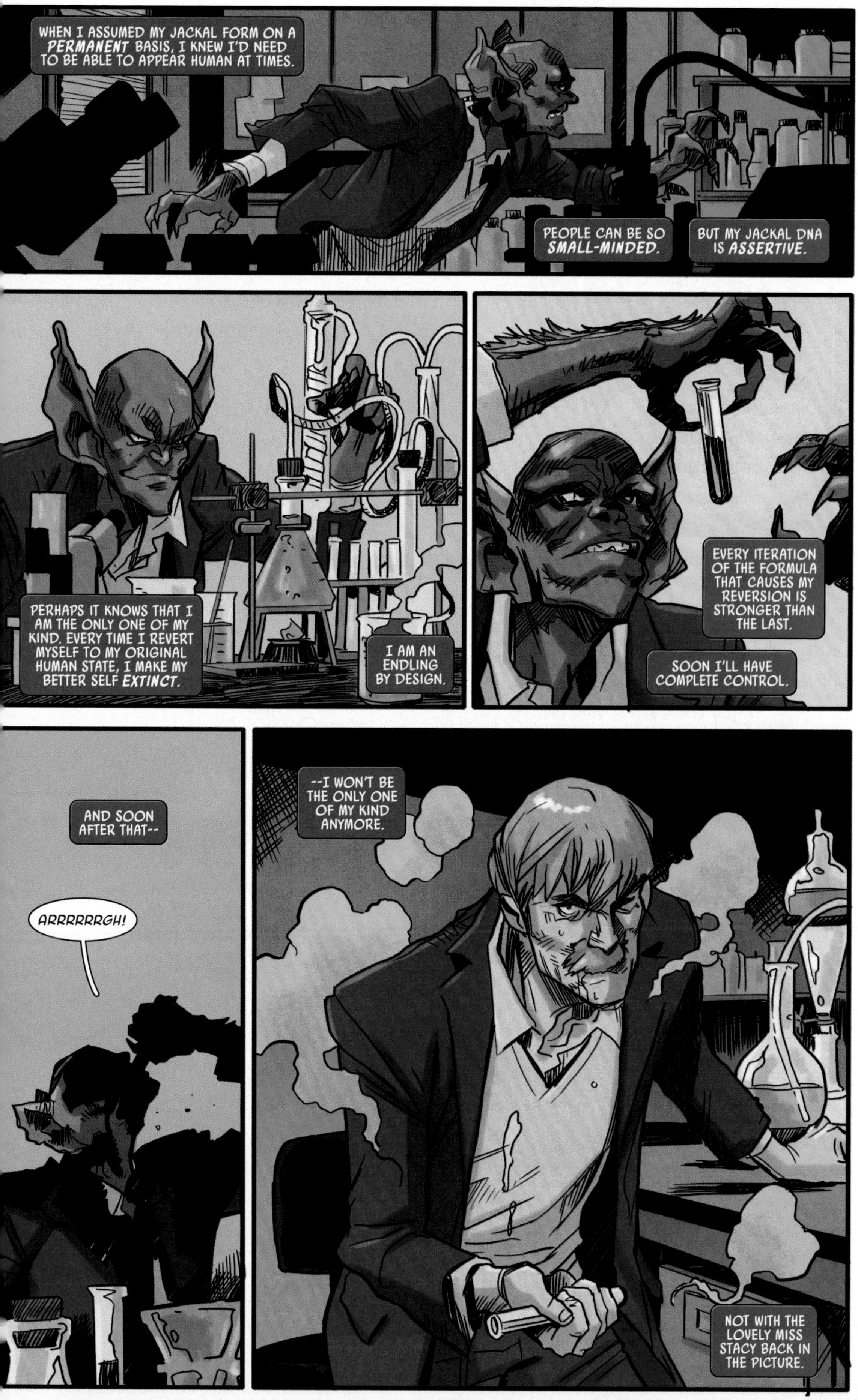
WHEN I ASSUMED MY JACKAL FORM ON A PERMANENT BASIS, I KNEW I'D NEED TO BE ABLE TO APPEAR HUMAN AT TIMES.
PEOPLE CAN BE SO SMALL-MINDED.
BUT MY JACKAL DNA IS ASSERTIVE.
PERHAPS IT KNOWS THAT I AM THE ONLY ONE OF MY KIND. EVERY TIME I REVERT MYSELF TO MY ORIGINAL HUMAN STATE, I MAKE MY BETTER SELF EXTINCT.
I AM AN ENDLING BY DESIGN.
EVERY ITERATION OF THE FORMULA THAT CAUSES MY REVERSION IS STRONGER THAN THE LAST.
SOON I'LL HAVE COMPLETE CONTROL.
AND SOON AFTER THAT--
ARRRRRRGH!
--I WON'T BE THE ONLY ONE OF MY KIND ANYMORE.
NOT WITH THE LOVELY MISS STACY BACK IN THE PICTURE.

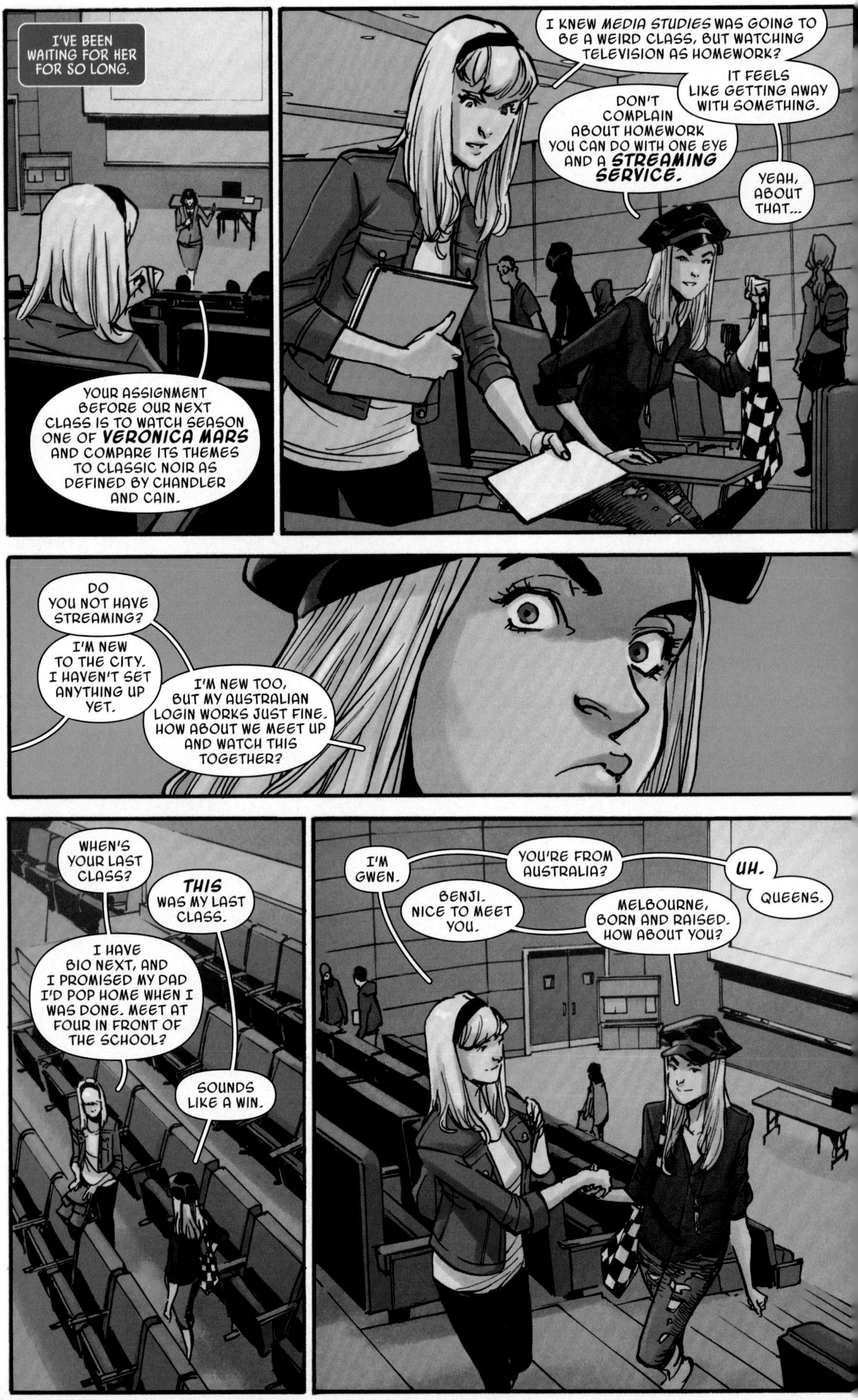
I'VE BEEN WAITING FOR HER FOR SO LONG.
YOUR ASSIGNMENT BEFORE OUR NEXT CLASS IS TO WATCH SEASON ONE OF VERONICA MARS AND COMPARE ITS THEMES TO CLASSIC NOIR AS DEFINED BY CHANDLER AND CAIN.
I KNEW MEDIA STUDIES WAS GOING TO BE A WEIRD CLASS, BUT WATCHING TELEVISION AS HOMEWORK?
IT FEELS LIKE GETTING AWAY WITH SOMETHING.
DON'T COMPLAIN ABOUT HOMEWORK YOU CAN DO WITH ONE EYE AND A STREAMING SERVICE.
YEAH, ABOUT THAT...
DO YOU NOT HAVE STREAMING?
I'M NEW TO THE CITY. I HAVEN'T SET ANYTHING UP YET.
I'M NEW TOO, BUT MY AUSTRALIAN LOGIN WORKS JUST FINE. HOW ABOUT WE MEET UP AND WATCH THIS TOGETHER?
WHEN'S YOUR LAST CLASS?
THIS WAS MY LAST CLASS.
I HAVE BIO NEXT, AND I PROMISED MY DAD I'D POP HOME WHEN I WAS DONE. MEET AT FOUR IN FRONT OF THE SCHOOL?
SOUNDS LIKE A WIN.
I'M GWEN.
BENJI. NICE TO MEET YOU.
YOU'RE FROM AUSTRALIA?
MELBOURNE, BORN AND RAISED. HOW ABOUT YOU?
UH.
QUEENS.

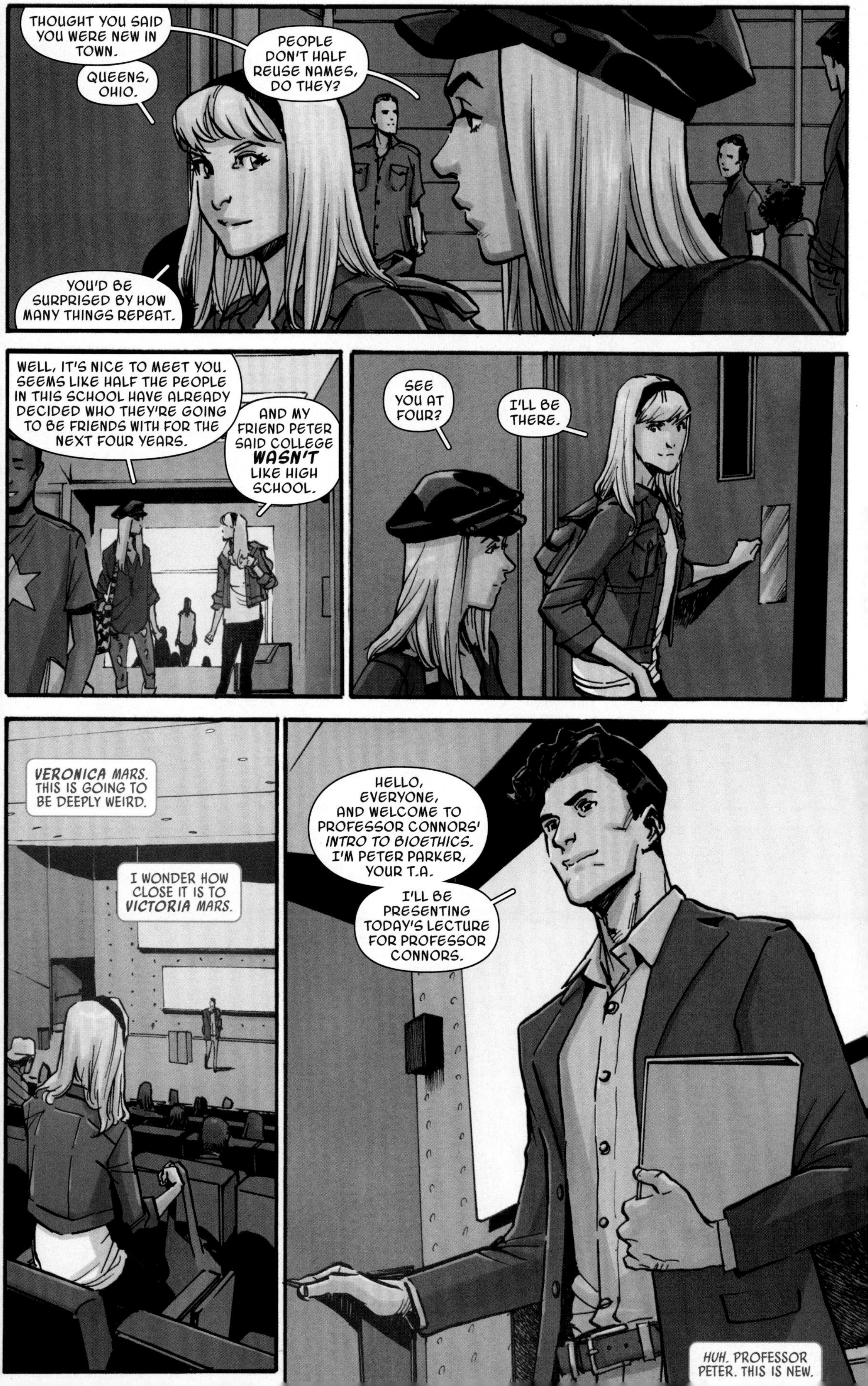
THOUGHT YOU SAID YOU WERE NEW IN TOWN.
PEOPLE DON'T HALF REUSE NAMES, DO THEY?
QUEENS, OHIO.
YOU'D BE SURPRISED BY HOW MANY THINGS REPEAT.
WELL, IT'S NICE TO MEET YOU. SEEMS LIKE HALF THE PEOPLE IN THIS SCHOOL HAVE ALREADY DECIDED WHO THEY'RE GOING TO BE FRIENDS WITH FOR THE NEXT FOUR YEARS.
AND MY FRIEND PETER SAID COLLEGE WASN'T LIKE HIGH SCHOOL.
SEE YOU AT FOUR?
I'LL BE THERE.
VERONICA MARS. THIS IS GOING TO BE DEEPLY WEIRD.
I WONDER HOW CLOSE IT IS TO VICTORIA MARS.
HELLO, EVERYONE, AND WELCOME TO PROFESSOR CONNORS' INTRO TO BIOETHICS. I'M PETER PARKER, YOUR T.A.
I'LL BE PRESENTING TODAY'S LECTURE FOR PROFESSOR CONNORS.
HUH. PROFESSOR PETER. THIS IS NEW.

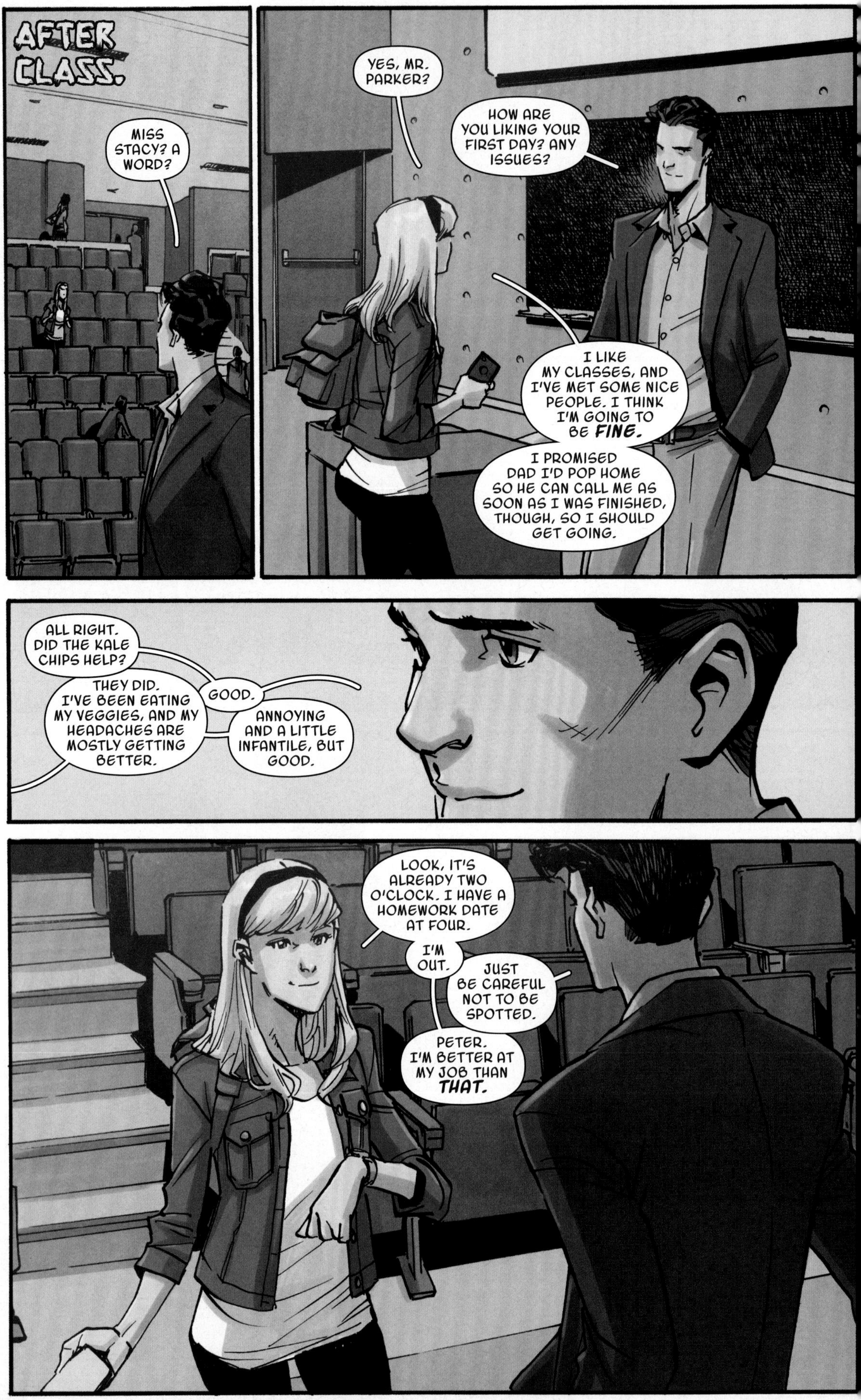
AFTER CLASS.
MISS STACY? A WORD?
YES, MR. PARKER?
HOW ARE YOU LIKING YOUR FIRST DAY? ANY ISSUES?
I LIKE MY CLASSES, AND I'VE MET SOME NICE PEOPLE. I THINK I'M GOING TO BE FINE.
I PROMISED DAD I'D POP HOME SO HE CAN CALL ME AS SOON AS I WAS FINISHED, THOUGH, SO I SHOULD GET GOING.
ALL RIGHT. DID THE KALE CHIPS HELP?
THEY DID. I'VE BEEN EATING MY VEGGIES, AND MY HEADACHES ARE MOSTLY GETTING BETTER.
GOOD.
ANNOYING AND A LITTLE INFANTILE, BUT GOOD.
LOOK, IT'S ALREADY TWO O'CLOCK. I HAVE A HOMEWORK DATE AT FOUR.
I'M OUT.
JUST BE CAREFUL NOT TO BE SPOTTED.
PETER. I'M BETTER AT MY JOB THAN THAT.

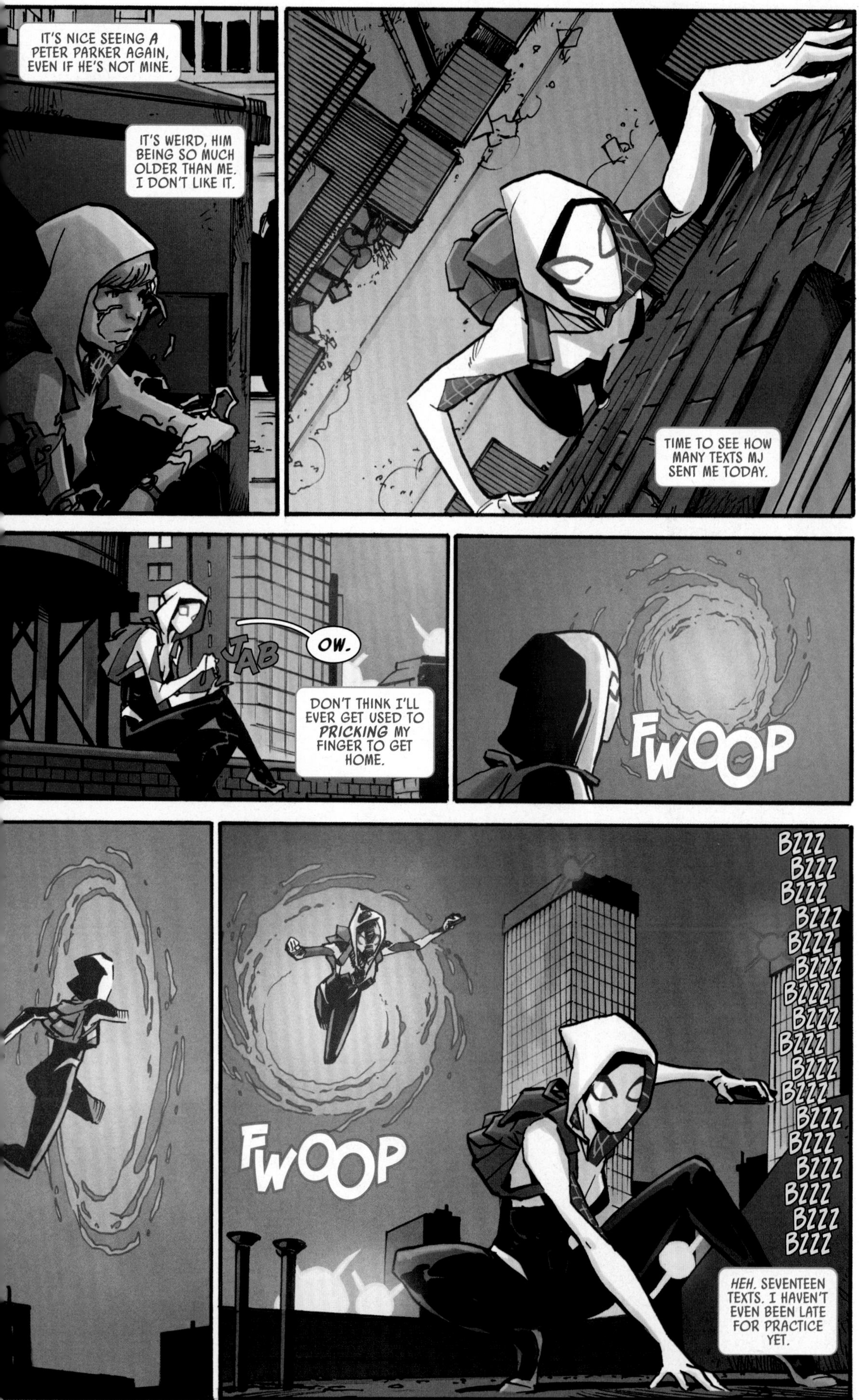
IT'S NICE SEEING A PETER PARKER AGAIN, EVEN IF HE'S NOT MINE.
IT'S WEIRD, HIM BEING SO MUCH OLDER THAN ME. I DON'T LIKE IT.
TIME TO SEE HOW MANY TEXTS MJ SENT ME TODAY.
JAB
OW.
DON'T THINK I'LL EVER GET USED TO PRICKING MY FINGER TO GET HOME.
FWOOP
FWOOP
BZZZ BZZZ BZZZ BZZZ BZZZ BZZZ BZZZ BZZZ BZZZ BZZZ BZZZ BZZZ BZZZ BZZZ BZZZ BZZZ BZZZ
HEH. SEVENTEEN TEXTS. I HAVEN'T EVEN BEEN LATE FOR PRACTICE YET.

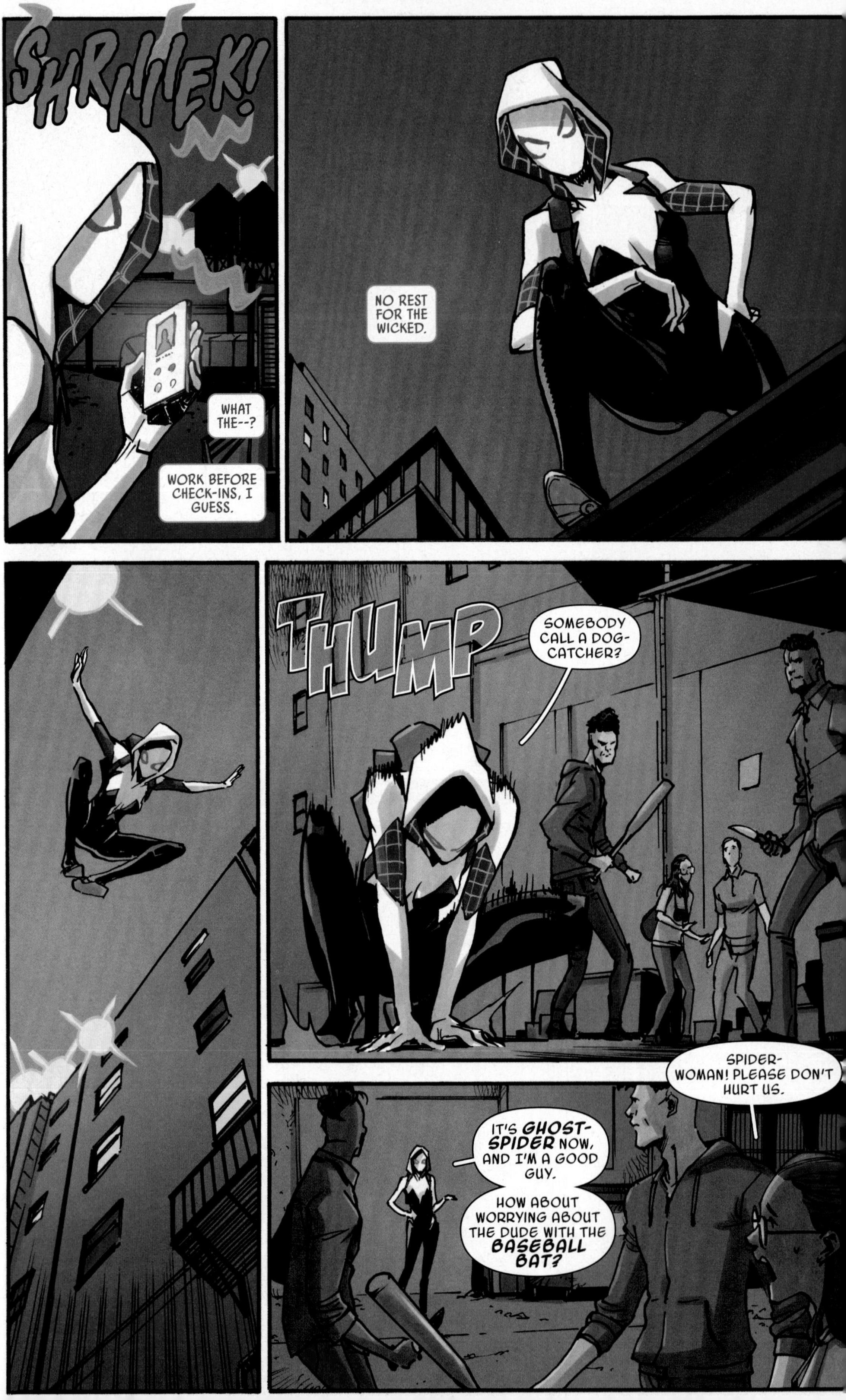
SHRIIIEK!
WHAT THE--?
WORK BEFORE CHECK-INS, I GUESS.
NO REST FOR THE WICKED.
THUMP
SOMEBODY CALL A DOG-CATCHER?
SPIDER-WOMAN! PLEASE DON'T HURT US.
IT'S GHOST-SPIDER NOW, AND I'M A GOOD GUY.
HOW ABOUT WORRYING ABOUT THE DUDE WITH THE BASEBALL BAT?

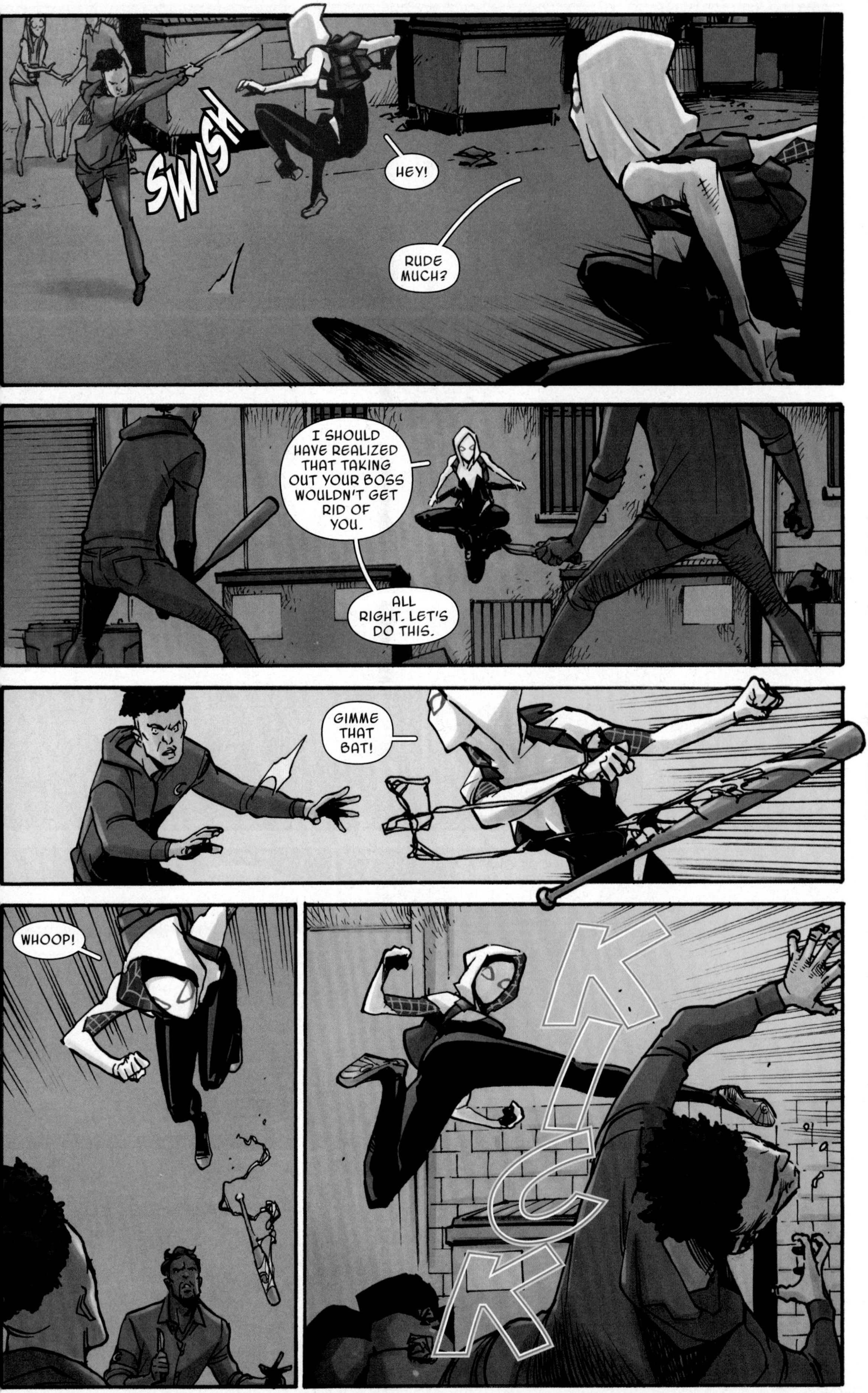
SWISH
HEY!
RUDE MUCH?
I SHOULD HAVE REALIZED THAT TAKING OUT YOUR BOSS WOULDN'T GET RID OF YOU.
ALL RIGHT. LET'S DO THIS.
GIMME THAT BAT!
WHOOP!
KICK

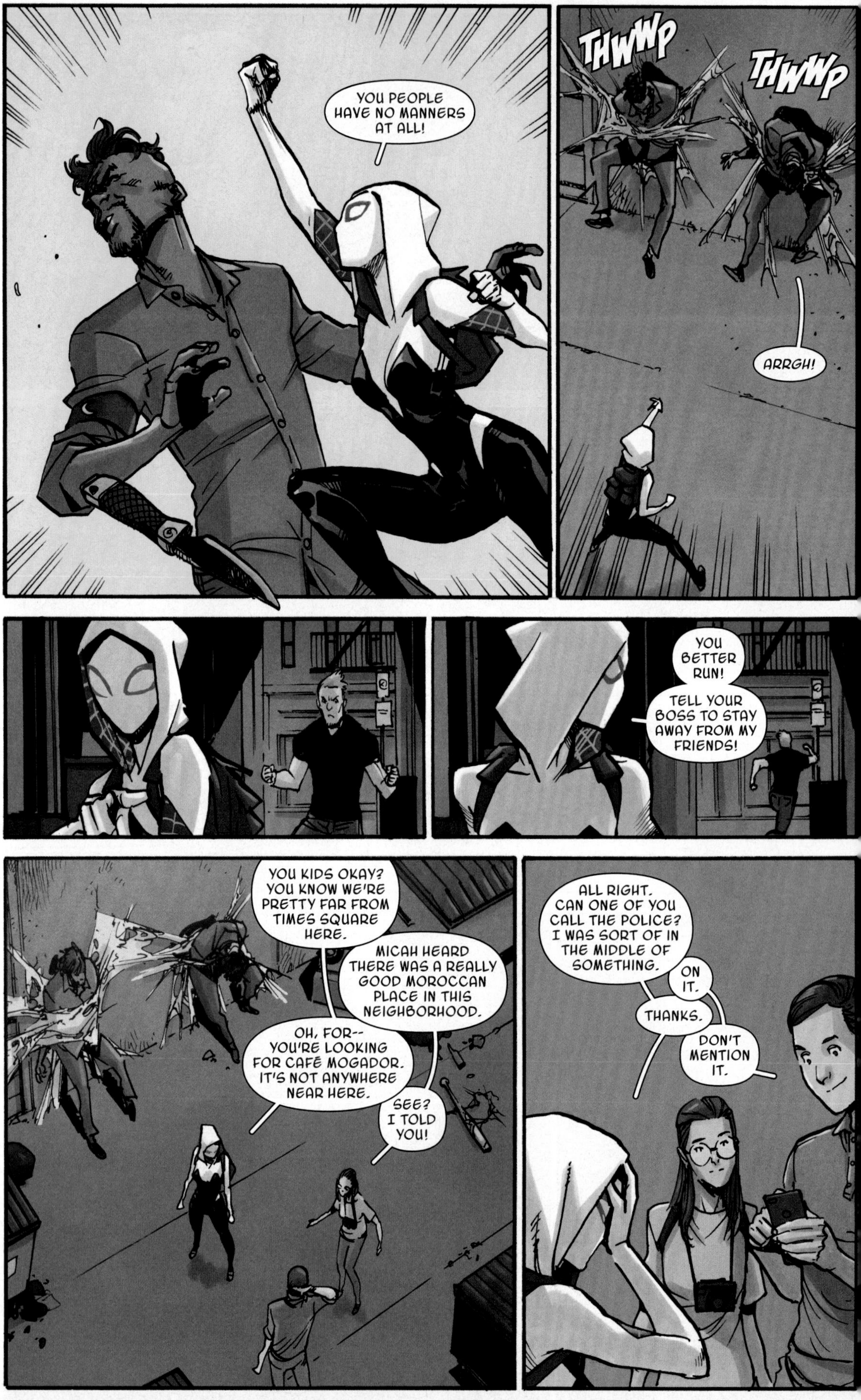
YOU PEOPLE HAVE NO MANNERS AT ALL!
THWWP
THWWP
ARRGH!
YOU BETTER RUN!
TELL YOUR BOSS TO STAY AWAY FROM MY FRIENDS!
YOU KIDS OKAY? YOU KNOW WE'RE PRETTY FAR FROM TIMES SQUARE HERE.
MICAH HEARD THERE WAS A REALLY GOOD MOROCCAN PLACE IN THIS NEIGHBORHOOD.
OH, FOR-- YOU'RE LOOKING FOR CAFÉ MOGADOR. IT'S NOT ANYWHERE NEAR HERE.
SEE? I TOLD YOU!
ALL RIGHT. CAN ONE OF YOU CALL THE POLICE? I WAS SORT OF IN THE MIDDLE OF SOMETHING.
ON IT.
THANKS.
DON'T MENTION IT.

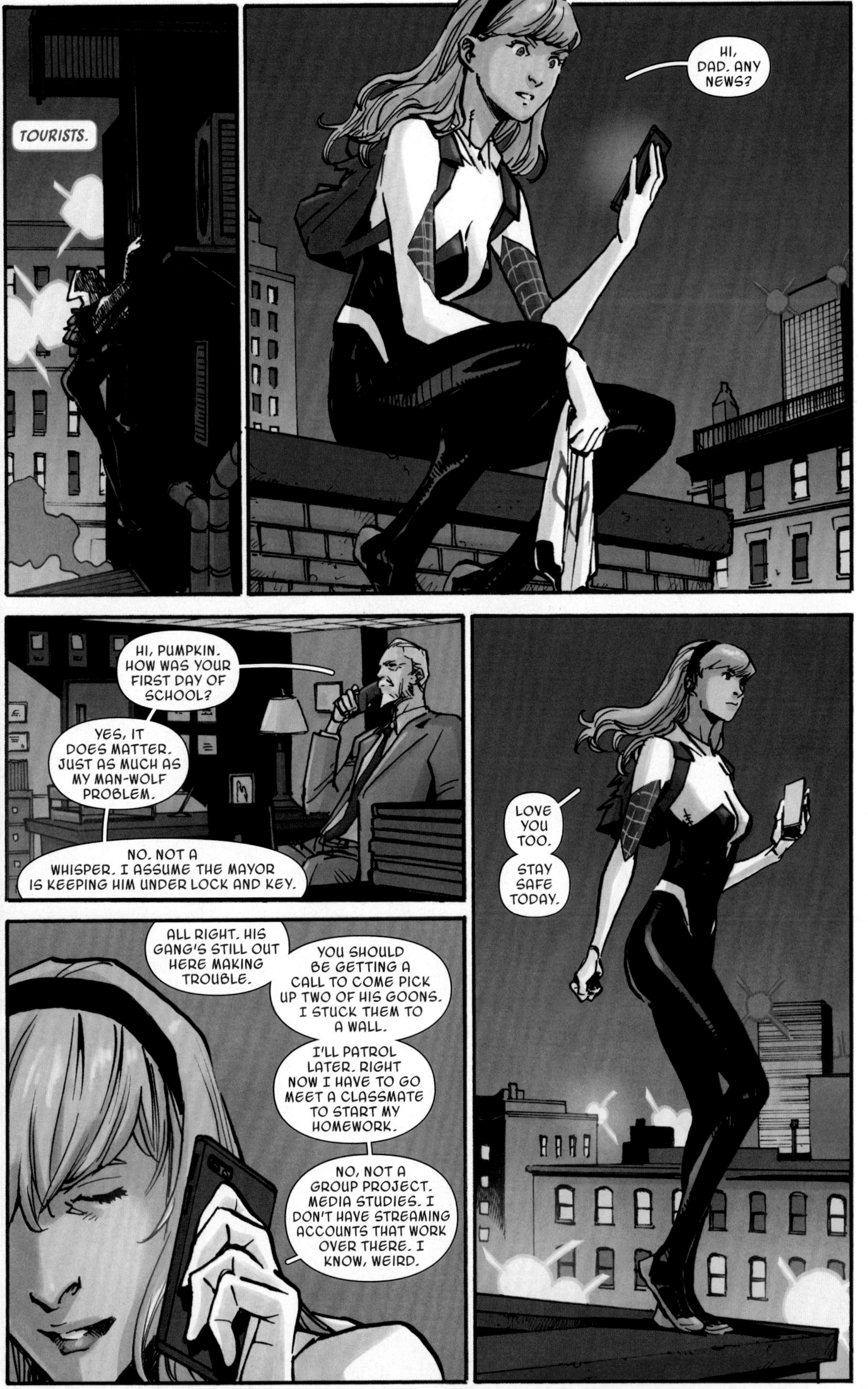
TOURISTS.
HI, DAD. ANY NEWS?
HI, PUMPKIN. HOW WAS YOUR FIRST DAY OF SCHOOL?
YES, IT DOES MATTER. JUST AS MUCH AS MY MAN-WOLF PROBLEM.
NO. NOT A WHISPER. I ASSUME THE MAYOR IS KEEPING HIM UNDER LOCK AND KEY.
ALL RIGHT. HIS GANG'S STILL OUT HERE MAKING TROUBLE.
YOU SHOULD BE GETTING A CALL TO COME PICK UP TWO OF HIS GOONS. I STUCK THEM TO A WALL.
I'LL PATROL LATER. RIGHT NOW I HAVE TO GO MEET A CLASSMATE TO START MY HOMEWORK.
NO, NOT A GROUP PROJECT. MEDIA STUDIES. I DON'T HAVE STREAMING ACCOUNTS THAT WORK OVER THERE. I KNOW, WEIRD.
LOVE YOU TOO.
STAY SAFE TODAY.

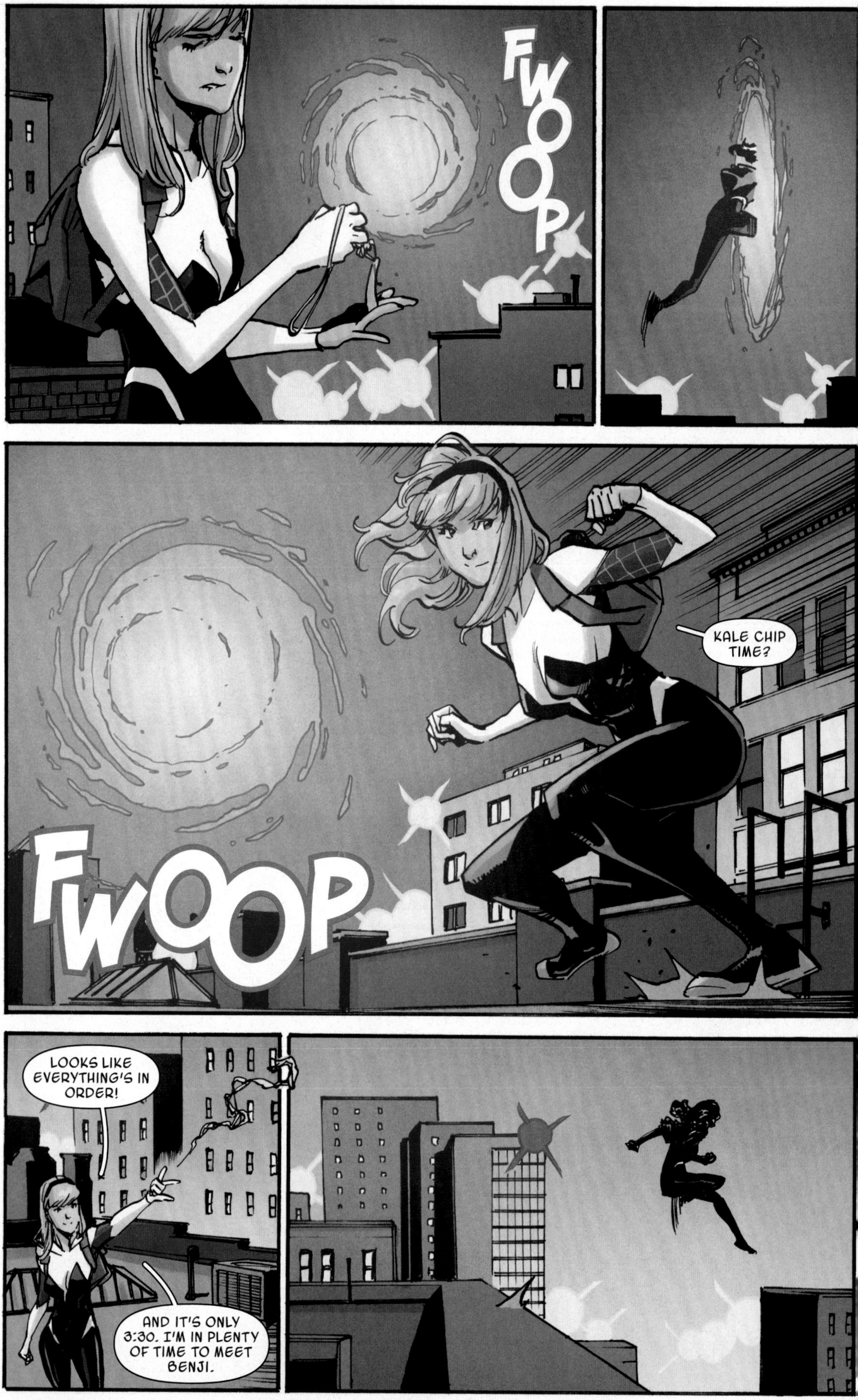
FWOOP
FWOOP
KALE CHIP TIME?
LOOKS LIKE EVERYTHING'S IN ORDER!
AND IT'S ONLY 3:30. I'M IN PLENTY OF TIME TO MEET BENJI.

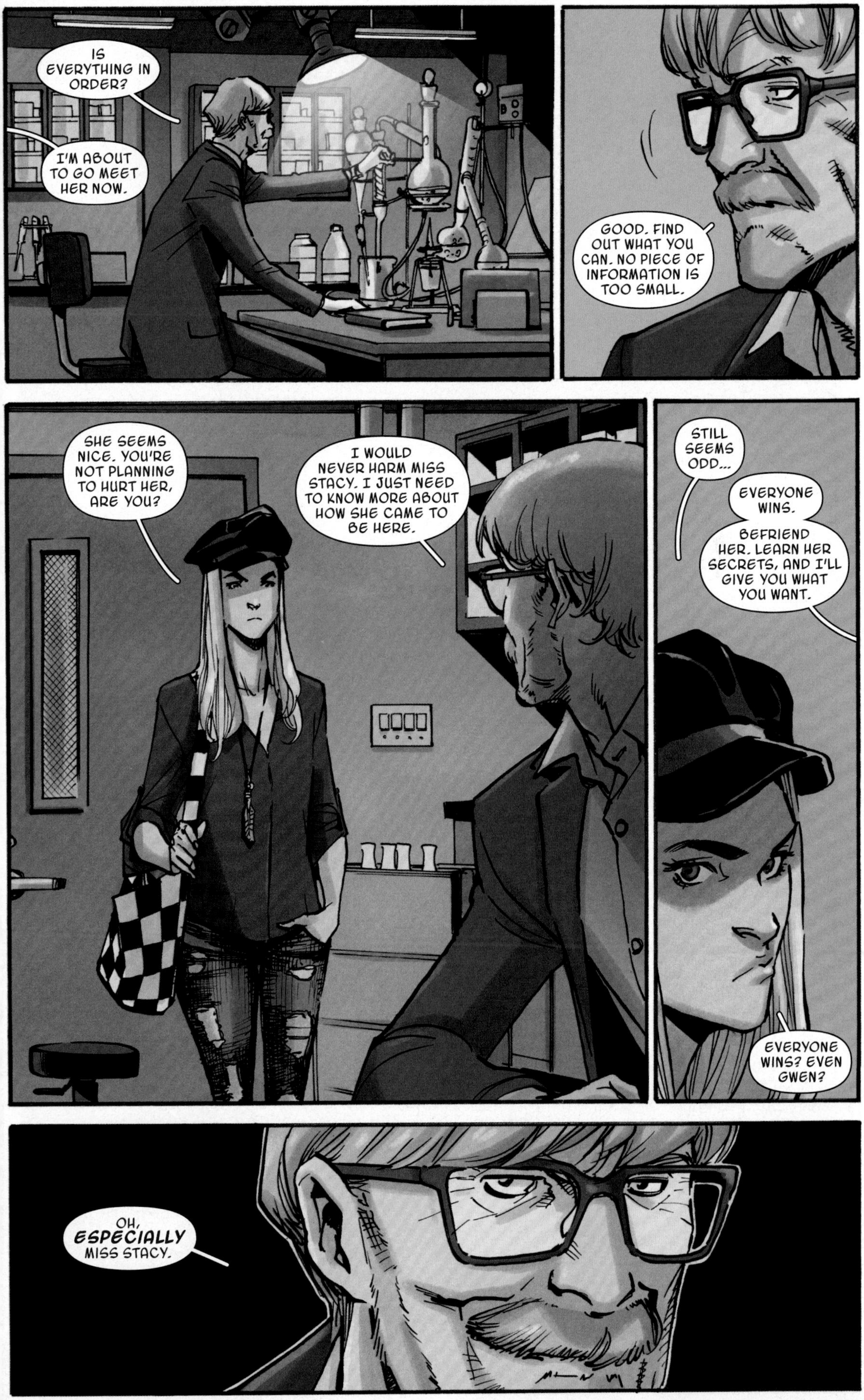
IS EVERYTHING IN ORDER?
I'M ABOUT TO GO MEET HER NOW.
GOOD. FIND OUT WHAT YOU CAN. NO PIECE OF INFORMATION IS TOO SMALL.
SHE SEEMS NICE. YOU'RE NOT PLANNING TO HURT HER, ARE YOU?
I WOULD NEVER HARM MISS STACY. I JUST NEED TO KNOW MORE ABOUT HOW SHE CAME TO BE HERE.
STILL SEEMS ODD...
EVERYONE WINS.
BEFRIEND HER. LEARN HER SECRETS, AND I'LL GIVE YOU WHAT YOU WANT.
EVERYONE WINS? EVEN GWEN?
OH, *ESPECIALLY* MISS STACY.

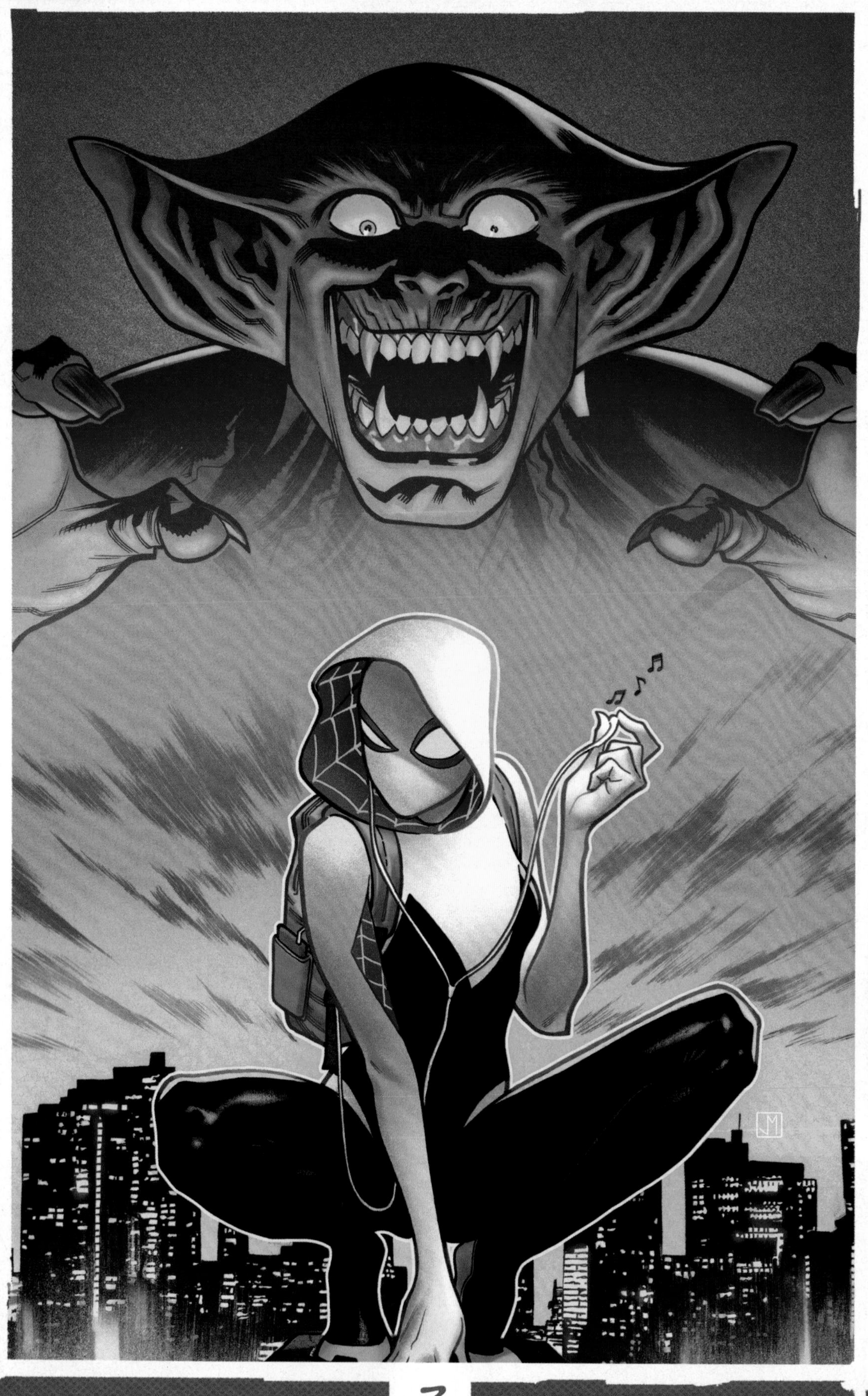

3

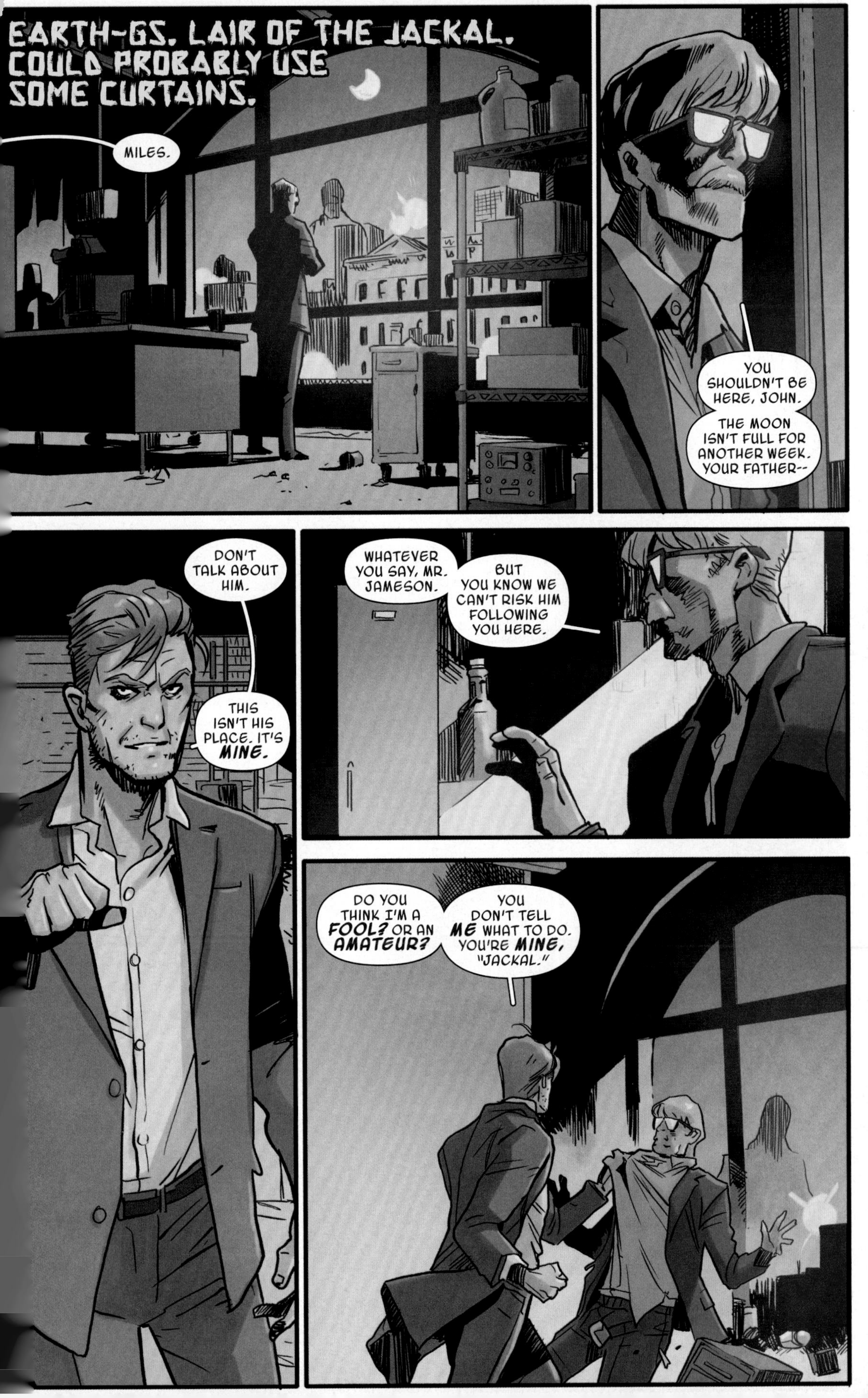
EARTH-65. LAIR OF THE JACKAL. COULD PROBABLY USE SOME CURTAINS.
MILES.
YOU SHOULDN'T BE HERE, JOHN.
THE MOON ISN'T FULL FOR ANOTHER WEEK. YOUR FATHER--
DON'T TALK ABOUT HIM.
THIS ISN'T HIS PLACE. IT'S MINE.
WHATEVER YOU SAY, MR. JAMESON.
BUT YOU KNOW WE CAN'T RISK HIM FOLLOWING YOU HERE.
DO YOU THINK I'M A FOOL? OR AN AMATEUR?
YOU DON'T TELL ME WHAT TO DO. YOU'RE MINE, "JACKAL."

YOU'RE MORE FRIGHTENING WHEN YOU'RE **BIGGER** THAN ME.

WHY YOU LITTLE--

THE MOON IS WAXING! SOON, THIS CITY WILL ONCE MORE KNOW THE WRATH OF THE **MAN-WOLF!**

WELL, PERHAPS THE MAN-WOLF'S WRATH COULD RESIST THE URGE TO **BLOW UP** ANYTHING ELSE?

GHOST-SPIDER WOULDN'T HAVE FELT THE NEED TO GET INVOLVED IF YOU HADN'T DONE THAT.

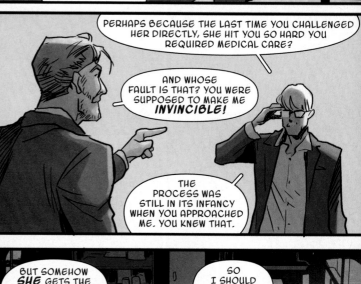

PERHAPS BECAUSE THE LAST TIME YOU CHALLENGED HER DIRECTLY, SHE HIT YOU SO HARD YOU REQUIRED MEDICAL CARE?

AND WHOSE FAULT IS THAT? YOU WERE SUPPOSED TO MAKE ME **INVINCIBLE!**

THE PROCESS WAS STILL IN ITS INFANCY WHEN YOU APPROACHED ME. YOU KNEW THAT.

WEREN'T YOU **LISTENING**, WARREN? THIS IS **MY** CITY. NOT MY FATHER'S, AND NOT **HERS.**

WHY SHOULD I CONSTRAIN MYSELF ON HER BEHALF?

BUT SOMEHOW **SHE** GETS THE POWERS THAT WORK ALL MONTH LONG.

GHOST-SPIDER ISN'T MY WORK. YOU KNOW THAT.

SO I SHOULD HAVE GONE TO ANOTHER MAD SCIENTIST?

NO. NO, THAT WOULDN'T HAVE WORKED EITHER--

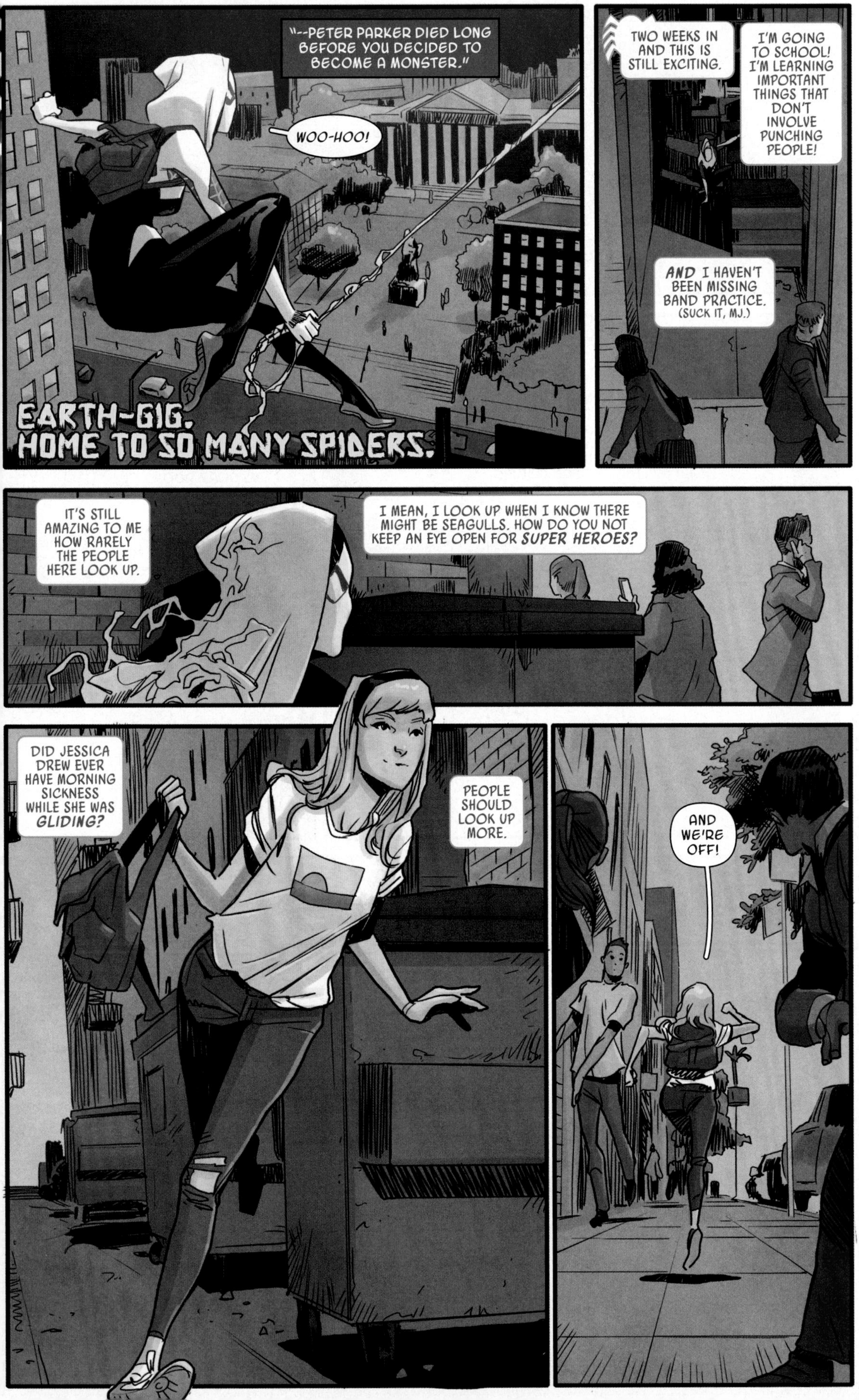
"--PETER PARKER DIED LONG BEFORE YOU DECIDED TO BECOME A MONSTER."
WOO-HOO!
EARTH-65. HOME TO SO MANY SPIDERS.
TWO WEEKS IN AND THIS IS STILL EXCITING.
I'M GOING TO SCHOOL! I'M LEARNING IMPORTANT THINGS THAT DON'T INVOLVE PUNCHING PEOPLE!
AND I HAVEN'T BEEN MISSING BAND PRACTICE. (SUCK IT, MJ.)
IT'S STILL AMAZING TO ME HOW RARELY THE PEOPLE HERE LOOK UP.
I MEAN, I LOOK UP WHEN I KNOW THERE MIGHT BE SEAGULLS. HOW DO YOU NOT KEEP AN EYE OPEN FOR SUPER HEROES?
DID JESSICA DREW EVER HAVE MORNING SICKNESS WHILE SHE WAS GLIDING?
PEOPLE SHOULD LOOK UP MORE.
AND WE'RE OFF!

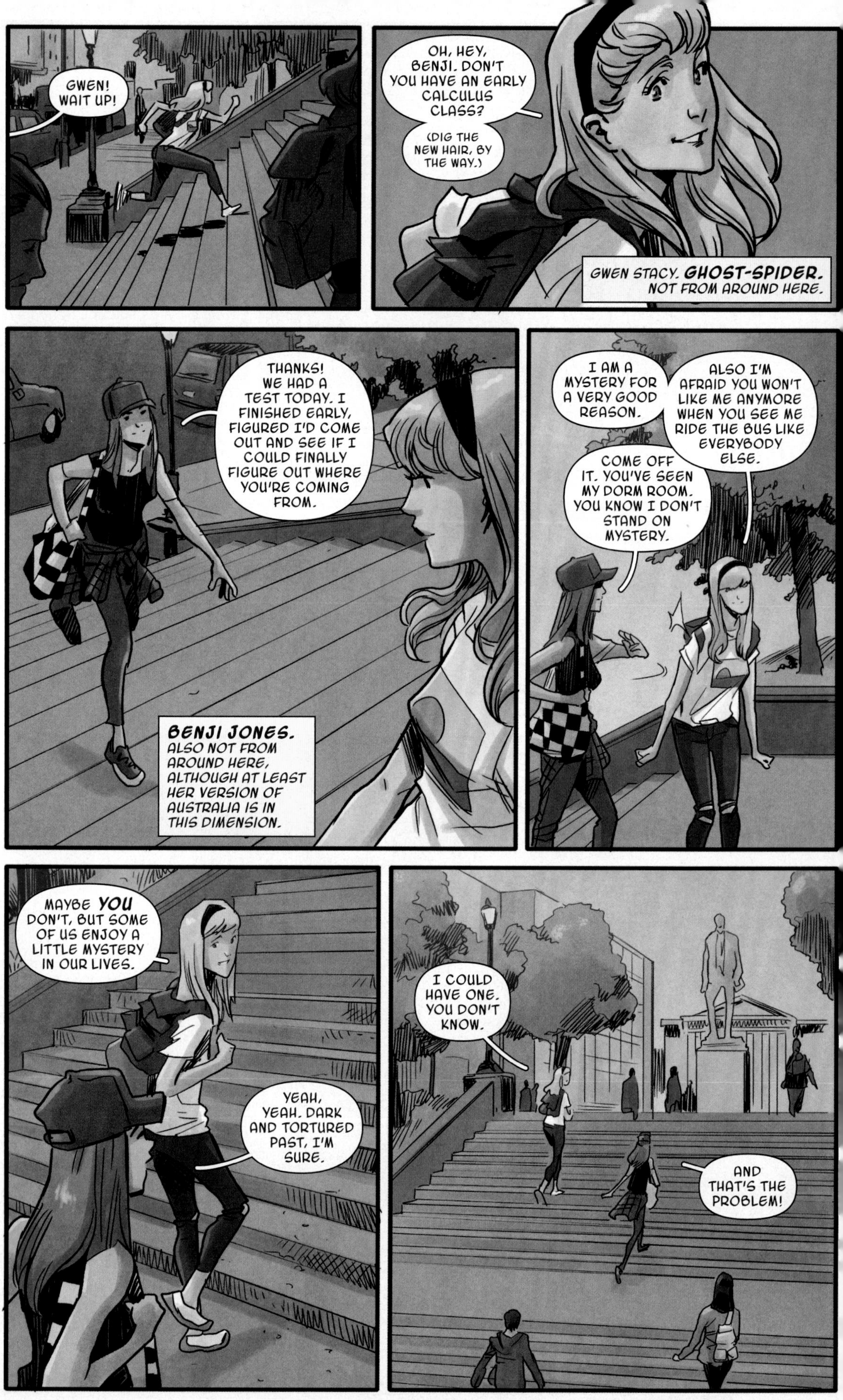
GWEN! WAIT UP!
OH, HEY, BENJI. DON'T YOU HAVE AN EARLY CALCULUS CLASS?
(DIG THE NEW HAIR, BY THE WAY.)
GWEN STACY. GHOST-SPIDER. NOT FROM AROUND HERE.
THANKS! WE HAD A TEST TODAY. I FINISHED EARLY, FIGURED I'D COME OUT AND SEE IF I COULD FINALLY FIGURE OUT WHERE YOU'RE COMING FROM.
BENJI JONES. ALSO NOT FROM AROUND HERE, ALTHOUGH AT LEAST HER VERSION OF AUSTRALIA IS IN THIS DIMENSION.
I AM A MYSTERY FOR A VERY GOOD REASON.
ALSO I'M AFRAID YOU WON'T LIKE ME ANYMORE WHEN YOU SEE ME RIDE THE BUS LIKE EVERYBODY ELSE.
COME OFF IT. YOU'VE SEEN MY DORM ROOM. YOU KNOW I DON'T STAND ON MYSTERY.
MAYBE YOU DON'T, BUT SOME OF US ENJOY A LITTLE MYSTERY IN OUR LIVES.
YEAH, YEAH. DARK AND TORTURED PAST, I'M SURE.
I COULD HAVE ONE. YOU DON'T KNOW.
AND THAT'S THE PROBLEM!

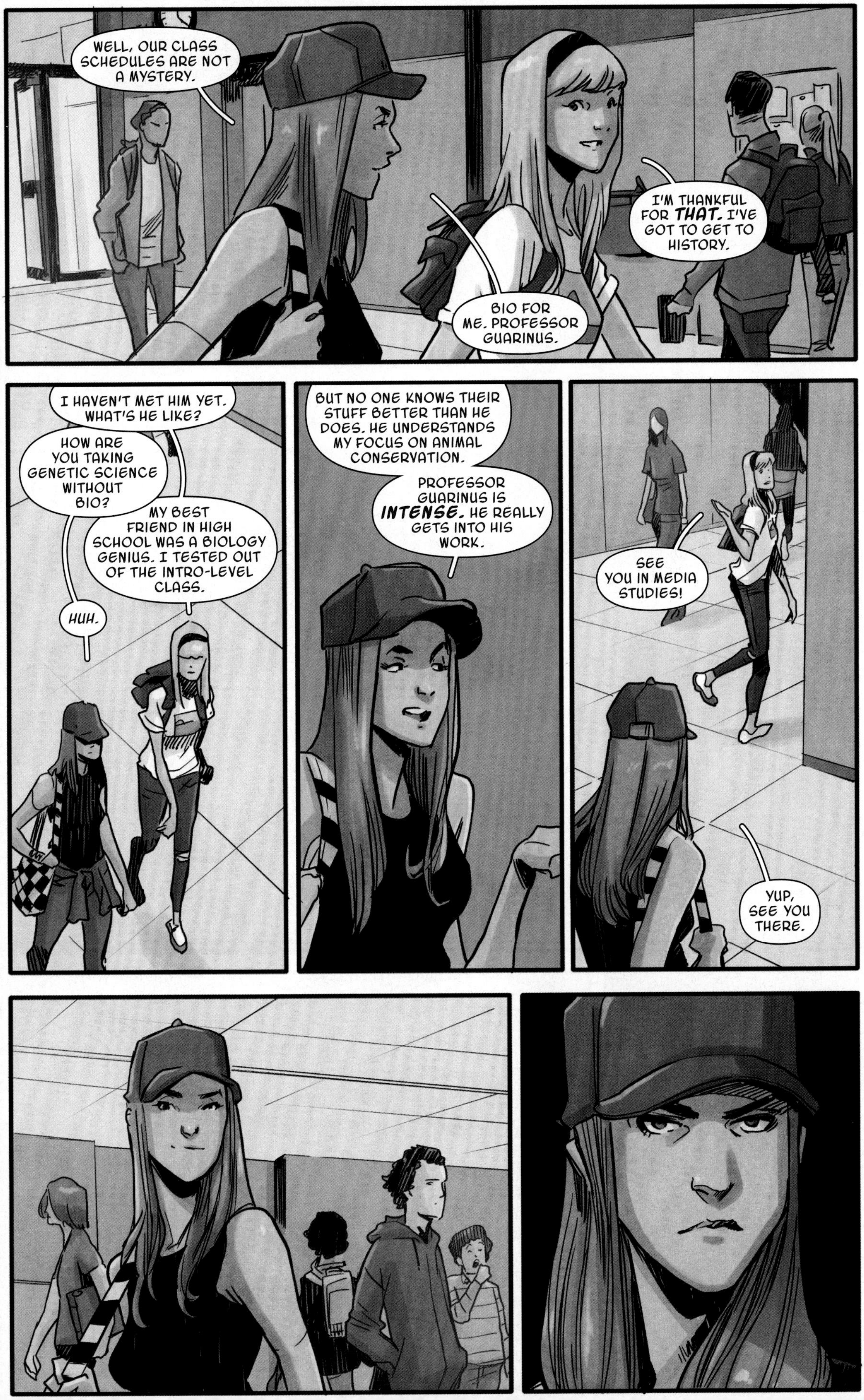
WELL, OUR CLASS SCHEDULES ARE NOT A MYSTERY.
I'M THANKFUL FOR THAT. I'VE GOT TO GET TO HISTORY.
BIO FOR ME. PROFESSOR GUARINUS.
I HAVEN'T MET HIM YET. WHAT'S HE LIKE?
HOW ARE YOU TAKING GENETIC SCIENCE WITHOUT BIO?
MY BEST FRIEND IN HIGH SCHOOL WAS A BIOLOGY GENIUS. I TESTED OUT OF THE INTRO-LEVEL CLASS.
HUH.
BUT NO ONE KNOWS THEIR STUFF BETTER THAN HE DOES. HE UNDERSTANDS MY FOCUS ON ANIMAL CONSERVATION.
PROFESSOR GUARINUS IS INTENSE. HE REALLY GETS INTO HIS WORK.
SEE YOU IN MEDIA STUDIES!
YUP, SEE YOU THERE.

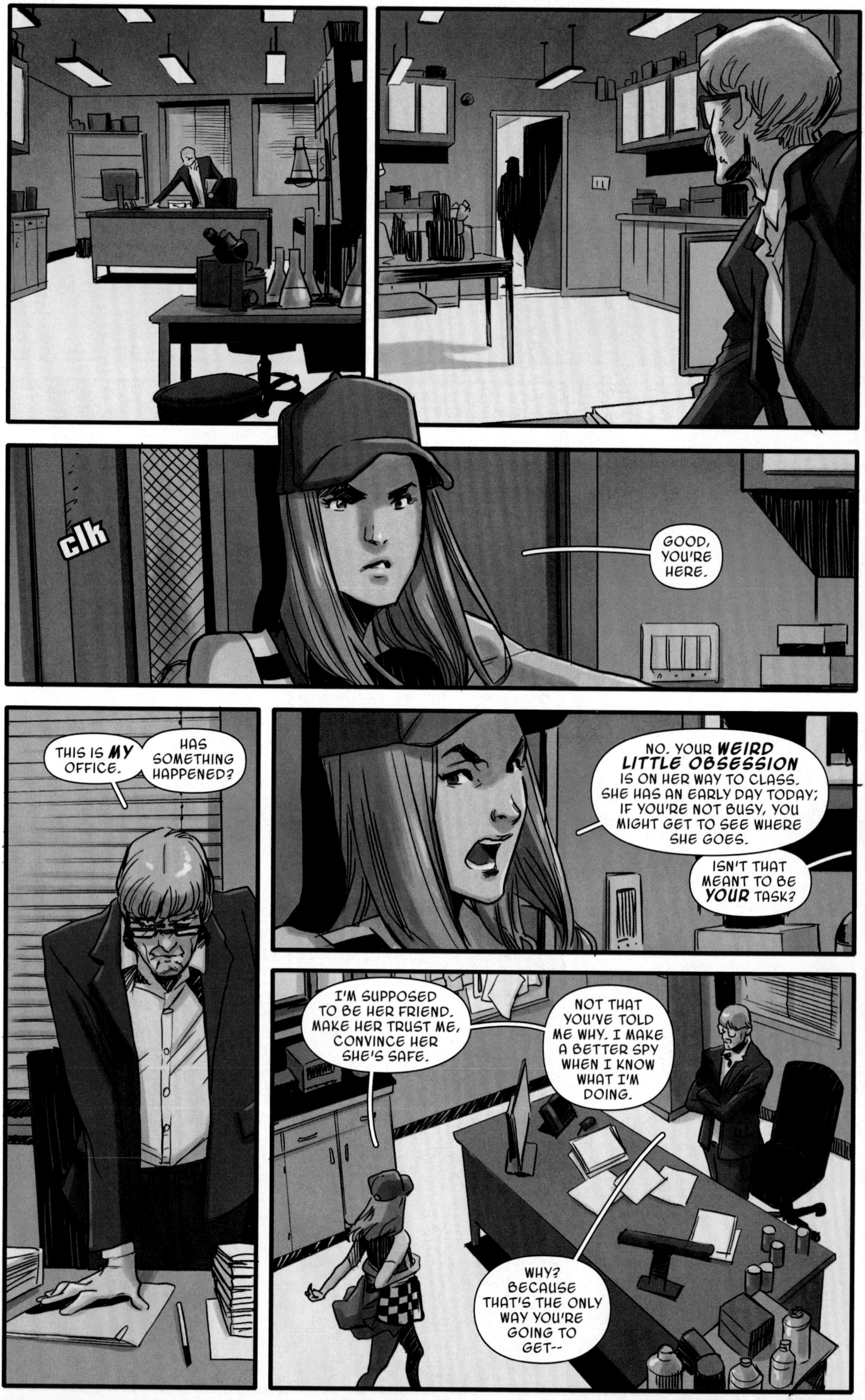
clk
GOOD, YOU'RE HERE.
THIS IS MY OFFICE.
HAS SOMETHING HAPPENED?
NO. YOUR WEIRD LITTLE OBSESSION IS ON HER WAY TO CLASS. SHE HAS AN EARLY DAY TODAY; IF YOU'RE NOT BUSY, YOU MIGHT GET TO SEE WHERE SHE GOES.
ISN'T THAT MEANT TO BE YOUR TASK?
I'M SUPPOSED TO BE HER FRIEND. MAKE HER TRUST ME, CONVINCE HER SHE'S SAFE.
NOT THAT YOU'VE TOLD ME WHY. I MAKE A BETTER SPY WHEN I KNOW WHAT I'M DOING.
WHY? BECAUSE THAT'S THE ONLY WAY YOU'RE GOING TO GET--

--THIS!

IT'S READY? IT'S REALLY READY?

YOU KNOW MY CAPABILITIES. IT WAS ONLY EVER A MATTER OF TIME.

GIVE IT--GIVE IT TO ME!

WHY SHOULD I? YOU HAVEN'T UPHELD YOUR PART OF THE BARGAIN.

I WAS IMPRESSED WITH YOU IN THE BEGINNING, MISS JONES. YOU SUSSED OUT MY TRUE IDENTITY. TRACKED ME DOWN LIKE A PROPER PREDATOR. YOU SEEMED TO GENUINELY WANT THIS.

BUT YOU'VE SINCE BEEN DISAPPOINTING ME. I ASKED YOU TO DO ONE SIMPLE THING...

I KNOW WHERE SHE GOES WHEN CLASS LETS OUT. IF YOU GIVE IT TO ME, I CAN FOLLOW HER. I CAN BRING HER BACK--

WITHOUT HARMING HER?

I WOULD NEVER.

I BELIEVE YOU MEAN THAT. I'M NOT SURE YOU FULLY GRASP WHAT YOU'RE ASKING FOR.

I KNEW WHO YOU WERE WHEN I CAME TO FIND YOU. I KNOW EXACTLY WHAT I WANT.

VERY WELL, THEN. ONE TIME TO PROVE YOURSELF. WE'LL DISCUSS PERMANENCE LATER.

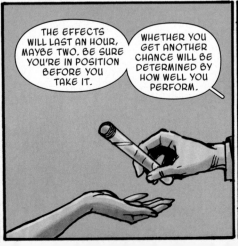

THE EFFECTS WILL LAST AN HOUR, MAYBE TWO. BE SURE YOU'RE IN POSITION BEFORE YOU TAKE IT.

WHETHER YOU GET ANOTHER CHANCE WILL BE DETERMINED BY HOW WELL YOU PERFORM.

I WON'T LET YOU DOWN. YOU KNOW I WON'T.

YOU SHOULD CERTAINLY HOPE NOT. FAILURE HAS CONSEQUENCES.

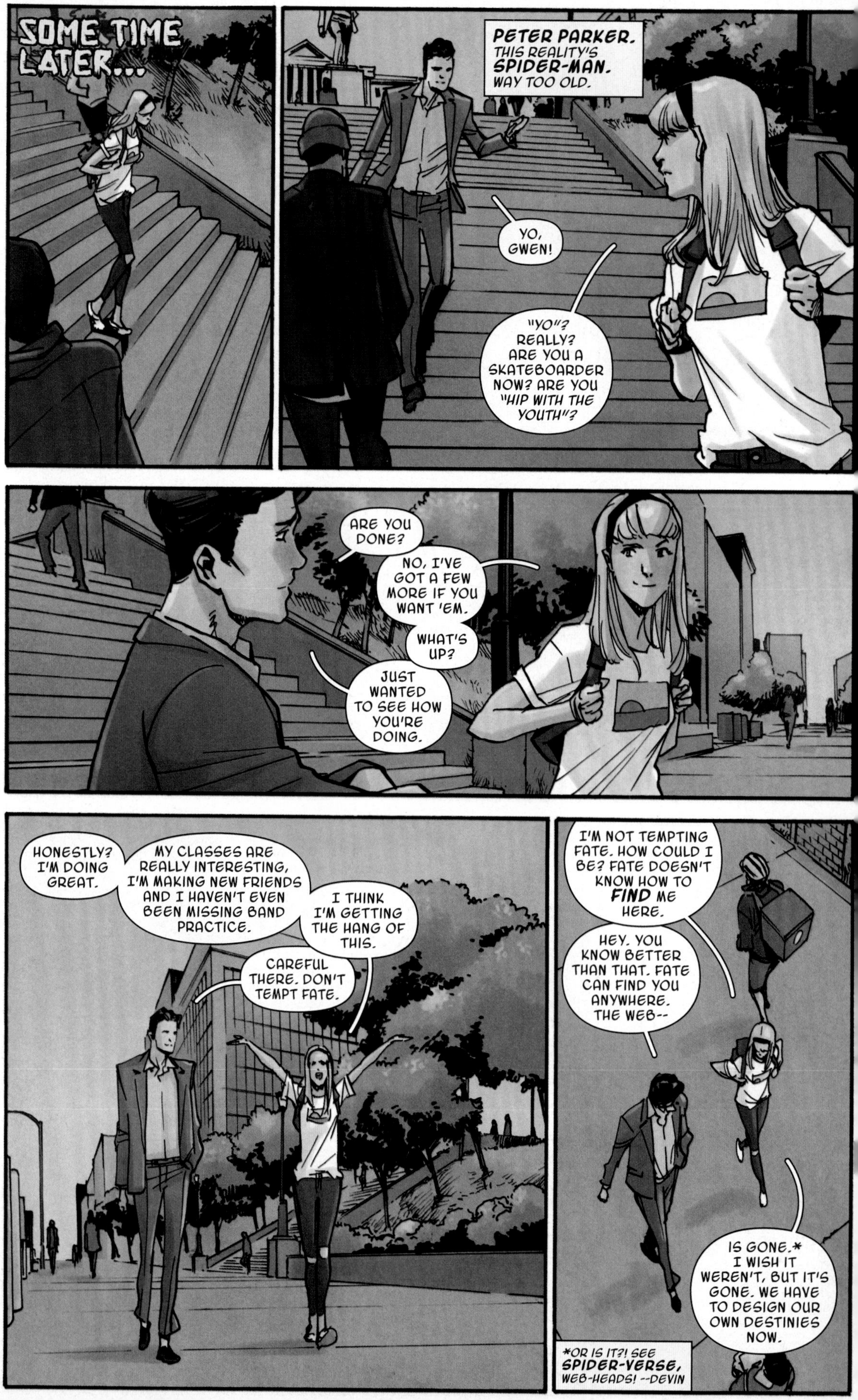
SOME TIME LATER...
PETER PARKER. THIS REALITY'S SPIDER-MAN. WAY TOO OLD.
YO, GWEN!
"YO"? REALLY? ARE YOU A SKATEBOARDER NOW? ARE YOU "HIP WITH THE YOUTH"?
ARE YOU DONE?
NO, I'VE GOT A FEW MORE IF YOU WANT 'EM.
WHAT'S UP?
JUST WANTED TO SEE HOW YOU'RE DOING.
HONESTLY? I'M DOING GREAT.
MY CLASSES ARE REALLY INTERESTING, I'M MAKING NEW FRIENDS AND I HAVEN'T EVEN BEEN MISSING BAND PRACTICE.
I THINK I'M GETTING THE HANG OF THIS.
CAREFUL THERE. DON'T TEMPT FATE.
I'M NOT TEMPTING FATE. HOW COULD I BE? FATE DOESN'T KNOW HOW TO FIND ME HERE.
HEY. YOU KNOW BETTER THAN THAT. FATE CAN FIND YOU ANYWHERE. THE WEB--
IS GONE.* I WISH IT WEREN'T, BUT IT'S GONE. WE HAVE TO DESIGN OUR OWN DESTINIES NOW.
*OR IS IT?! SEE SPIDER-VERSE, WEB-HEADS! --DEVIN

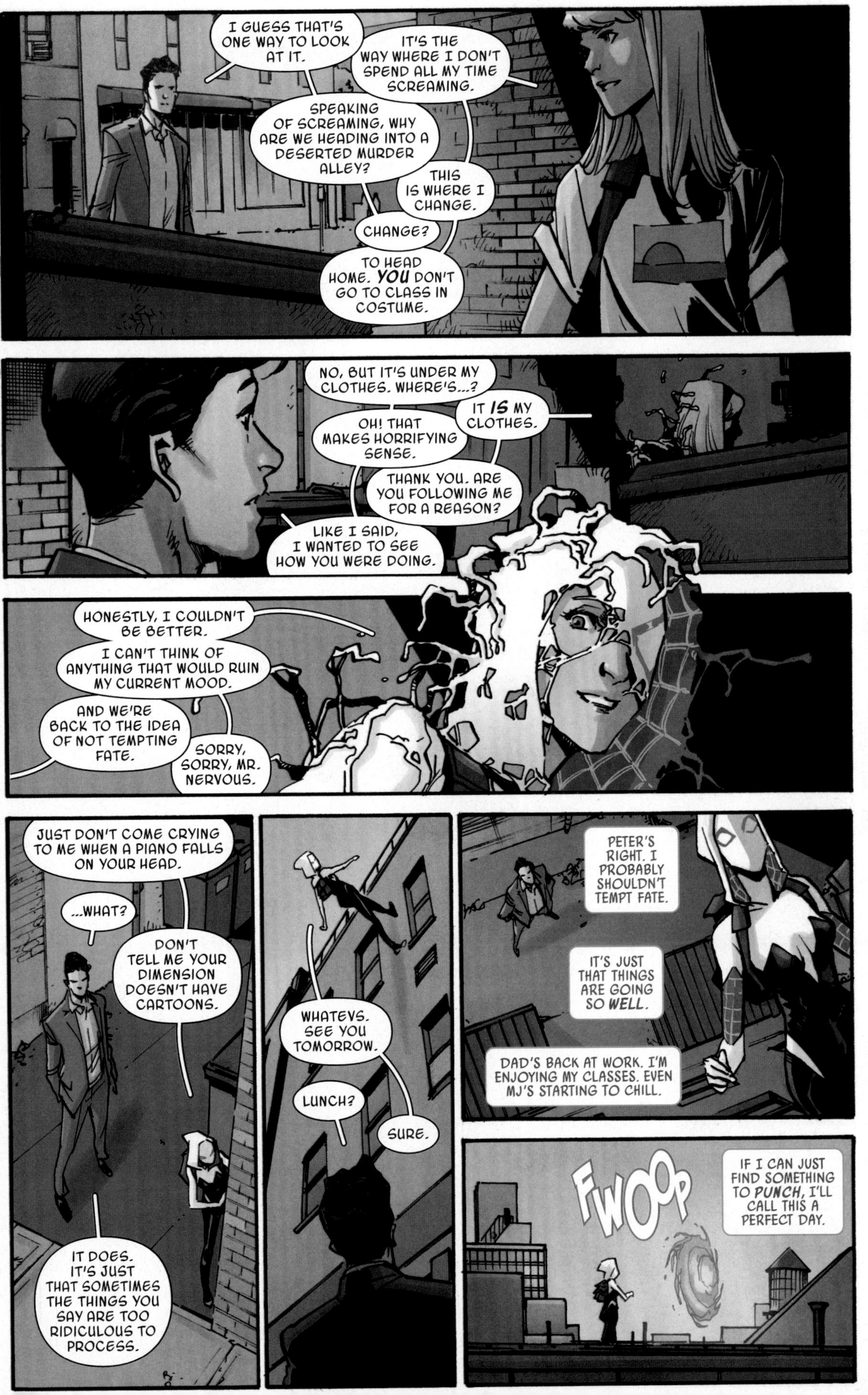
I GUESS THAT'S ONE WAY TO LOOK AT IT.
IT'S THE WAY WHERE I DON'T SPEND ALL MY TIME SCREAMING.
SPEAKING OF SCREAMING, WHY ARE WE HEADING INTO A DESERTED MURDER ALLEY?
THIS IS WHERE I CHANGE.
CHANGE?
TO HEAD HOME. YOU DON'T GO TO CLASS IN COSTUME.
NO, BUT IT'S UNDER MY CLOTHES. WHERE'S...?
IT IS MY CLOTHES.
OH! THAT MAKES HORRIFYING SENSE.
THANK YOU. ARE YOU FOLLOWING ME FOR A REASON?
LIKE I SAID, I WANTED TO SEE HOW YOU WERE DOING.
HONESTLY, I COULDN'T BE BETTER.
I CAN'T THINK OF ANYTHING THAT WOULD RUIN MY CURRENT MOOD.
AND WE'RE BACK TO THE IDEA OF NOT TEMPTING FATE.
SORRY, SORRY, MR. NERVOUS.
JUST DON'T COME CRYING TO ME WHEN A PIANO FALLS ON YOUR HEAD.
...WHAT?
DON'T TELL ME YOUR DIMENSION DOESN'T HAVE CARTOONS.
IT DOES. IT'S JUST THAT SOMETIMES THE THINGS YOU SAY ARE TOO RIDICULOUS TO PROCESS.
WHATEVS. SEE YOU TOMORROW.
LUNCH?
SURE.
PETER'S RIGHT. I PROBABLY SHOULDN'T TEMPT FATE.
IT'S JUST THAT THINGS ARE GOING SO WELL.
DAD'S BACK AT WORK. I'M ENJOYING MY CLASSES. EVEN MJ'S STARTING TO CHILL.
FWOOP
IF I CAN JUST FIND SOMETHING TO PUNCH, I'LL CALL THIS A PERFECT DAY.

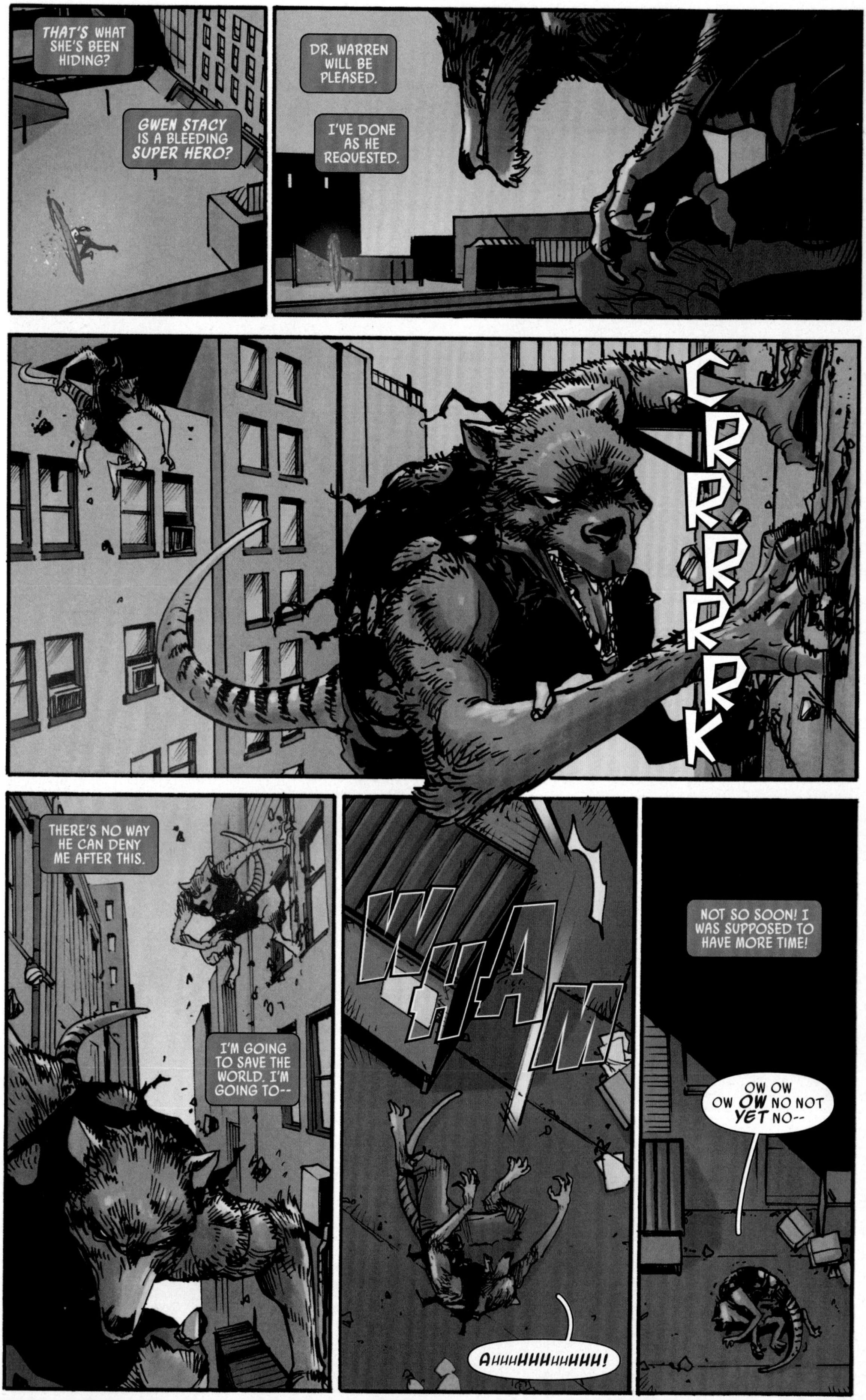

THAT'S WHAT SHE'S BEEN HIDING?
GWEN STACY IS A BLEEDING SUPER HERO?
DR. WARREN WILL BE PLEASED.
I'VE DONE AS HE REQUESTED.
CRRRRK
THERE'S NO WAY HE CAN DENY ME AFTER THIS.
I'M GOING TO SAVE THE WORLD. I'M GOING TO--
WHAM
AHHHHHHHHHHH!
NOT SO SOON! I WAS SUPPOSED TO HAVE MORE TIME!
OW OW OW OW NO NOT YET NO--

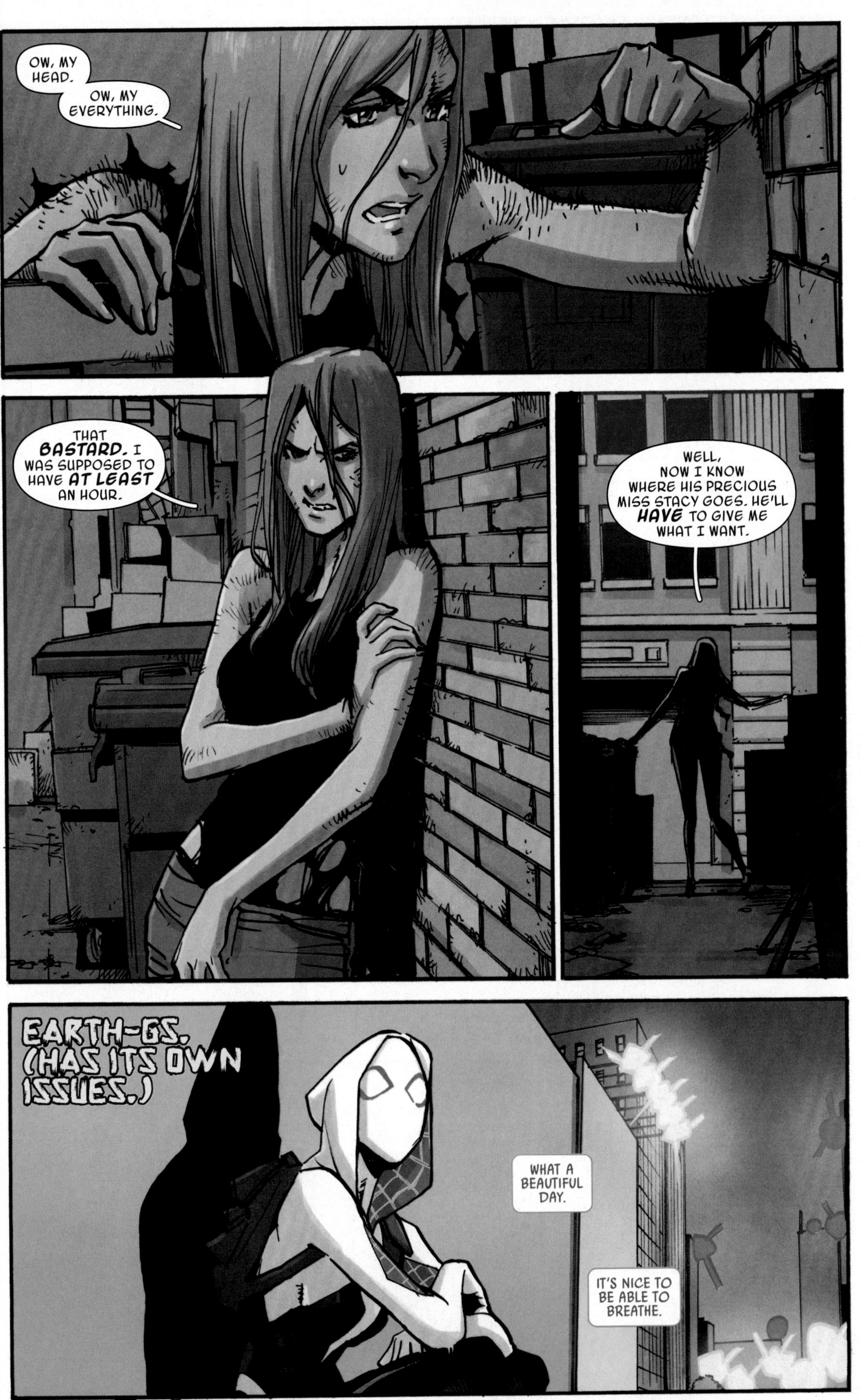
OW, MY HEAD.
OW, MY EVERYTHING.
THAT **BASTARD.** I WAS SUPPOSED TO HAVE **AT LEAST** AN HOUR.
WELL, NOW I KNOW WHERE HIS PRECIOUS MISS STACY GOES. HE'LL **HAVE** TO GIVE ME WHAT I WANT.
EARTH-65. (HAS ITS OWN ISSUES.)
WHAT A BEAUTIFUL DAY.
IT'S NICE TO BE ABLE TO BREATHE.

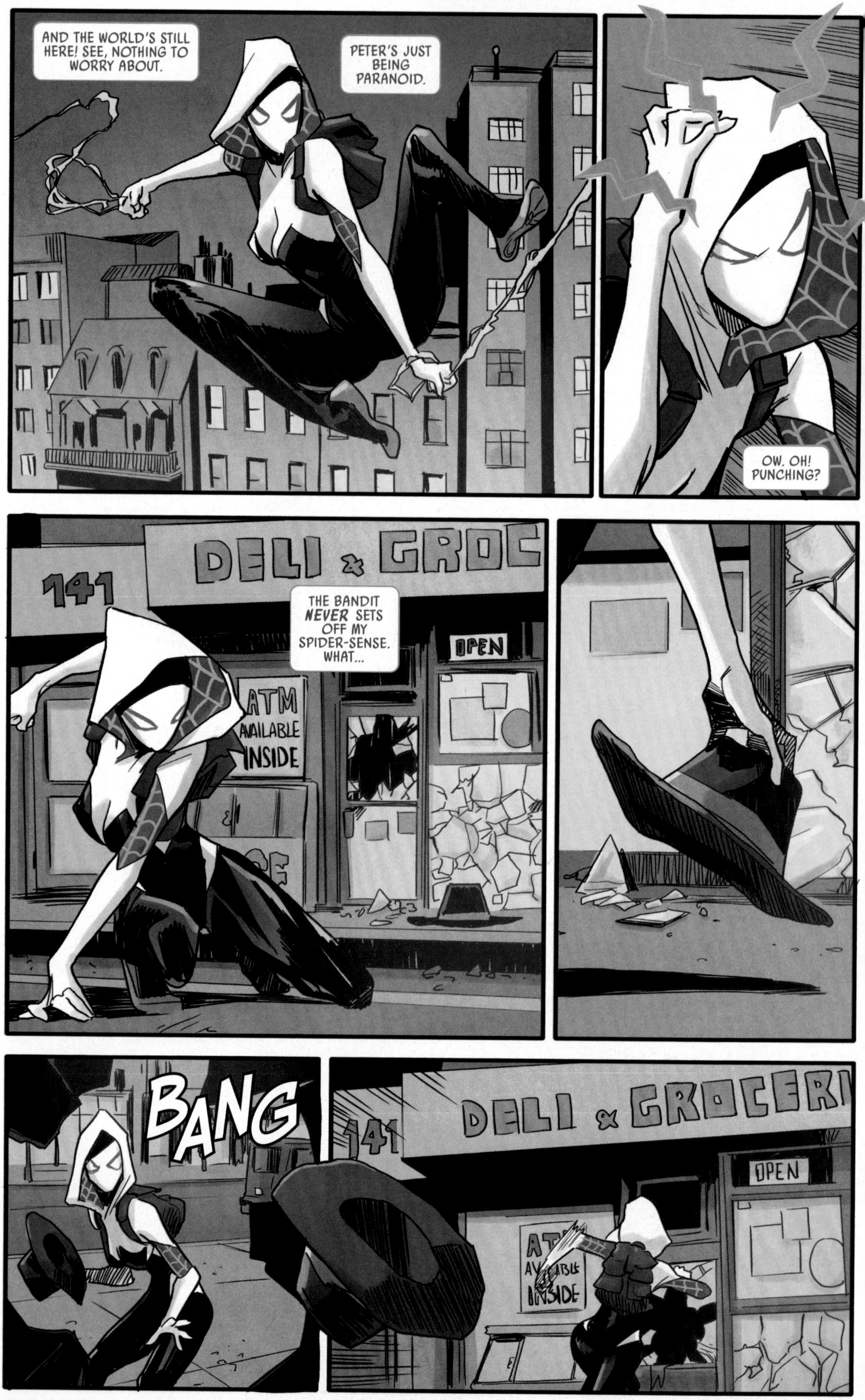
AND THE WORLD'S STILL HERE! SEE, NOTHING TO WORRY ABOUT.
PETER'S JUST BEING PARANOID.
OW. OH! PUNCHING?
DELI & GROC
141
THE BANDIT NEVER SETS OFF MY SPIDER-SENSE. WHAT...
ATM AVAILABLE INSIDE
OPEN
BANG
141
DELI & GROCERI
OPEN
ATM AVAILABLE INSIDE

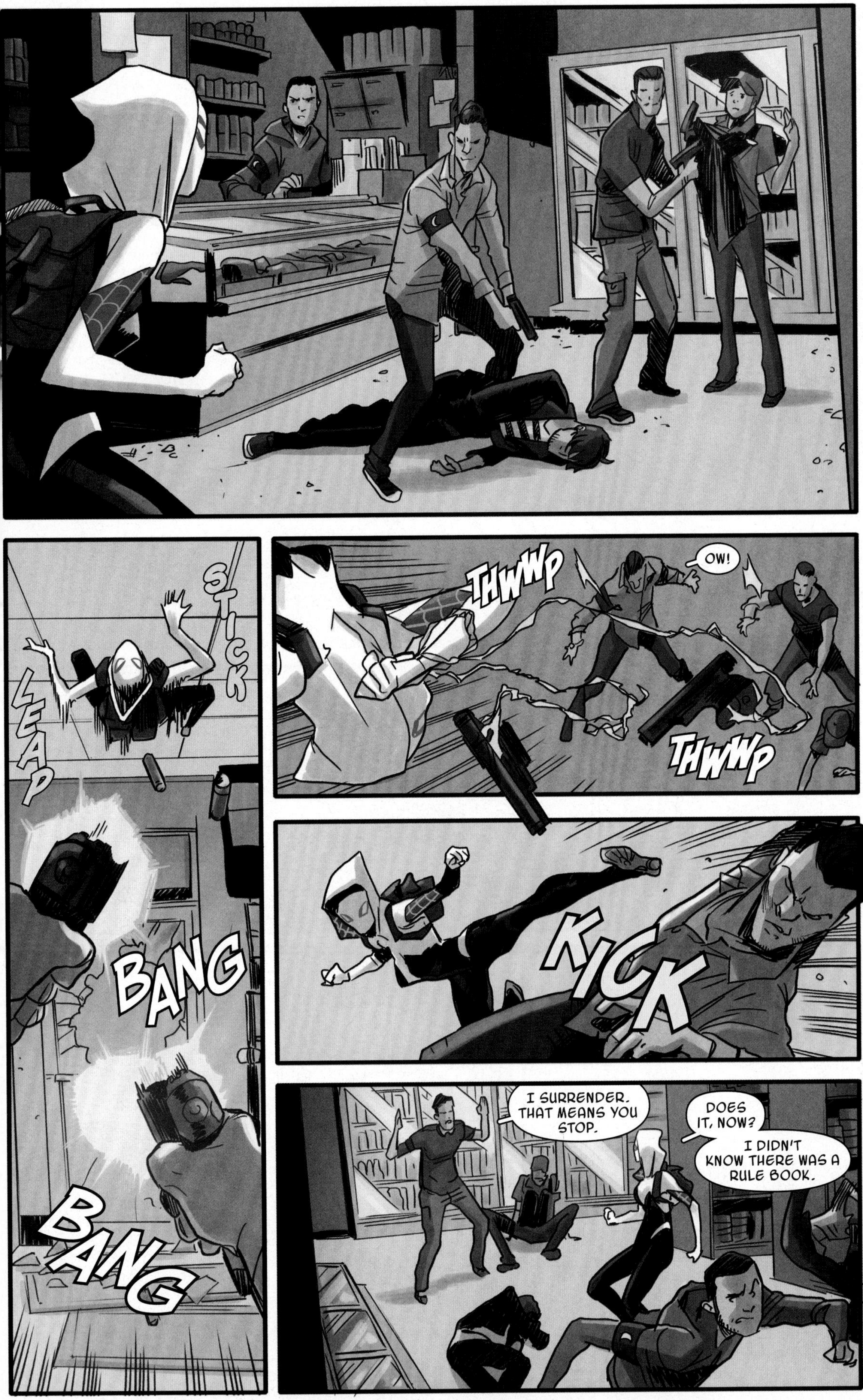

STICK
LEAP
BANG
BANG
THWWP
OW!
THWWP
KICK
I SURRENDER. THAT MEANS YOU STOP.
DOES IT, NOW?
I DIDN'T KNOW THERE WAS A RULE BOOK.

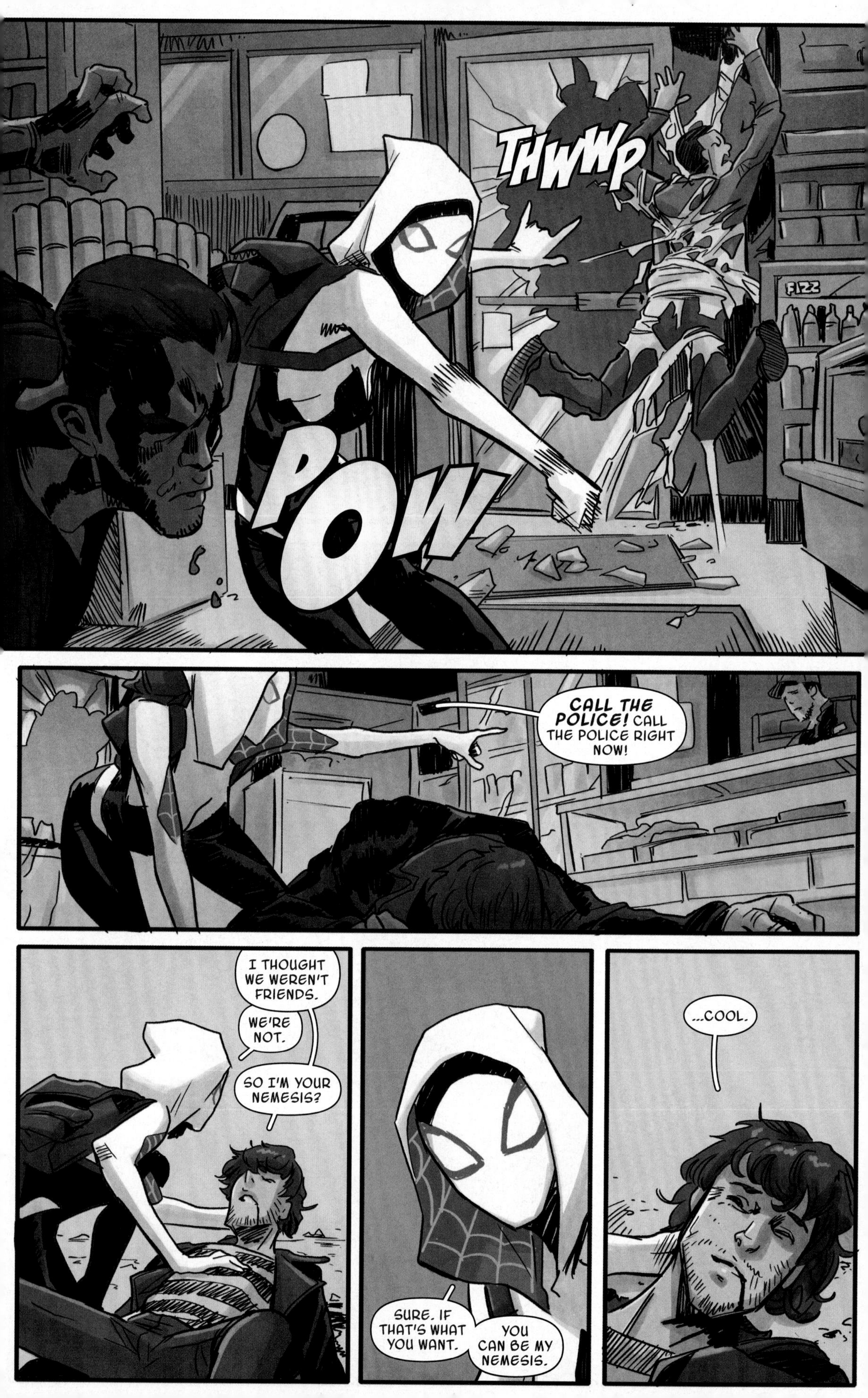
THWWP
POW
CALL THE POLICE! CALL THE POLICE RIGHT NOW!
I THOUGHT WE WEREN'T FRIENDS.
WE'RE NOT.
SO I'M YOUR NEMESIS?
SURE. IF THAT'S WHAT YOU WANT.
YOU CAN BE MY NEMESIS.
...COOL.

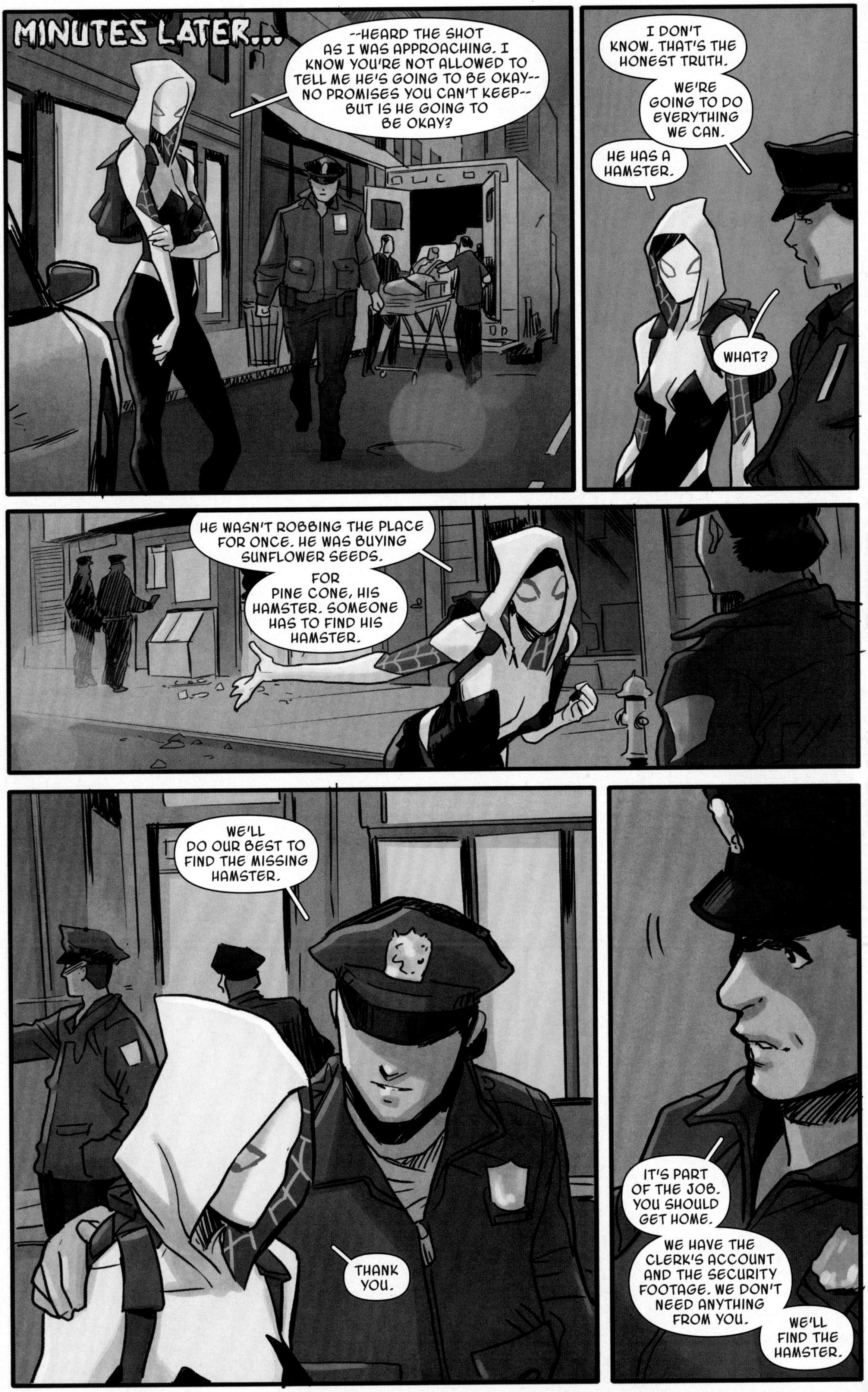
MINUTES LATER...
--HEARD THE SHOT AS I WAS APPROACHING. I KNOW YOU'RE NOT ALLOWED TO TELL ME HE'S GOING TO BE OKAY-- NO PROMISES YOU CAN'T KEEP-- BUT IS HE GOING TO BE OKAY?
I DON'T KNOW. THAT'S THE HONEST TRUTH.
WE'RE GOING TO DO EVERYTHING WE CAN.
HE HAS A HAMSTER.
WHAT?
HE WASN'T ROBBING THE PLACE FOR ONCE. HE WAS BUYING SUNFLOWER SEEDS.
FOR PINE CONE, HIS HAMSTER. SOMEONE HAS TO FIND HIS HAMSTER.
WE'LL DO OUR BEST TO FIND THE MISSING HAMSTER.
THANK YOU.
IT'S PART OF THE JOB. YOU SHOULD GET HOME.
WE HAVE THE CLERK'S ACCOUNT AND THE SECURITY FOOTAGE. WE DON'T NEED ANYTHING FROM YOU.
WE'LL FIND THE HAMSTER.

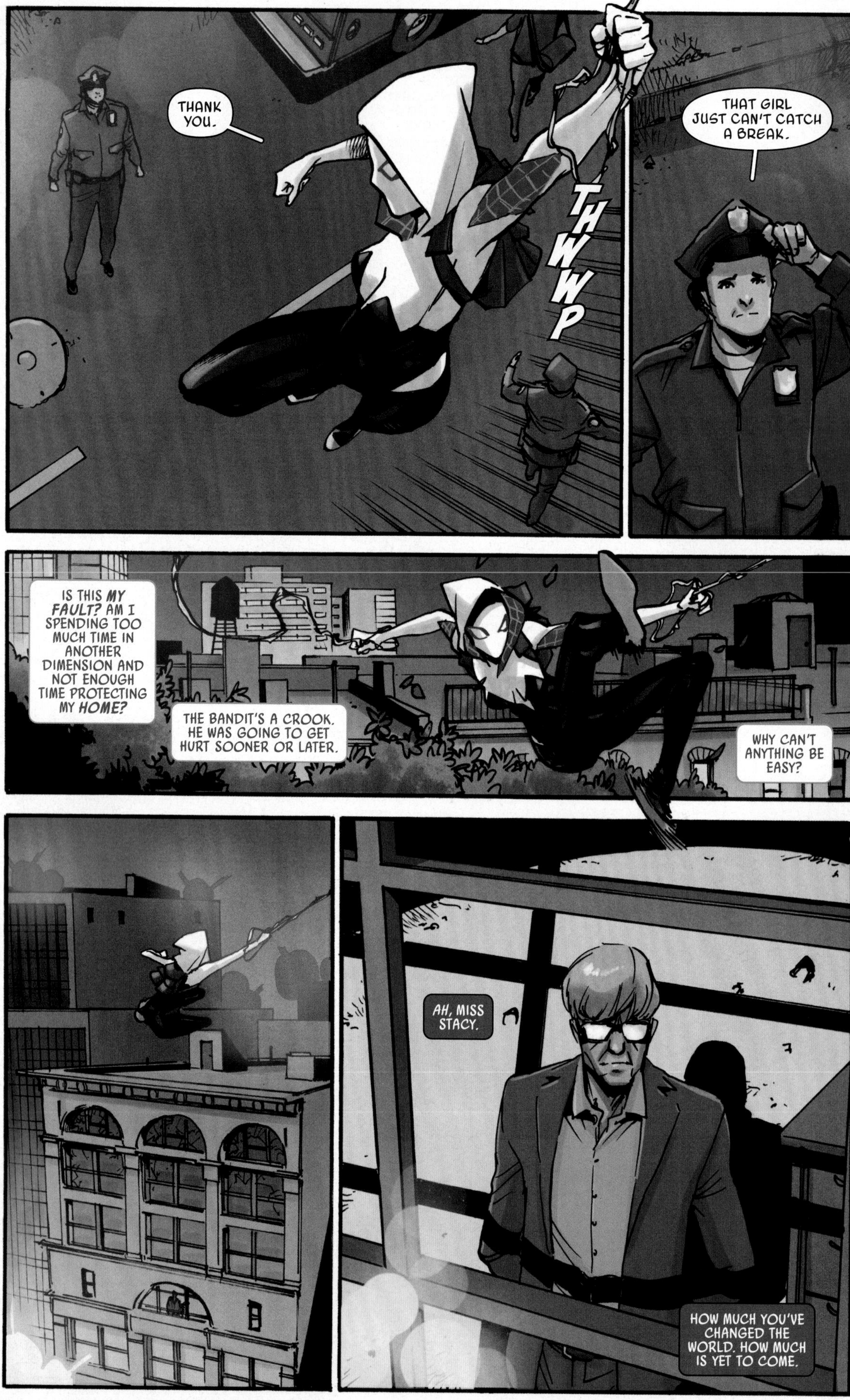
THANK YOU.
THWWP
THAT GIRL JUST CAN'T CATCH A BREAK.
IS THIS MY FAULT? AM I SPENDING TOO MUCH TIME IN ANOTHER DIMENSION AND NOT ENOUGH TIME PROTECTING MY HOME?
THE BANDIT'S A CROOK. HE WAS GOING TO GET HURT SOONER OR LATER.
WHY CAN'T ANYTHING BE EASY?
AH, MISS STACY.
HOW MUCH YOU'VE CHANGED THE WORLD. HOW MUCH IS YET TO COME.

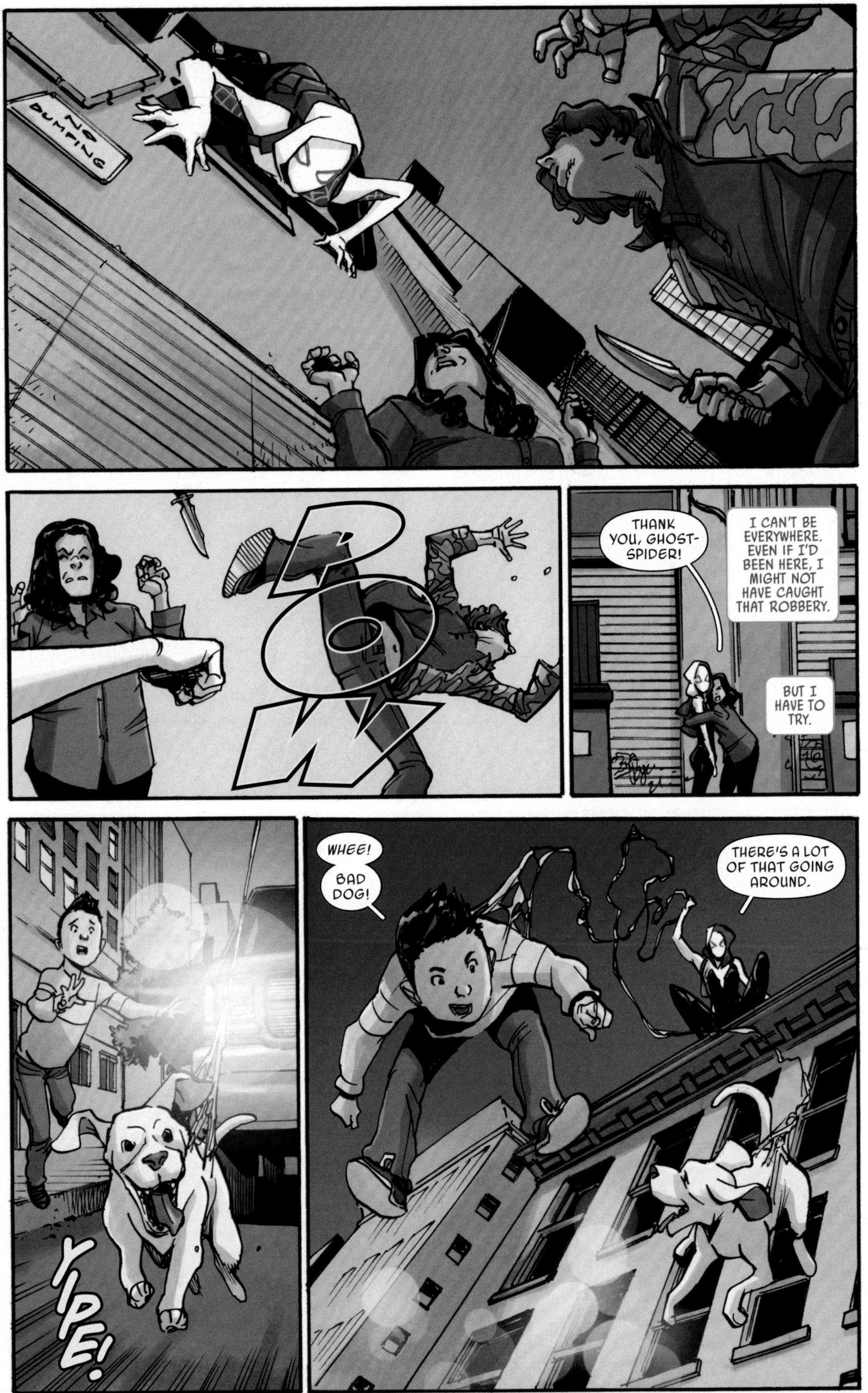
NO DUMPING
POW
THANK YOU, GHOST-SPIDER!
I CAN'T BE EVERYWHERE. EVEN IF I'D BEEN HERE, I MIGHT NOT HAVE CAUGHT THAT ROBBERY.
BUT I HAVE TO TRY.
YIPE!
WHEE!
BAD DOG!
THERE'S A LOT OF THAT GOING AROUND.

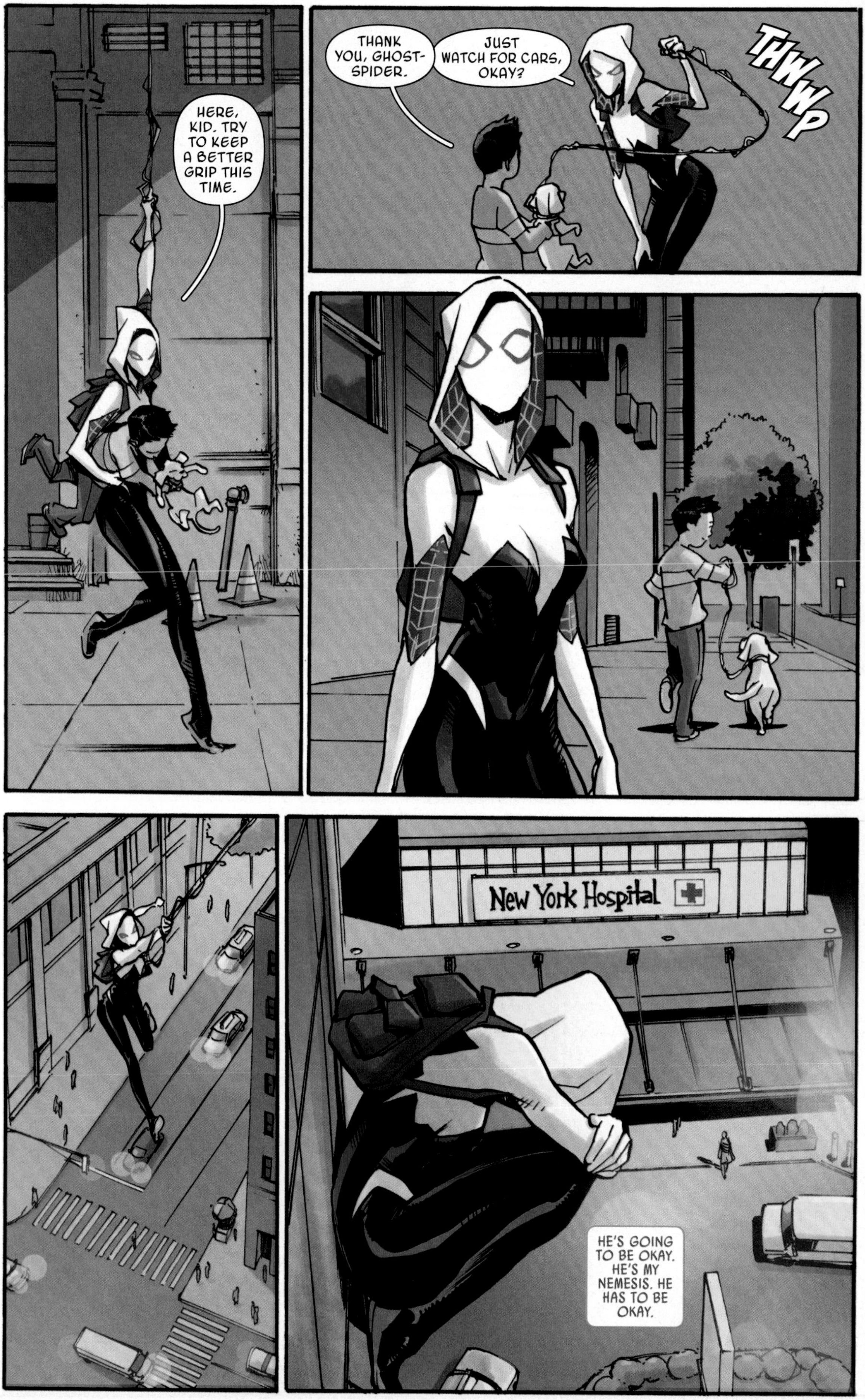
HERE, KID. TRY TO KEEP A BETTER GRIP THIS TIME.
THANK YOU, GHOST-SPIDER.
JUST WATCH FOR CARS, OKAY?
THWWP
New York Hospital
HE'S GOING TO BE OKAY. HE'S MY NEMESIS. HE HAS TO BE OKAY.

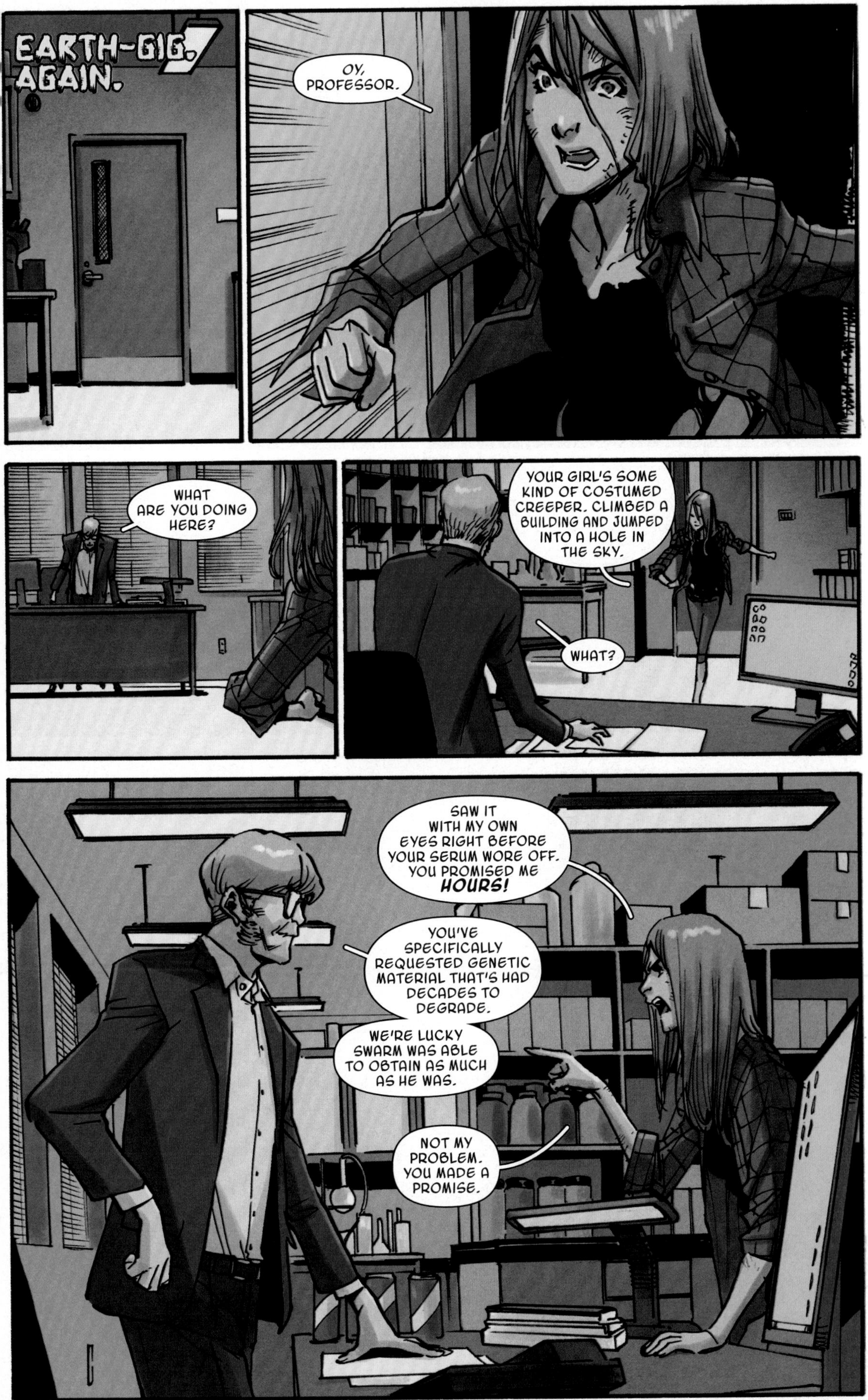
EARTH-616. AGAIN.
OY, PROFESSOR.
WHAT ARE YOU DOING HERE?
YOUR GIRL'S SOME KIND OF COSTUMED CREEPER. CLIMBED A BUILDING AND JUMPED INTO A HOLE IN THE SKY.
WHAT?
SAW IT WITH MY OWN EYES RIGHT BEFORE YOUR SERUM WORE OFF. YOU PROMISED ME HOURS!
YOU'VE SPECIFICALLY REQUESTED GENETIC MATERIAL THAT'S HAD DECADES TO DEGRADE.
WE'RE LUCKY SWARM WAS ABLE TO OBTAIN AS MUCH AS HE WAS.
NOT MY PROBLEM. YOU MADE A PROMISE.

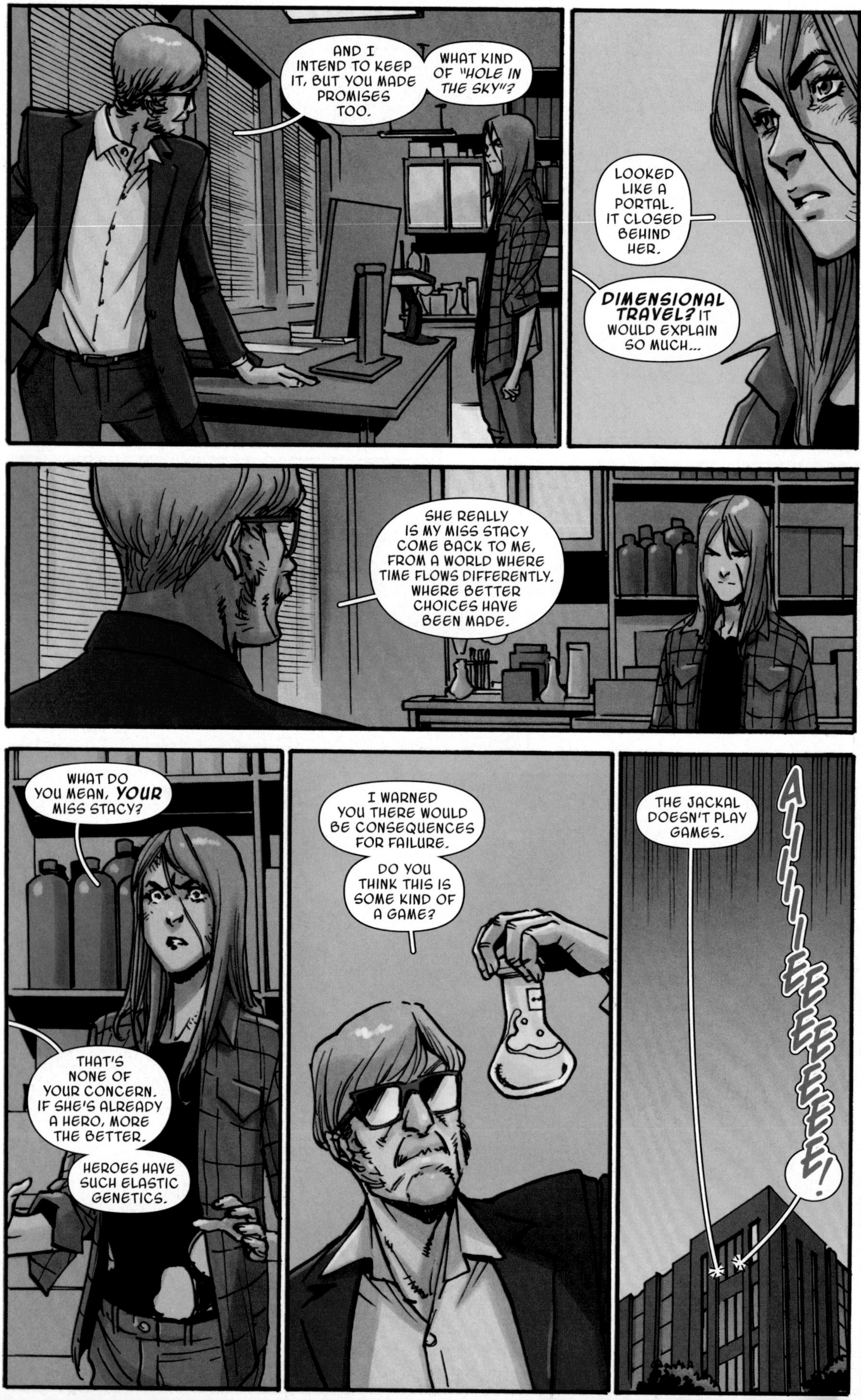
AND I INTEND TO KEEP IT, BUT YOU MADE PROMISES TOO.
WHAT KIND OF "HOLE IN THE SKY"?
LOOKED LIKE A PORTAL. IT CLOSED BEHIND HER.
DIMENSIONAL TRAVEL? IT WOULD EXPLAIN SO MUCH...
SHE REALLY IS MY MISS STACY COME BACK TO ME, FROM A WORLD WHERE TIME FLOWS DIFFERENTLY. WHERE BETTER CHOICES HAVE BEEN MADE.
WHAT DO YOU MEAN, YOUR MISS STACY?
THAT'S NONE OF YOUR CONCERN. IF SHE'S ALREADY A HERO, MORE THE BETTER.
HEROES HAVE SUCH ELASTIC GENETICS.
I WARNED YOU THERE WOULD BE CONSEQUENCES FOR FAILURE.
DO YOU THINK THIS IS SOME KIND OF A GAME?
THE JACKAL DOESN'T PLAY GAMES.
AIIIIIEEEEEEEE!

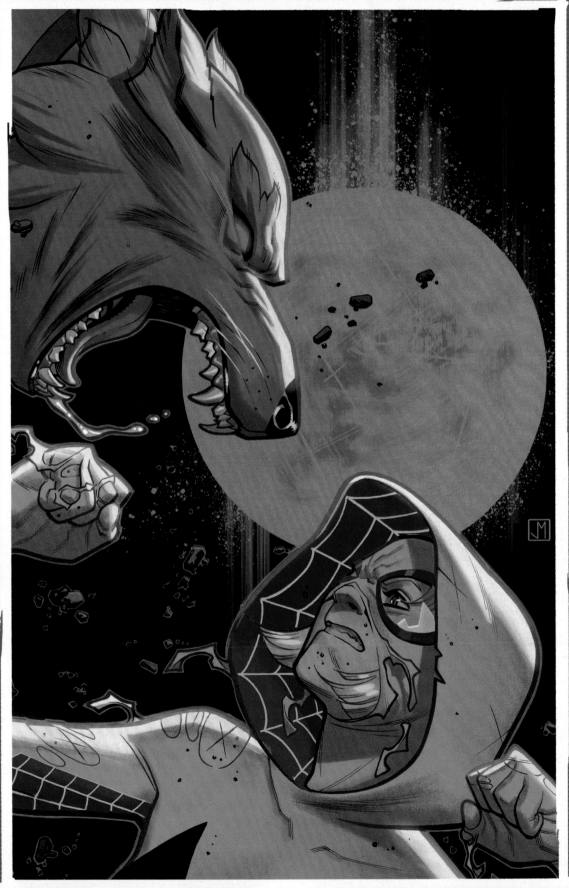

EARTH-GIG.
EMPIRE STATE
UNIVERSITY.

GWEN STACY.
THE HAUNTING
GHOST-SPIDER.
FEELING SORT OF
DITCHED.

WHERE *IS* SHE?

GWEN! WHAT ARE YOU DOING OUT HERE?

I'M SUPPOSED TO BE MEETING BENJI SO WE CAN REVIEW OUR MEDIA STUDIES PROJECT. HAVE YOU SEEN HER?

NOT TODAY.

UGH.

KOSEI SATO. ENGINEERING MAJOR. NOT A SUPER HERO.

BUT HEY, YOU'VE GOT ME! AREN'T I AN IMPROVEMENT?

NOT UNLESS YOU HAVE AN ENCYCLOPEDIC KNOWLEDGE OF *VERONICA MARS.*

ER, NO. I WAS ALWAYS MORE INTO *GAME OF THRONES.*

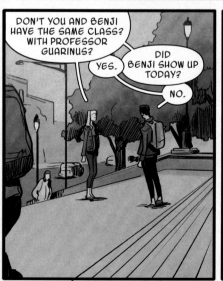

DON'T YOU AND BENJI HAVE THE SAME CLASS? WITH PROFESSOR GUARINUS?

YES.

DID BENJI SHOW UP TODAY?

NO.

I'M SURE SHE'S JUST TAKING A MENTAL HEALTH DAY. WE ALL NEED THOSE ONCE IN A WHILE.

I GUESS...

SHE'S A BIG GIRL. I'M SURE SHE'S FINE.

BUT--

I HAVE TO GO. SEE YOU TOMORROW!

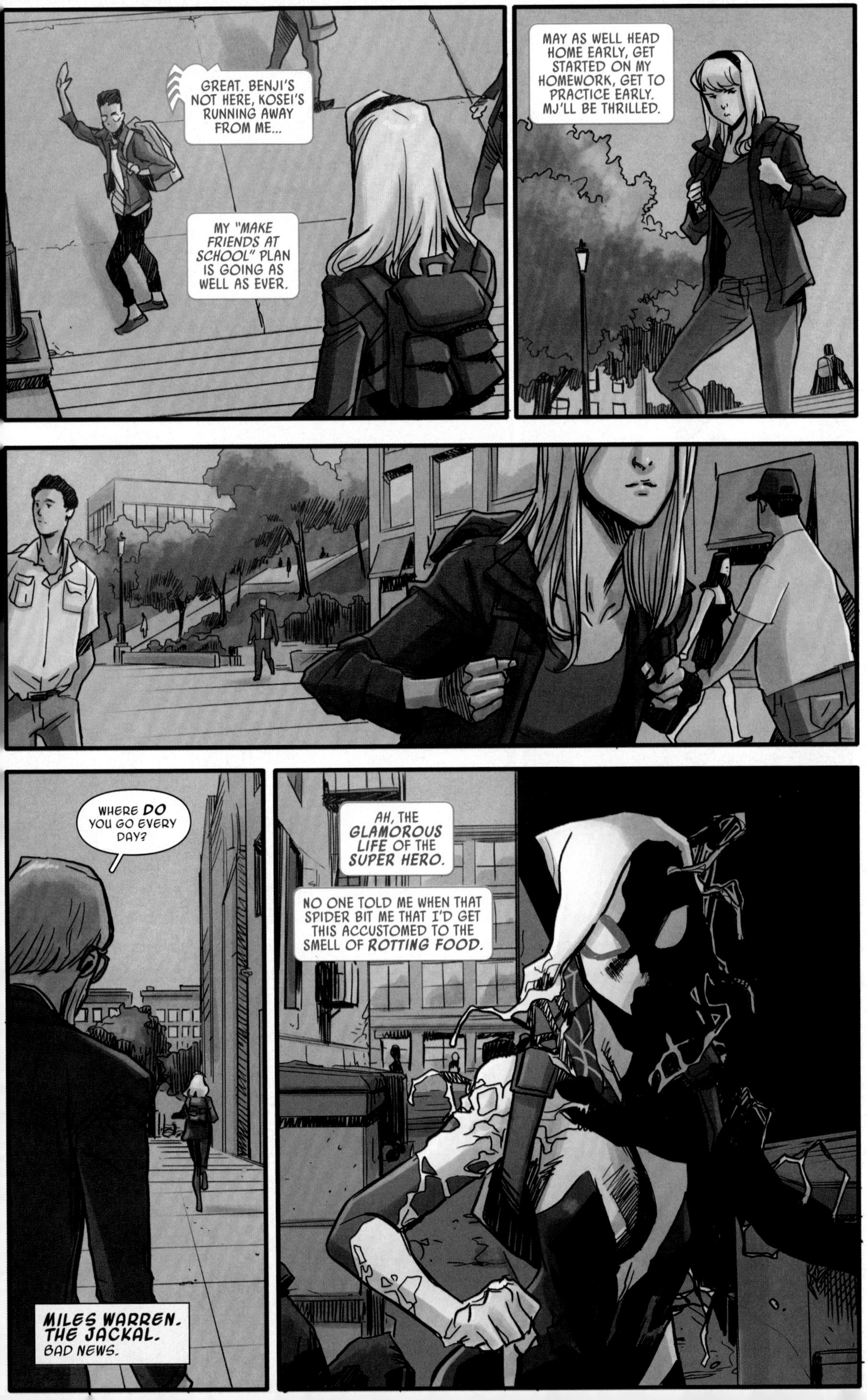
GREAT. BENJI'S NOT HERE, KOSEI'S RUNNING AWAY FROM ME...
MY "MAKE FRIENDS AT SCHOOL" PLAN IS GOING AS WELL AS EVER.
MAY AS WELL HEAD HOME EARLY, GET STARTED ON MY HOMEWORK, GET TO PRACTICE EARLY. MJ'LL BE THRILLED.
WHERE DO YOU GO EVERY DAY?
MILES WARREN. THE JACKAL. BAD NEWS.
AH, THE GLAMOROUS LIFE OF THE SUPER HERO.
NO ONE TOLD ME WHEN THAT SPIDER BIT ME THAT I'D GET THIS ACCUSTOMED TO THE SMELL OF ROTTING FOOD.

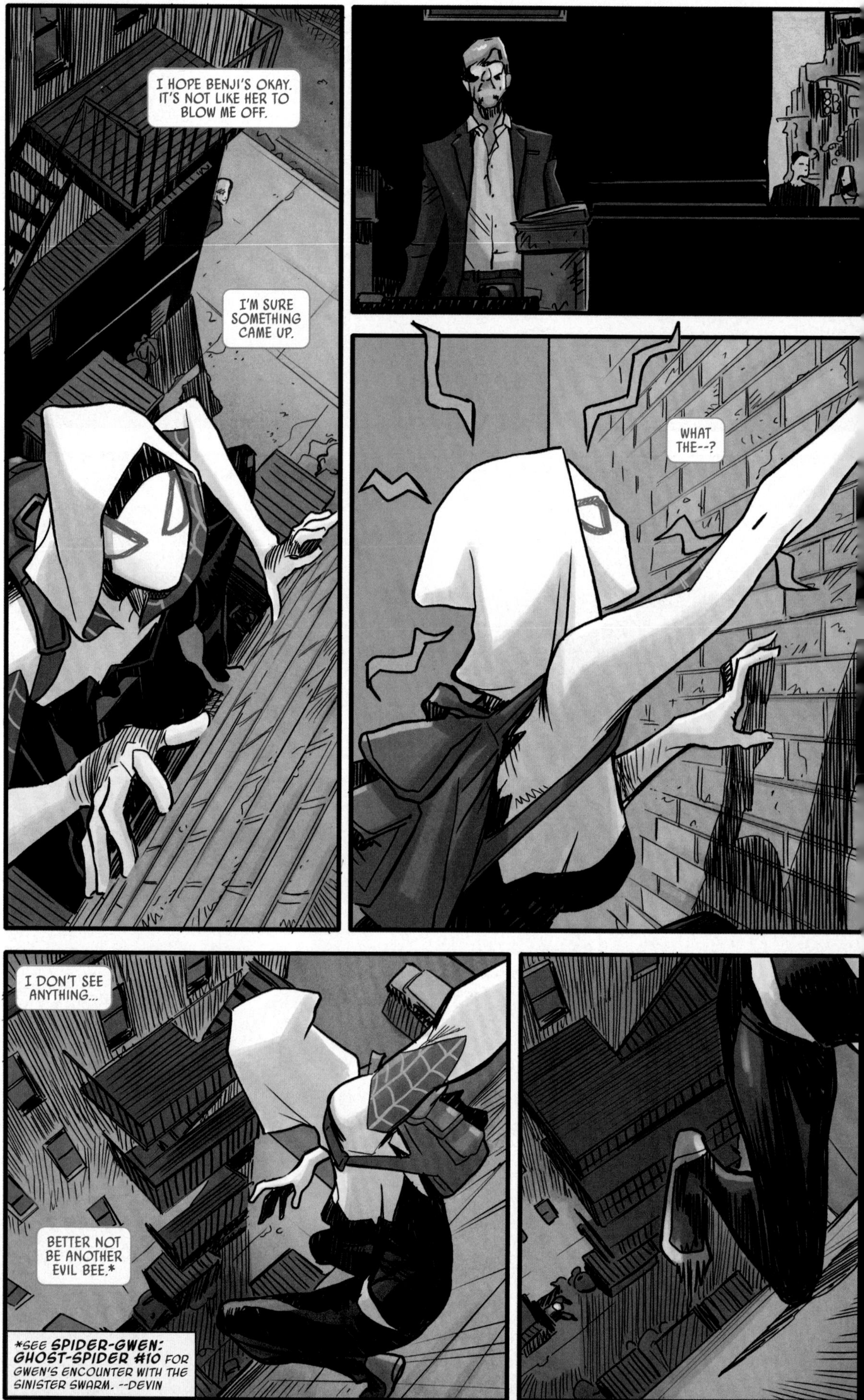
I HOPE BENJI'S OKAY. IT'S NOT LIKE HER TO BLOW ME OFF.
I'M SURE SOMETHING CAME UP.
WHAT THE--?
I DON'T SEE ANYTHING...
BETTER NOT BE ANOTHER EVIL BEE.*
*SEE SPIDER-GWEN: GHOST-SPIDER #10 FOR GWEN'S ENCOUNTER WITH THE SINISTER SWARM. --DEVIN

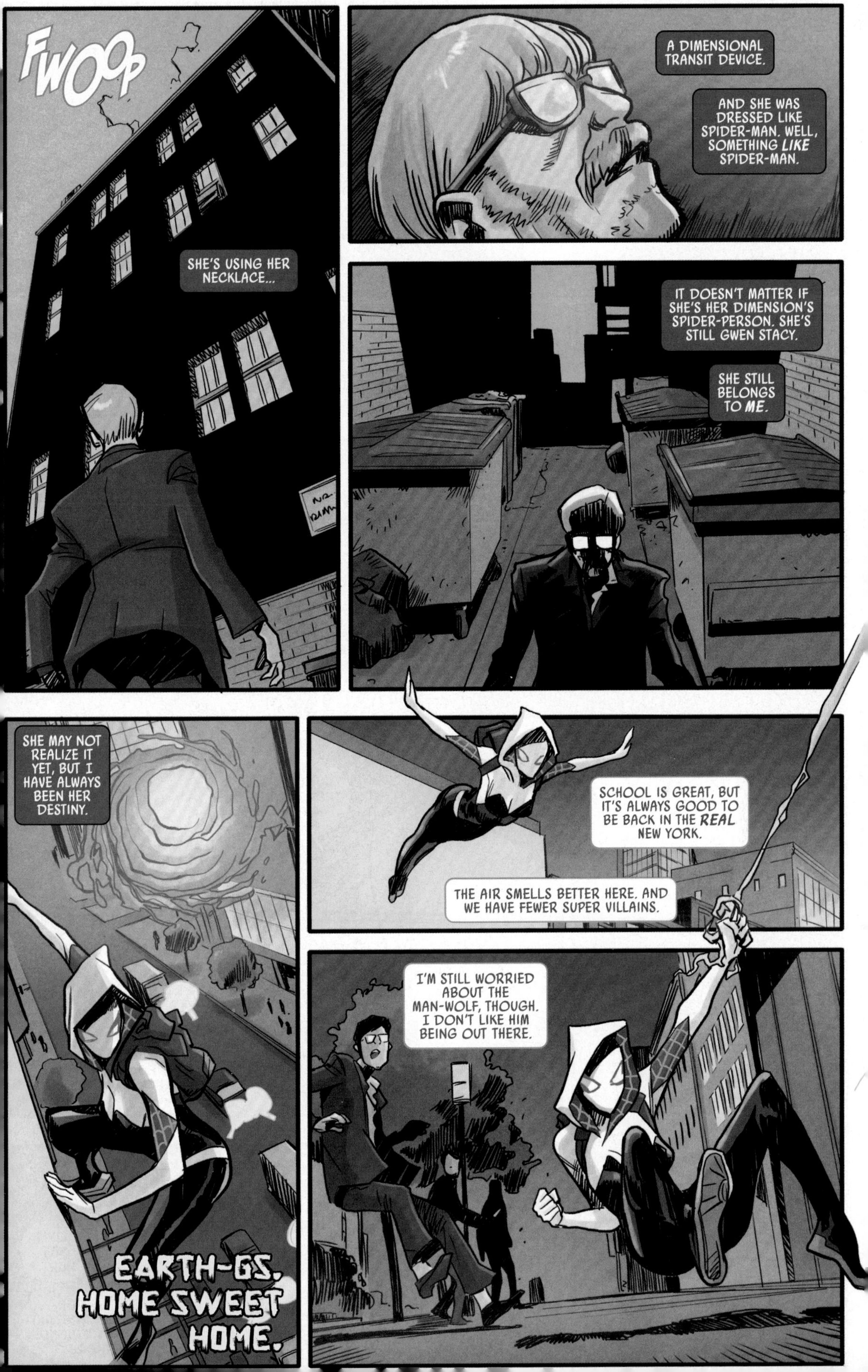
FWOOP
SHE'S USING HER NECKLACE...
A DIMENSIONAL TRANSIT DEVICE.
AND SHE WAS DRESSED LIKE SPIDER-MAN. WELL, SOMETHING LIKE SPIDER-MAN.
IT DOESN'T MATTER IF SHE'S HER DIMENSION'S SPIDER-PERSON. SHE'S STILL GWEN STACY.
SHE STILL BELONGS TO ME.
SHE MAY NOT REALIZE IT YET, BUT I HAVE ALWAYS BEEN HER DESTINY.
EARTH-65. HOME SWEET HOME.
SCHOOL IS GREAT, BUT IT'S ALWAYS GOOD TO BE BACK IN THE REAL NEW YORK.
THE AIR SMELLS BETTER HERE. AND WE HAVE FEWER SUPER VILLAINS.
I'M STILL WORRIED ABOUT THE MAN-WOLF, THOUGH. I DON'T LIKE HIM BEING OUT THERE.

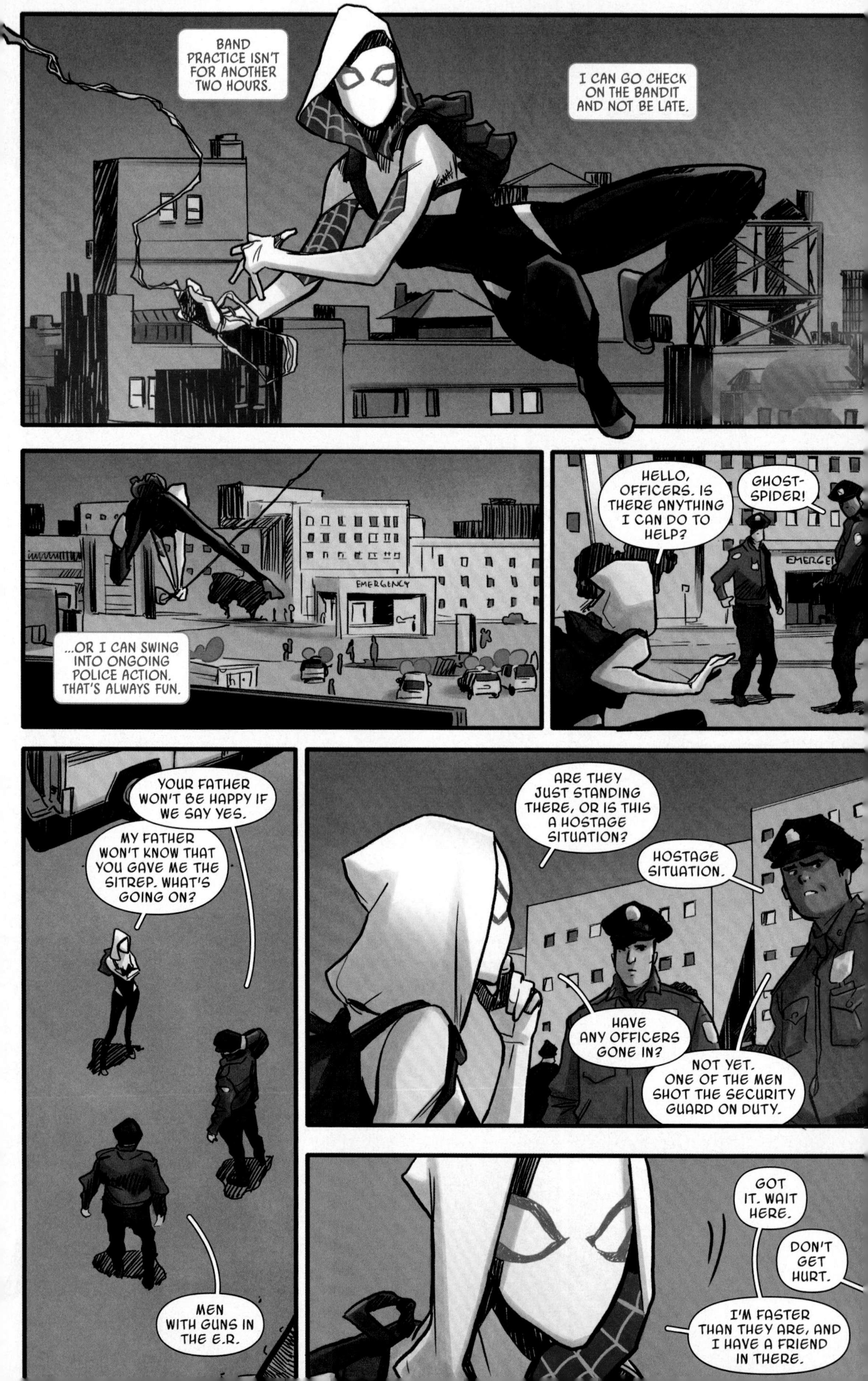
BAND PRACTICE ISN'T FOR ANOTHER TWO HOURS.
I CAN GO CHECK ON THE BANDIT AND NOT BE LATE.
...OR I CAN SWING INTO ONGOING POLICE ACTION. THAT'S ALWAYS FUN.
EMERGENCY
HELLO, OFFICERS. IS THERE ANYTHING I CAN DO TO HELP?
GHOST-SPIDER!
YOUR FATHER WON'T BE HAPPY IF WE SAY YES.
MY FATHER WON'T KNOW THAT YOU GAVE ME THE SITREP. WHAT'S GOING ON?
MEN WITH GUNS IN THE E.R.
ARE THEY JUST STANDING THERE, OR IS THIS A HOSTAGE SITUATION?
HOSTAGE SITUATION.
HAVE ANY OFFICERS GONE IN?
NOT YET. ONE OF THE MEN SHOT THE SECURITY GUARD ON DUTY.
GOT IT. WAIT HERE.
DON'T GET HURT.
I'M FASTER THAN THEY ARE, AND I HAVE A FRIEND IN THERE.

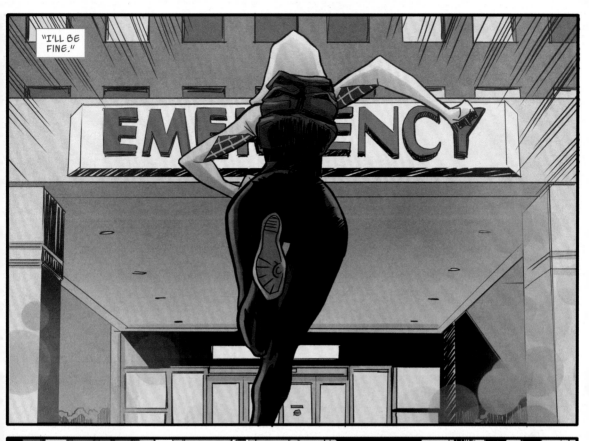

"I'LL BE FINE."

SHHHHHHHSSSH

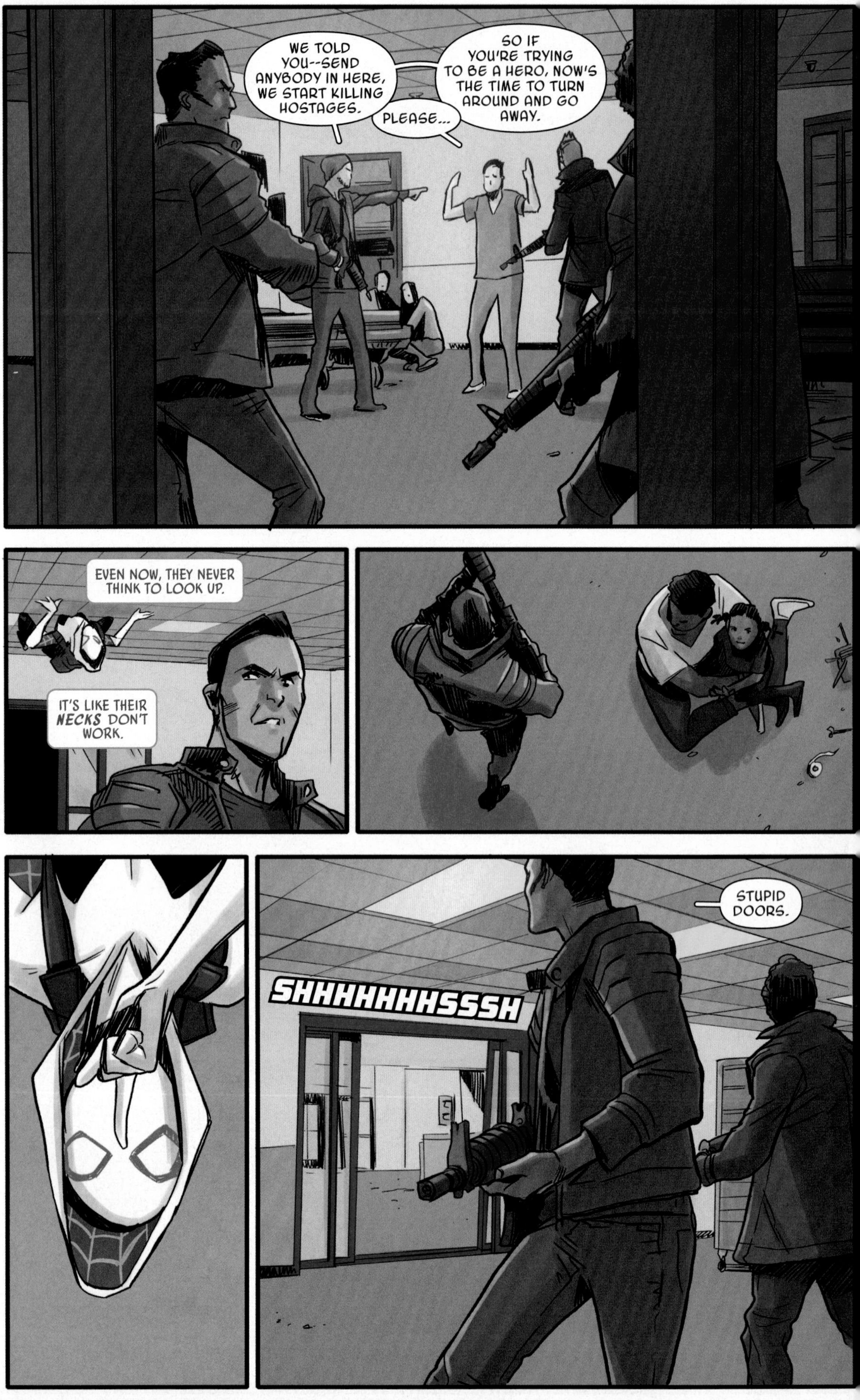
WE TOLD YOU--SEND ANYBODY IN HERE, WE START KILLING HOSTAGES.
SO IF YOU'RE TRYING TO BE A HERO, NOW'S THE TIME TO TURN AROUND AND GO AWAY.
PLEASE...
EVEN NOW, THEY NEVER THINK TO LOOK UP.
IT'S LIKE THEIR NECKS DON'T WORK.
SHHHHHHHHSSSH
STUPID DOORS.

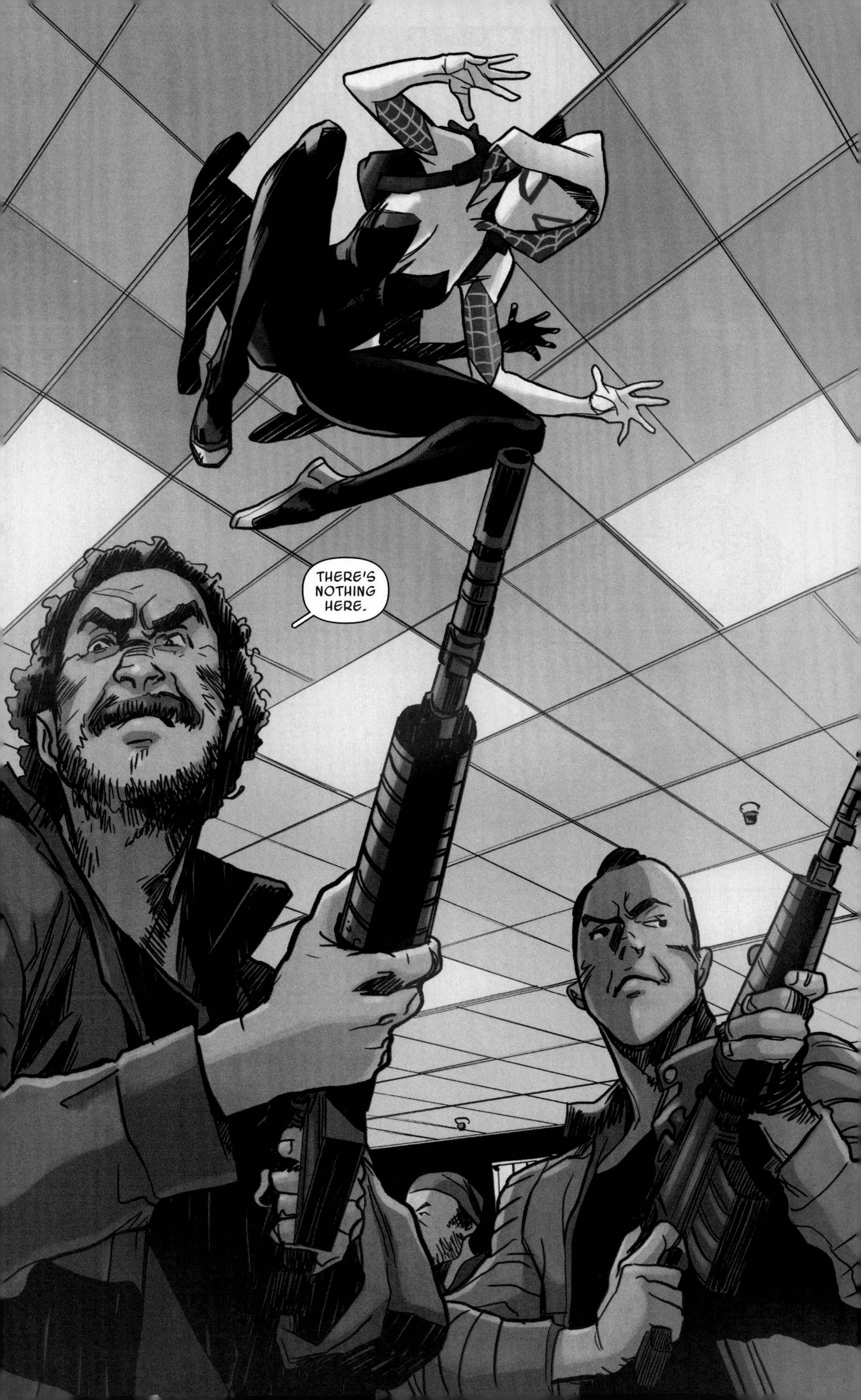
THERE'S NOTHING HERE.

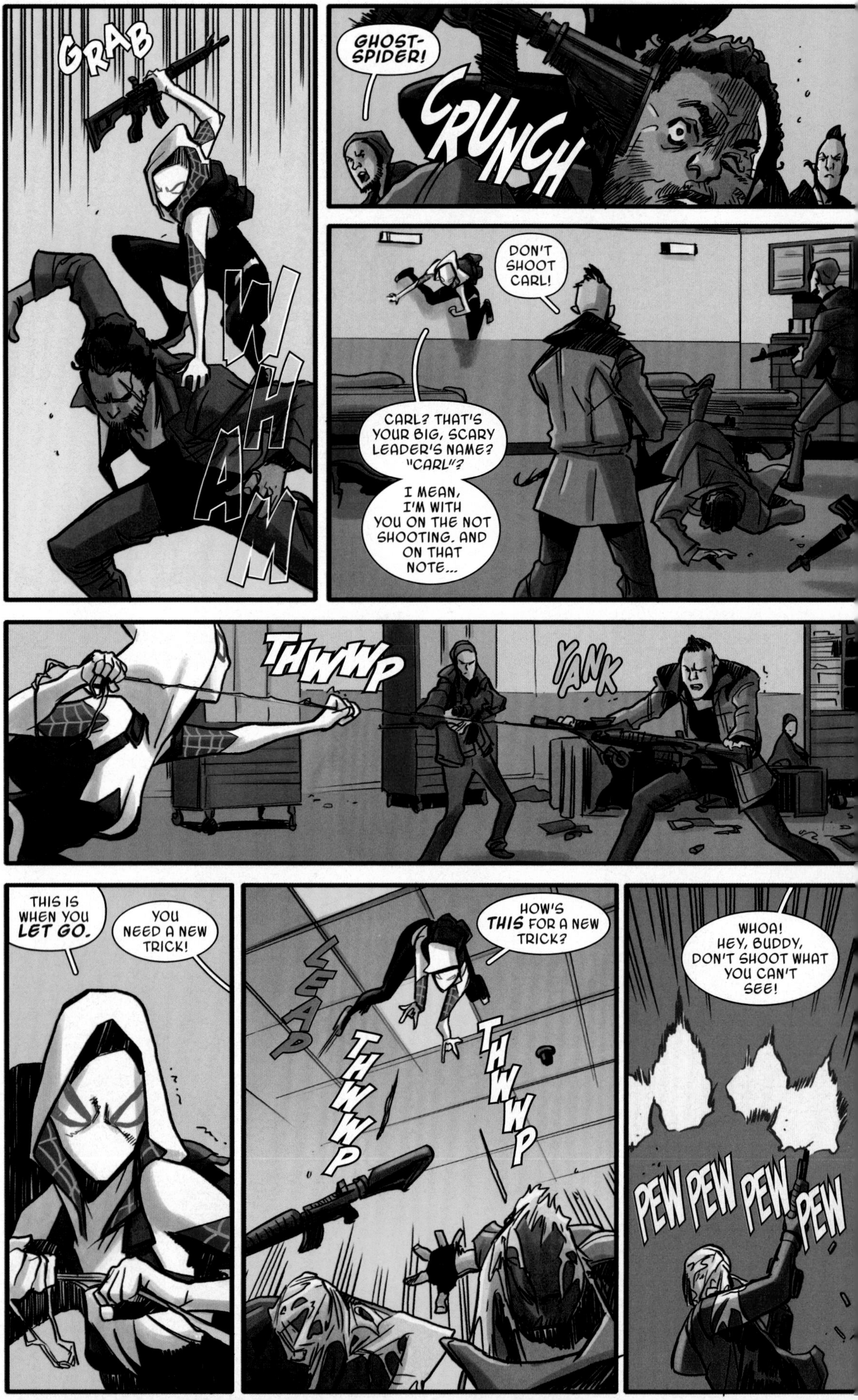
GRAB
WHAM
GHOST-SPIDER!
CRUNCH
DON'T SHOOT CARL!
CARL? THAT'S YOUR BIG, SCARY LEADER'S NAME? "CARL"?
I MEAN, I'M WITH YOU ON THE NOT SHOOTING. AND ON THAT NOTE...
THWWP
YANK
THIS IS WHEN YOU LET GO.
YOU NEED A NEW TRICK!
HOW'S THIS FOR A NEW TRICK?
LEAP
THWWP
THWWP
WHOA! HEY, BUDDY, DON'T SHOOT WHAT YOU CAN'T SEE!
PEW PEW PEW PEW

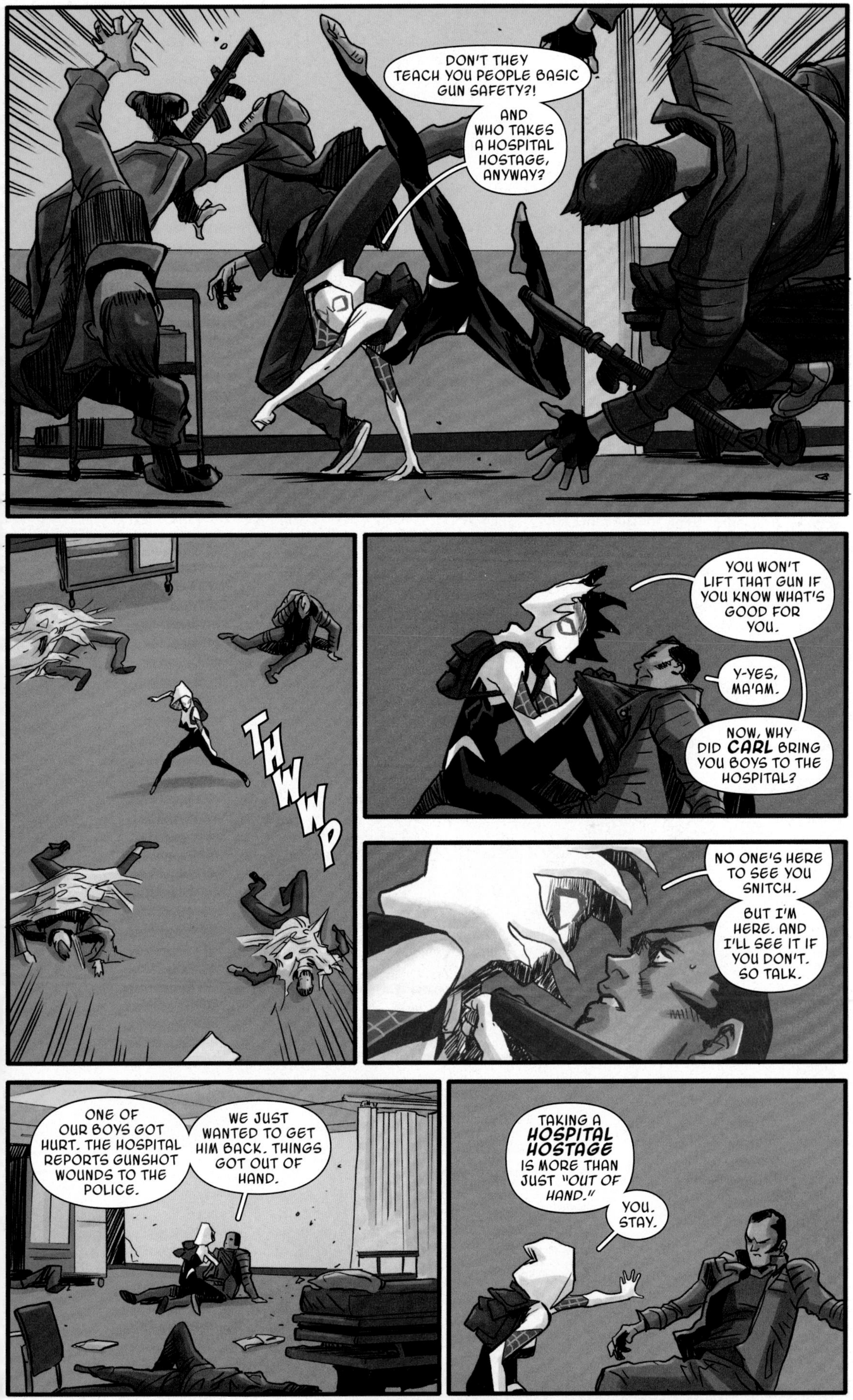
DON'T THEY TEACH YOU PEOPLE BASIC GUN SAFETY?!
AND WHO TAKES A HOSPITAL HOSTAGE, ANYWAY?
THWWP
YOU WON'T LIFT THAT GUN IF YOU KNOW WHAT'S GOOD FOR YOU.
Y-YES, MA'AM.
NOW, WHY DID CARL BRING YOU BOYS TO THE HOSPITAL?
NO ONE'S HERE TO SEE YOU SNITCH.
BUT I'M HERE. AND I'LL SEE IT IF YOU DON'T. SO TALK.
ONE OF OUR BOYS GOT HURT. THE HOSPITAL REPORTS GUNSHOT WOUNDS TO THE POLICE.
WE JUST WANTED TO GET HIM BACK. THINGS GOT OUT OF HAND.
TAKING A HOSPITAL HOSTAGE IS MORE THAN JUST "OUT OF HAND."
YOU. STAY.

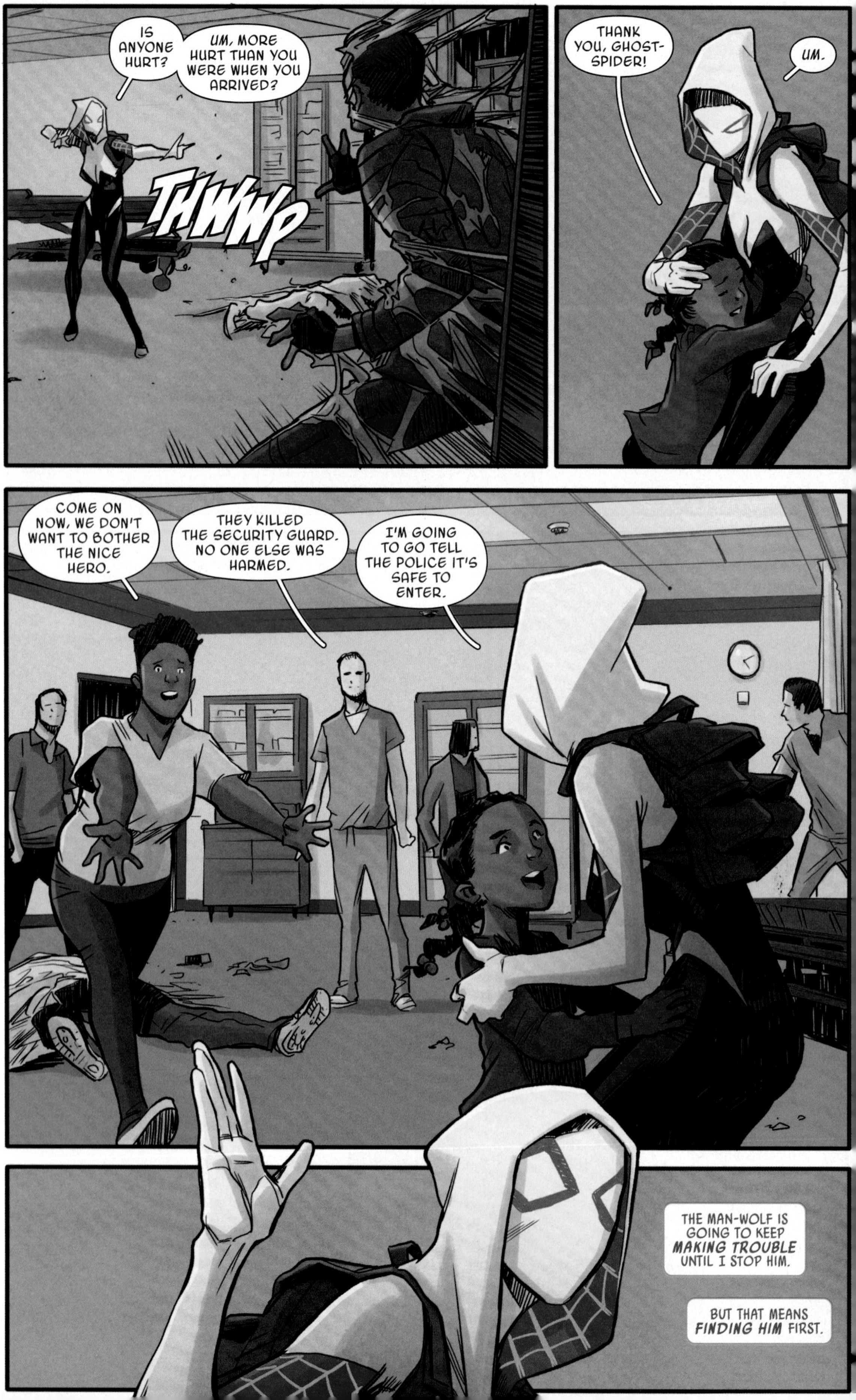
IS ANYONE HURT?
UM, MORE HURT THAN YOU WERE WHEN YOU ARRIVED?
THWWP
THANK YOU, GHOST-SPIDER!
UM.
COME ON NOW, WE DON'T WANT TO BOTHER THE NICE HERO.
THEY KILLED THE SECURITY GUARD. NO ONE ELSE WAS HARMED.
I'M GOING TO GO TELL THE POLICE IT'S SAFE TO ENTER.
THE MAN-WOLF IS GOING TO KEEP *MAKING TROUBLE* UNTIL I STOP HIM.
BUT THAT MEANS *FINDING HIM* FIRST.

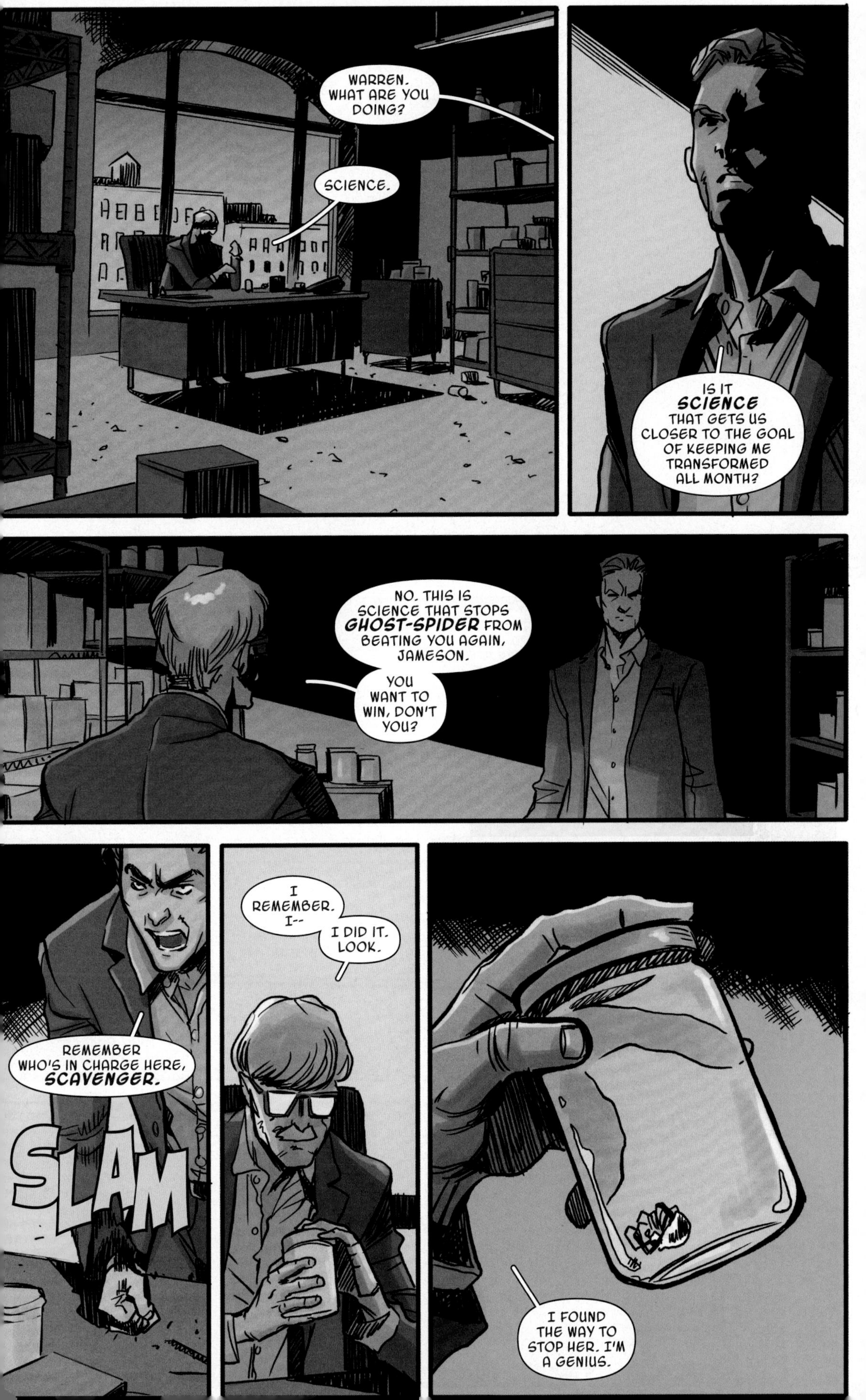

WARREN. WHAT ARE YOU DOING?
SCIENCE.
IS IT SCIENCE THAT GETS US CLOSER TO THE GOAL OF KEEPING ME TRANSFORMED ALL MONTH?
NO. THIS IS SCIENCE THAT STOPS GHOST-SPIDER FROM BEATING YOU AGAIN, JAMESON.
YOU WANT TO WIN, DON'T YOU?
REMEMBER WHO'S IN CHARGE HERE, SCAVENGER.
SLAM
I REMEMBER. I--
I DID IT. LOOK.
I FOUND THE WAY TO STOP HER. I'M A GENIUS.

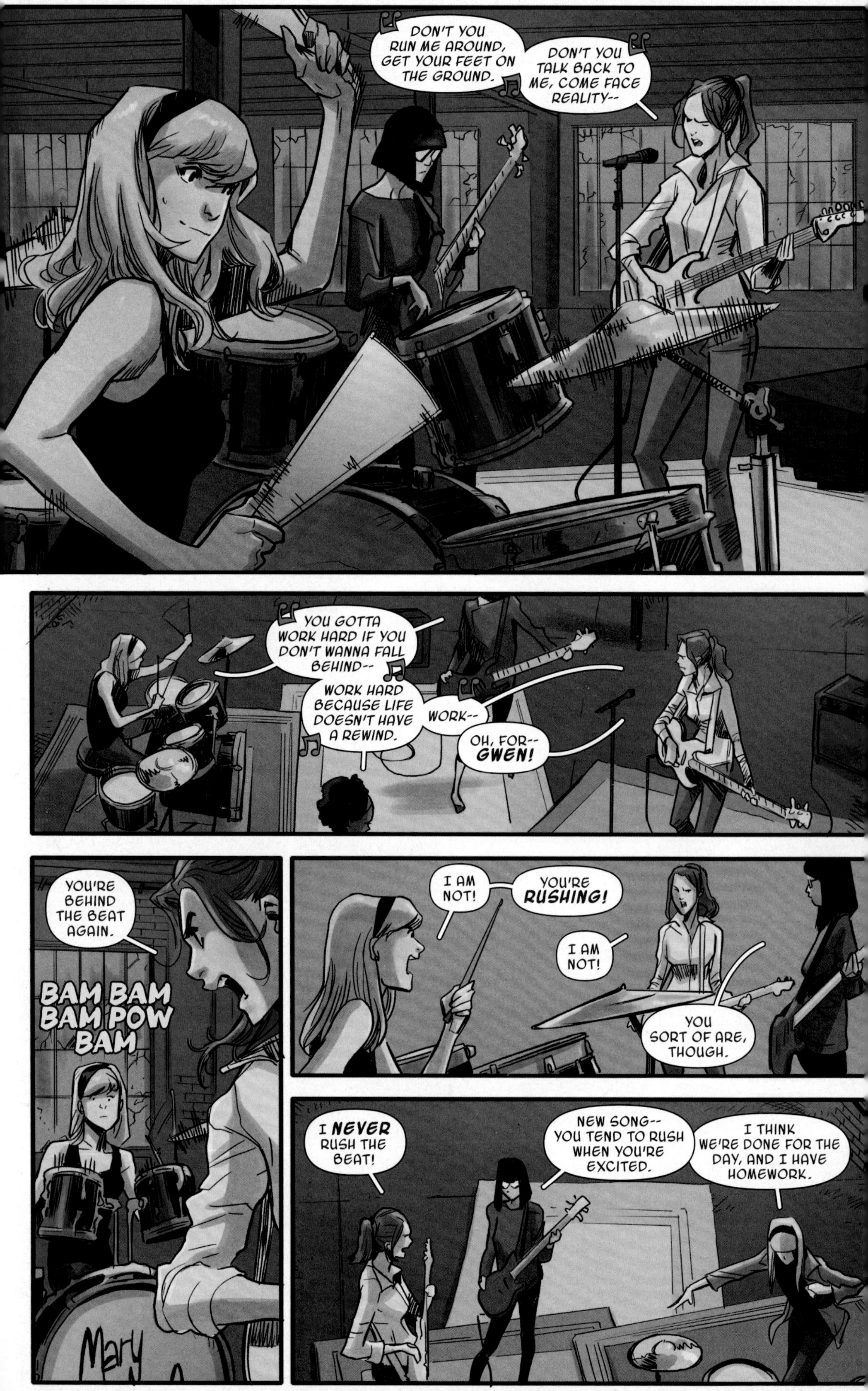
DON'T YOU RUN ME AROUND, GET YOUR FEET ON THE GROUND.
DON'T YOU TALK BACK TO ME, COME FACE REALITY--
YOU GOTTA WORK HARD IF YOU DON'T WANNA FALL BEHIND--
WORK HARD BECAUSE LIFE DOESN'T HAVE A REWIND.
WORK--
OH, FOR-- GWEN!
YOU'RE BEHIND THE BEAT AGAIN.
BAM BAM BAM POW BAM
I AM NOT!
YOU'RE RUSHING!
I AM NOT!
YOU SORT OF ARE, THOUGH.
I NEVER RUSH THE BEAT!
NEW SONG-- YOU TEND TO RUSH WHEN YOU'RE EXCITED.
I THINK WE'RE DONE FOR THE DAY, AND I HAVE HOMEWORK.

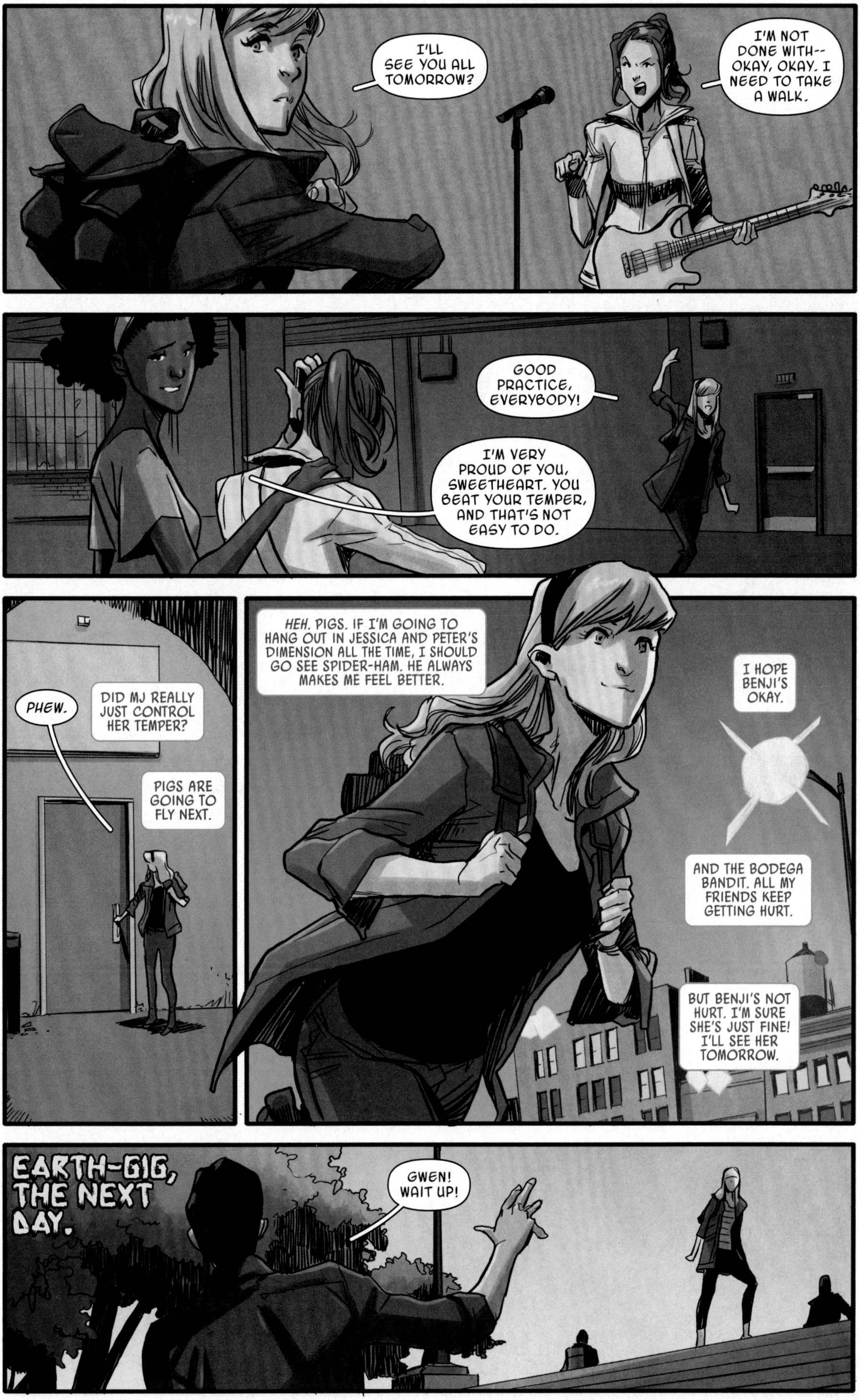
I'LL SEE YOU ALL TOMORROW?
I'M NOT DONE WITH-- OKAY, OKAY. I NEED TO TAKE A WALK.
GOOD PRACTICE, EVERYBODY!
I'M VERY PROUD OF YOU, SWEETHEART. YOU BEAT YOUR TEMPER, AND THAT'S NOT EASY TO DO.
PHEW.
DID MJ REALLY JUST CONTROL HER TEMPER?
PIGS ARE GOING TO FLY NEXT.
HEH. PIGS. IF I'M GOING TO HANG OUT IN JESSICA AND PETER'S DIMENSION ALL THE TIME, I SHOULD GO SEE SPIDER-HAM. HE ALWAYS MAKES ME FEEL BETTER.
I HOPE BENJI'S OKAY.
AND THE BODEGA BANDIT. ALL MY FRIENDS KEEP GETTING HURT.
BUT BENJI'S NOT HURT. I'M SURE SHE'S JUST FINE! I'LL SEE HER TOMORROW.
EARTH-GIG, THE NEXT DAY.
GWEN! WAIT UP!

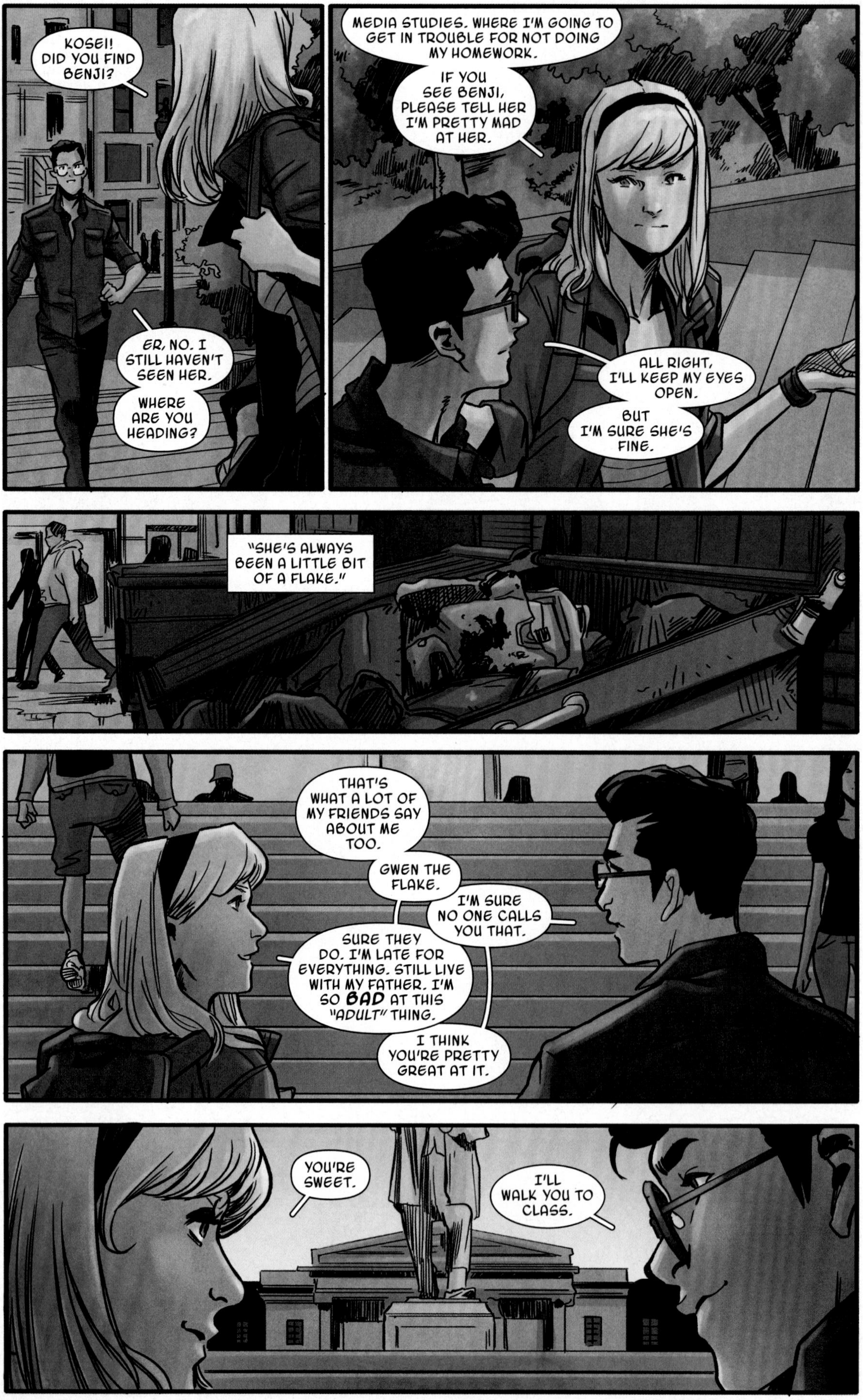
KOSEI! DID YOU FIND BENJI?
ER, NO. I STILL HAVEN'T SEEN HER.
WHERE ARE YOU HEADING?
MEDIA STUDIES. WHERE I'M GOING TO GET IN TROUBLE FOR NOT DOING MY HOMEWORK.
IF YOU SEE BENJI, PLEASE TELL HER I'M PRETTY MAD AT HER.
ALL RIGHT, I'LL KEEP MY EYES OPEN.
BUT I'M SURE SHE'S FINE.
"SHE'S ALWAYS BEEN A LITTLE BIT OF A FLAKE."
THAT'S WHAT A LOT OF MY FRIENDS SAY ABOUT ME TOO.
GWEN THE FLAKE.
I'M SURE NO ONE CALLS YOU THAT.
SURE THEY DO. I'M LATE FOR EVERYTHING. STILL LIVE WITH MY FATHER. I'M SO **BAD** AT THIS "ADULT" THING.
I THINK YOU'RE PRETTY GREAT AT IT.
YOU'RE SWEET.
I'LL WALK YOU TO CLASS.

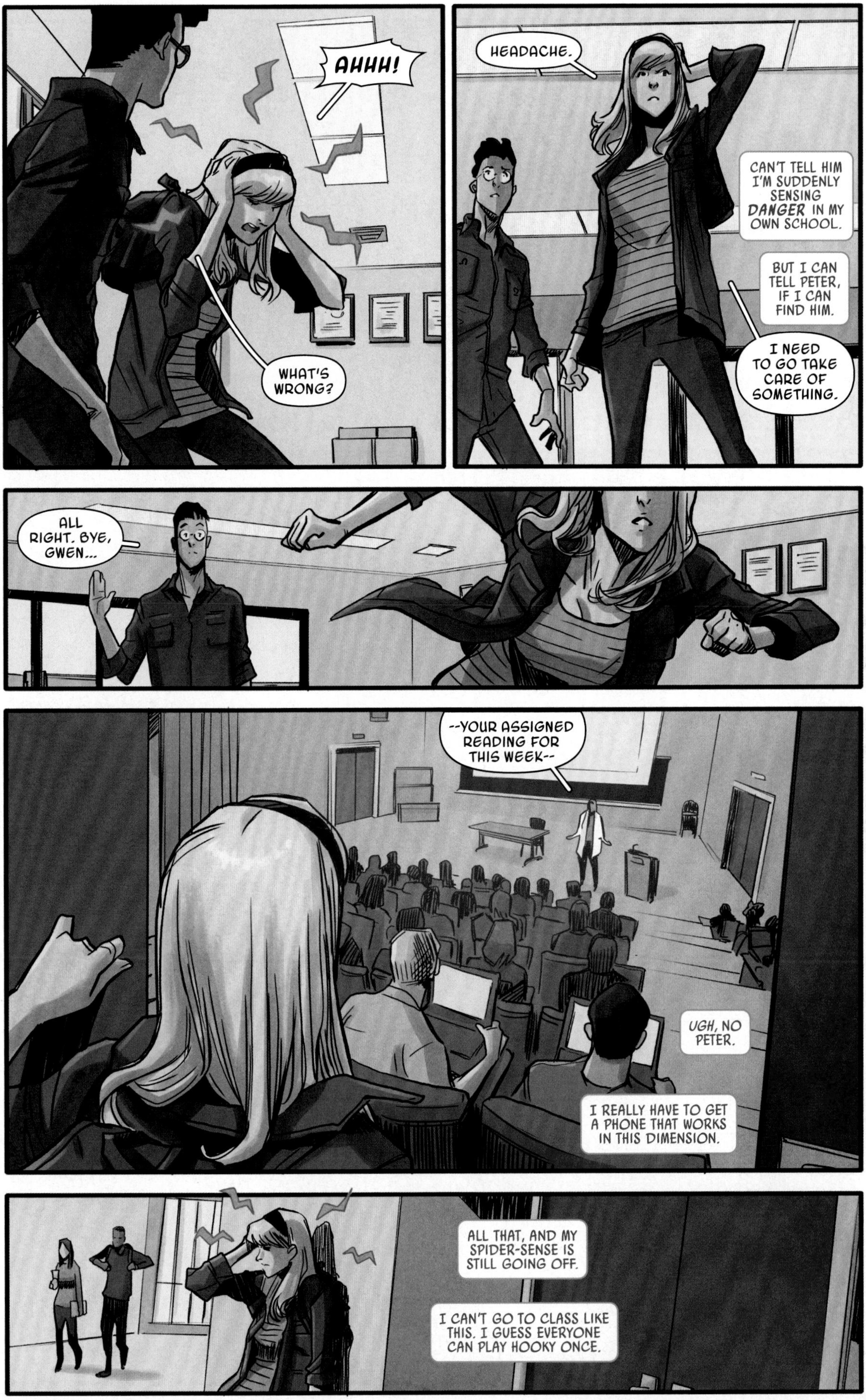
AHHH!
WHAT'S WRONG?
HEADACHE.
CAN'T TELL HIM I'M SUDDENLY SENSING DANGER IN MY OWN SCHOOL.
BUT I CAN TELL PETER, IF I CAN FIND HIM.
I NEED TO GO TAKE CARE OF SOMETHING.
ALL RIGHT. BYE, GWEN...
--YOUR ASSIGNED READING FOR THIS WEEK--
UGH, NO PETER.
I REALLY HAVE TO GET A PHONE THAT WORKS IN THIS DIMENSION.
ALL THAT, AND MY SPIDER-SENSE IS STILL GOING OFF.
I CAN'T GO TO CLASS LIKE THIS. I GUESS EVERYONE CAN PLAY HOOKY ONCE.

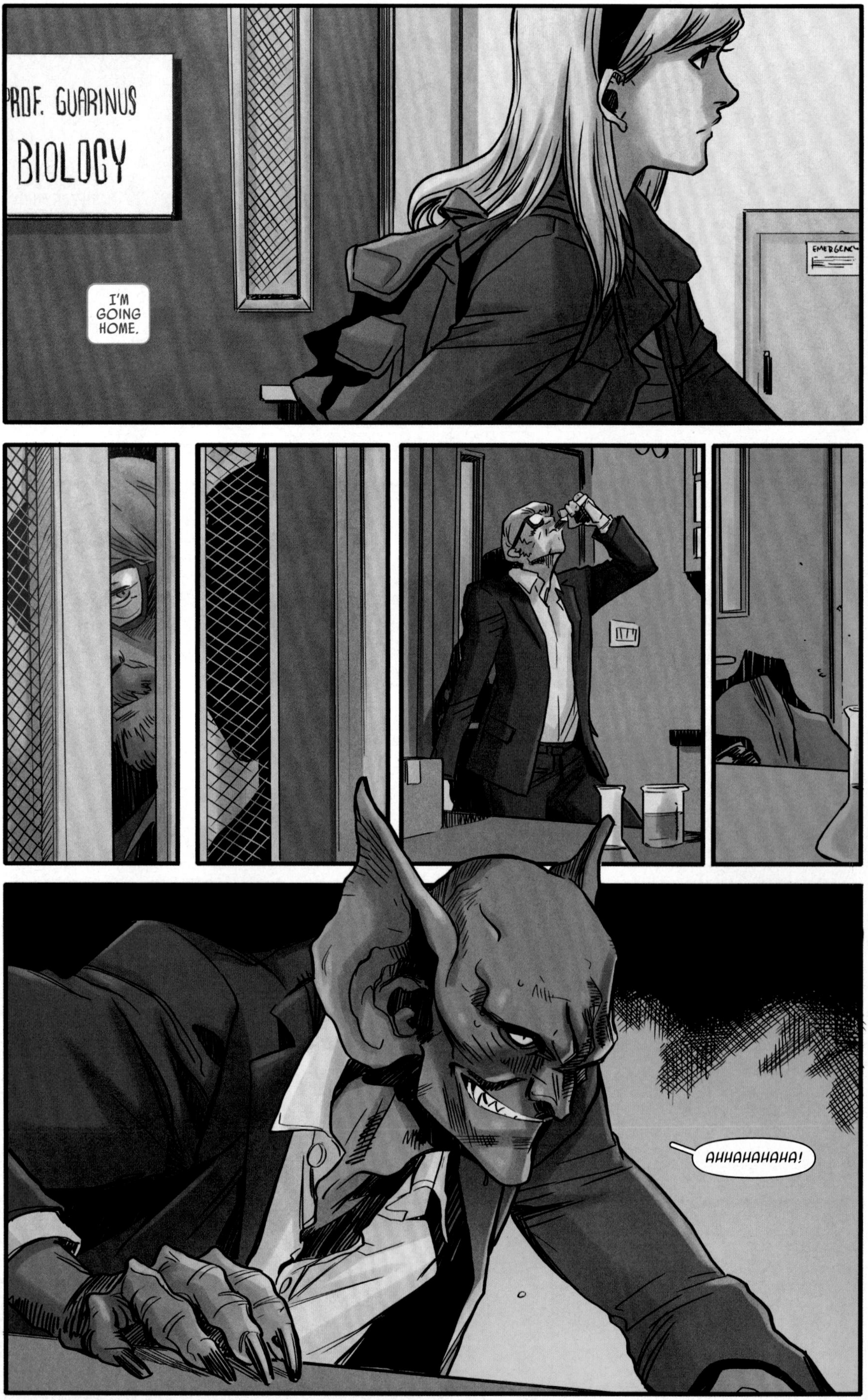
PROF. GUARINUS
BIOLOGY
I'M GOING HOME.
AHHAHAHAHA!

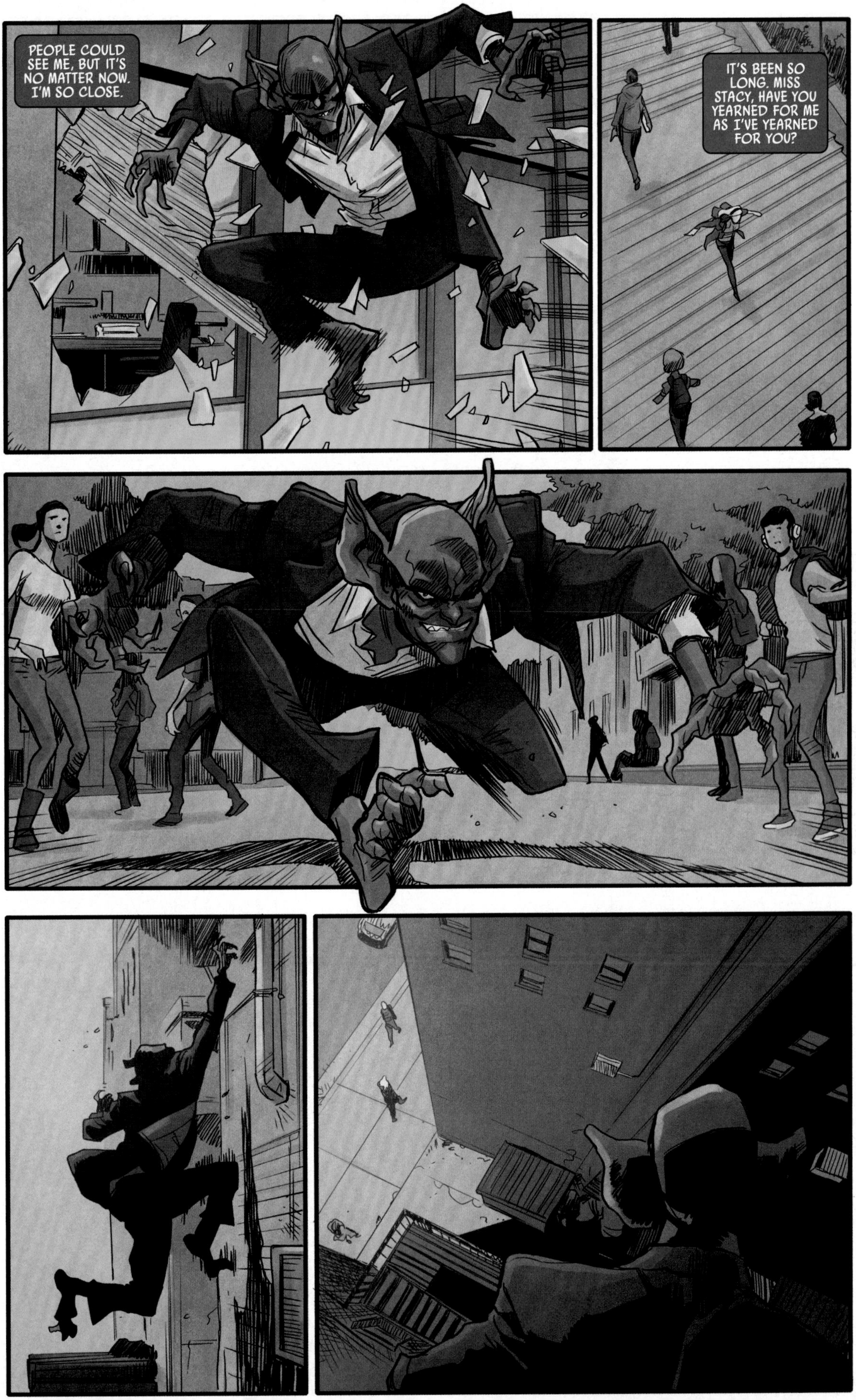
PEOPLE COULD SEE ME, BUT IT'S NO MATTER NOW. I'M SO CLOSE.
IT'S BEEN SO LONG. MISS STACY, HAVE YOU YEARNED FOR ME AS I'VE YEARNED FOR YOU?

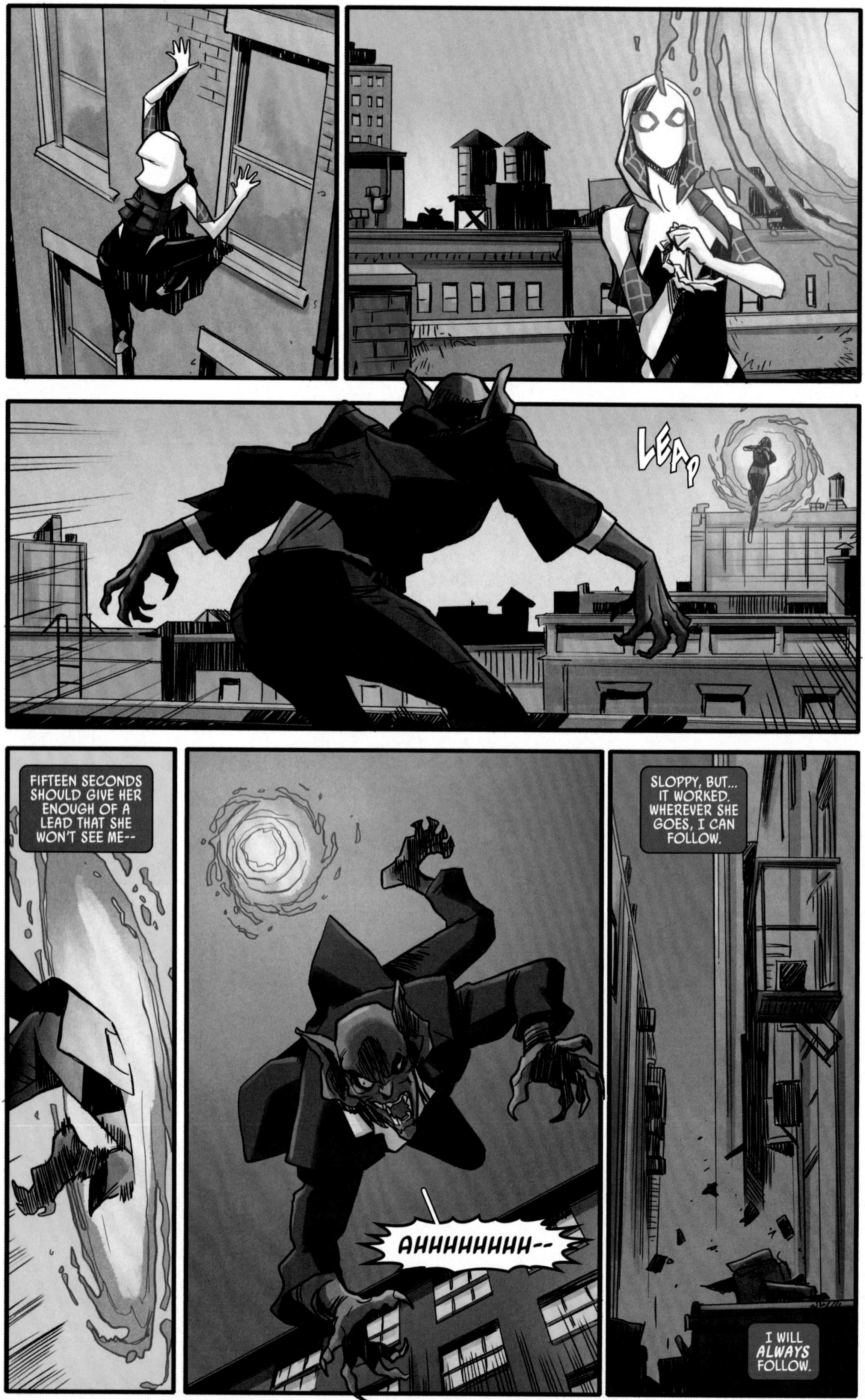
LEAP
FIFTEEN SECONDS SHOULD GIVE HER ENOUGH OF A LEAD THAT SHE WON'T SEE ME--
AHHHHHHHH--
SLOPPY, BUT... IT WORKED. WHEREVER SHE GOES, I CAN FOLLOW.
I WILL ALWAYS FOLLOW.

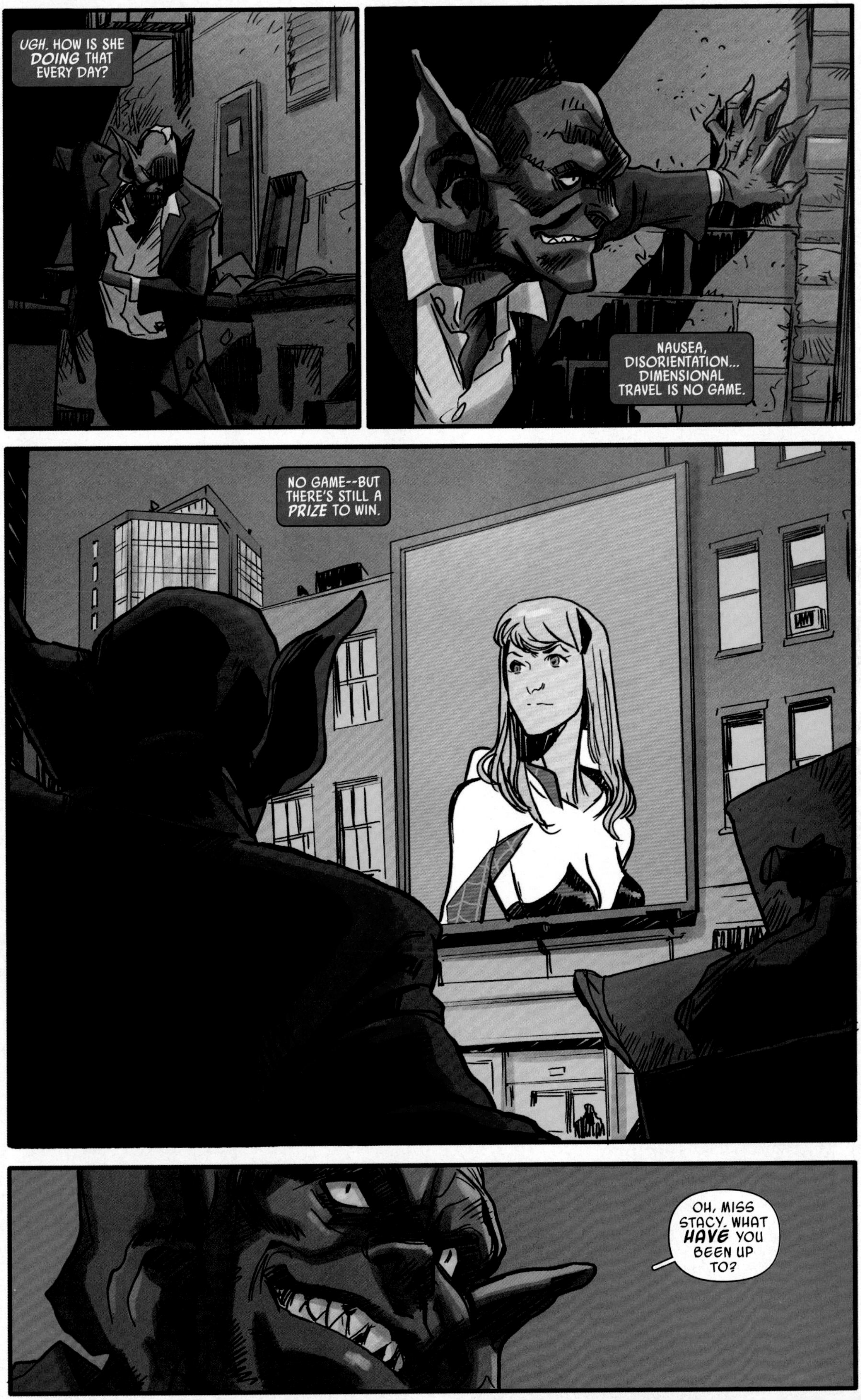
UGH. HOW IS SHE DOING THAT EVERY DAY?
NAUSEA, DISORIENTATION... DIMENSIONAL TRAVEL IS NO GAME.
NO GAME--BUT THERE'S STILL A PRIZE TO WIN.
OH, MISS STACY. WHAT HAVE YOU BEEN UP TO?

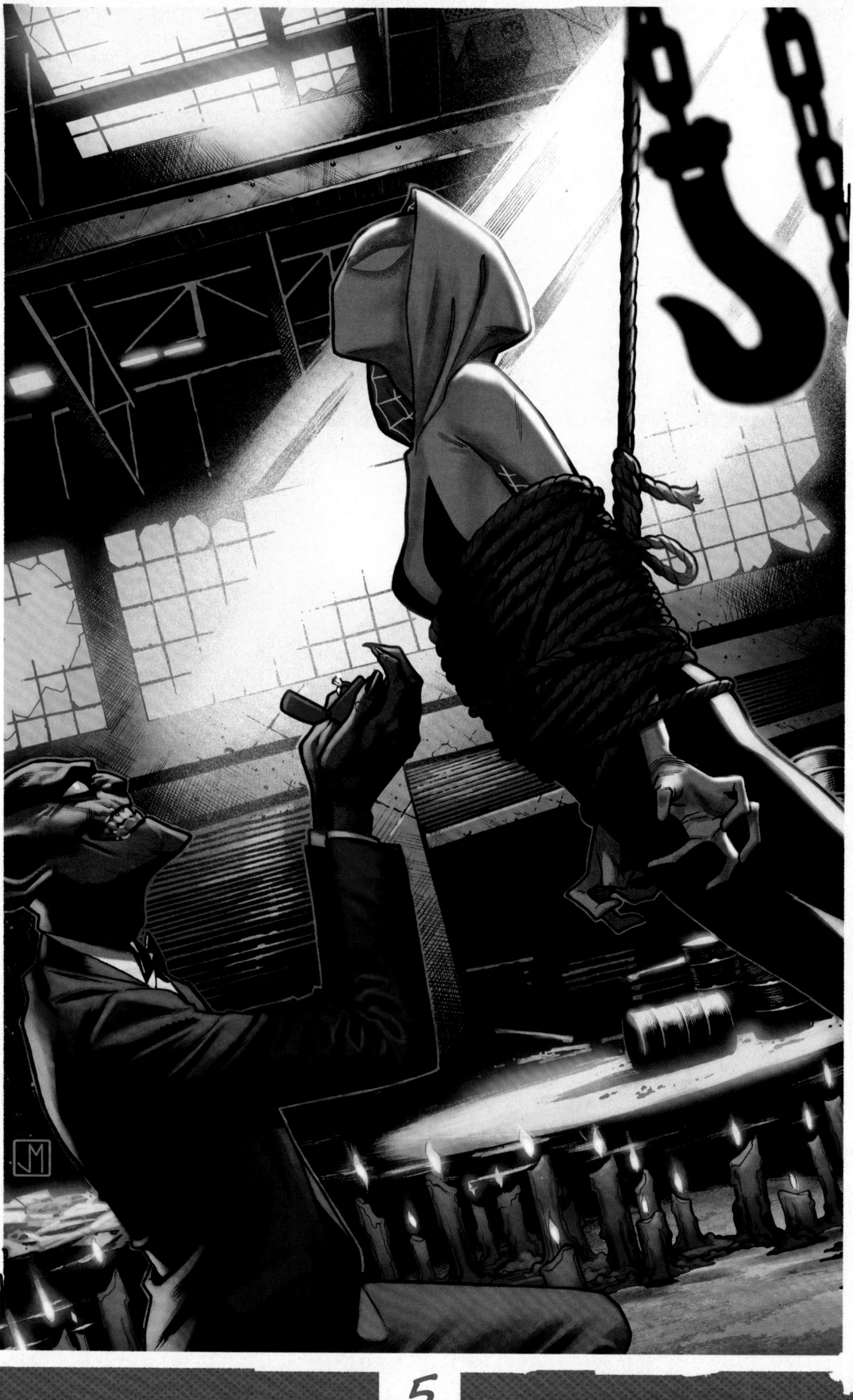
JM

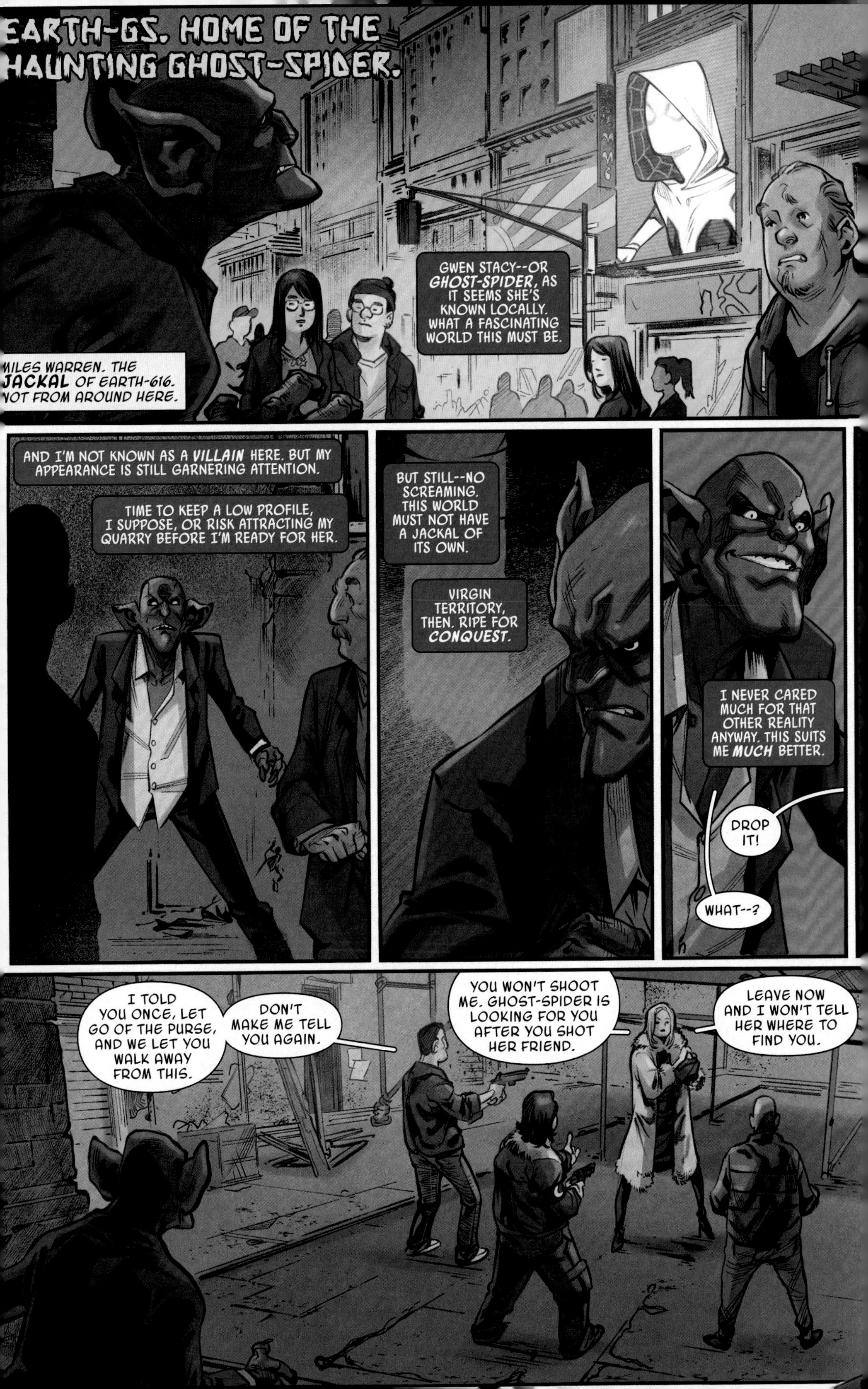
EARTH-GS. HOME OF THE HAUNTING GHOST-SPIDER.
MILES WARREN. THE JACKAL OF EARTH-616. NOT FROM AROUND HERE.
GWEN STACY--OR GHOST-SPIDER, AS IT SEEMS SHE'S KNOWN LOCALLY. WHAT A FASCINATING WORLD THIS MUST BE.
AND I'M NOT KNOWN AS A VILLAIN HERE. BUT MY APPEARANCE IS STILL GARNERING ATTENTION.
TIME TO KEEP A LOW PROFILE, I SUPPOSE, OR RISK ATTRACTING MY QUARRY BEFORE I'M READY FOR HER.
BUT STILL--NO SCREAMING. THIS WORLD MUST NOT HAVE A JACKAL OF ITS OWN.
VIRGIN TERRITORY, THEN. RIPE FOR CONQUEST.
I NEVER CARED MUCH FOR THAT OTHER REALITY ANYWAY. THIS SUITS ME MUCH BETTER.
DROP IT!
WHAT--?
I TOLD YOU ONCE, LET GO OF THE PURSE, AND WE LET YOU WALK AWAY FROM THIS.
DON'T MAKE ME TELL YOU AGAIN.
YOU WON'T SHOOT ME. GHOST-SPIDER IS LOOKING FOR YOU AFTER YOU SHOT HER FRIEND.
LEAVE NOW AND I WON'T TELL HER WHERE TO FIND YOU.

YOU KNOW WHERE TO FIND GHOST-SPIDER? AND WHERE, PRAY TELL, WOULD THAT BE?

I....

I'M WAITING.

...=÷

HMM. UNFORTUNATE.

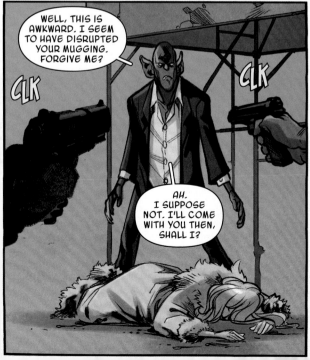

WELL, THIS IS AWKWARD. I SEEM TO HAVE DISRUPTED YOUR MUGGING. FORGIVE ME?

CLK

CLK

AH. I SUPPOSE NOT. I'LL COME WITH YOU THEN, SHALL I?

YES, YES, I AM YOUR CAPTIVE.

OF COURSE YOUR GUNS ARE ENOUGH TO STOP ME.

SHALL WE GO?

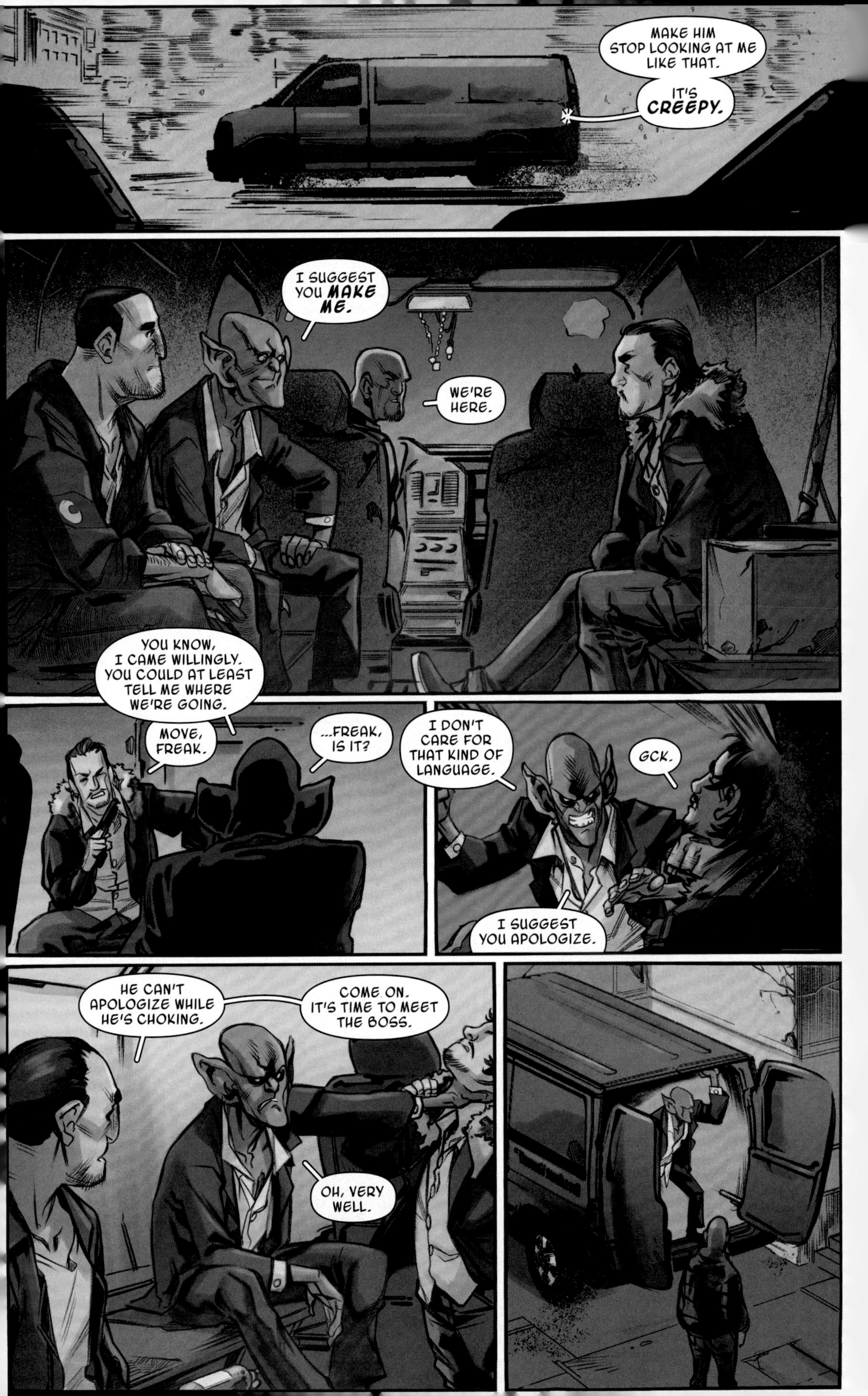
MAKE HIM STOP LOOKING AT ME LIKE THAT.
IT'S CREEPY.
I SUGGEST YOU MAKE ME.
WE'RE HERE.
YOU KNOW, I CAME WILLINGLY. YOU COULD AT LEAST TELL ME WHERE WE'RE GOING.
MOVE, FREAK.
...FREAK, IS IT?
I DON'T CARE FOR THAT KIND OF LANGUAGE.
GCK.
I SUGGEST YOU APOLOGIZE.
HE CAN'T APOLOGIZE WHILE HE'S CHOKING.
COME ON. IT'S TIME TO MEET THE BOSS.
OH, VERY WELL.

YO, BOSS! WE FOUND A--ER. WE FOUND SOMETHING INTERESTING.

WAY TO DODGE THE ISSUE.

SHUT UP.

...PLEASE.

MR. JAMESON IS CURRENTLY UNAVAILABLE. WHAT HAVE WE TOLD YOU ABOUT INVITING GUESTS OVER?

JAMESON? THIS IS NOT A SOCIAL CLUB.

HE WAS LOOKING FOR SPIDER-WOMAN.

YOU MEAN GHOST-SPIDER.

YEAH, THAT.

FORGIVE ME, GENTLEMEN, BUT WHAT IS THAT?

YOU DON'T KNOW ME, BUT I KNOW YOU.

THAT VOICE, THAT FACE...I'VE KNOWN YOU MY WHOLE LIFE. AND YOU'VE KNOWN ME...

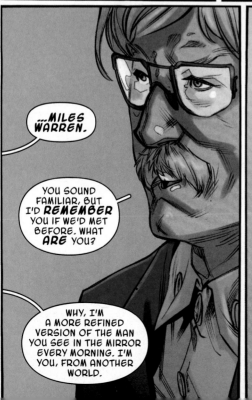

...MILES WARREN.

YOU SOUND FAMILIAR, BUT I'D REMEMBER YOU IF WE'D MET BEFORE. WHAT ARE YOU?

WHY, I'M A MORE REFINED VERSION OF THE MAN YOU SEE IN THE MIRROR EVERY MORNING. I'M YOU, FROM ANOTHER WORLD.

ANOTHER WORLD? I'VE THEORIZED ABOUT A MULTI-VERSE, BUT I NEVER EXPECTED TO BE CONFRONTED WITH PROOF.

ANOTHER WORLD.

AND YOU'RE GREEN BECAUSE...?

I'M A MAN OF SCIENCE.

AS AM I.

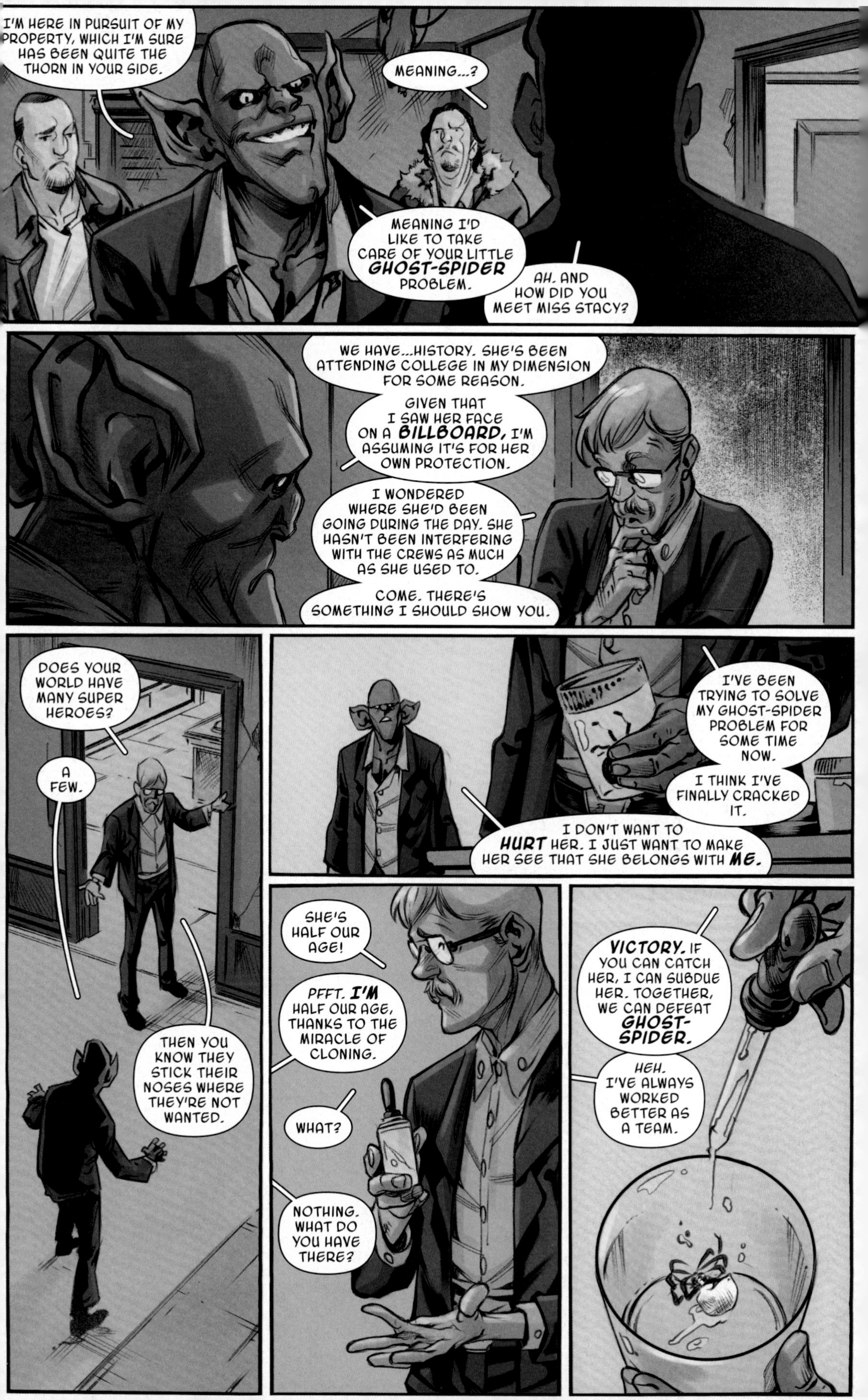
I'M HERE IN PURSUIT OF MY PROPERTY, WHICH I'M SURE HAS BEEN QUITE THE THORN IN YOUR SIDE.
MEANING...?
MEANING I'D LIKE TO TAKE CARE OF YOUR LITTLE GHOST-SPIDER PROBLEM.
AH. AND HOW DID YOU MEET MISS STACY?
WE HAVE...HISTORY. SHE'S BEEN ATTENDING COLLEGE IN MY DIMENSION FOR SOME REASON.
GIVEN THAT I SAW HER FACE ON A BILLBOARD, I'M ASSUMING IT'S FOR HER OWN PROTECTION.
I WONDERED WHERE SHE'D BEEN GOING DURING THE DAY. SHE HASN'T BEEN INTERFERING WITH THE CREWS AS MUCH AS SHE USED TO.
COME. THERE'S SOMETHING I SHOULD SHOW YOU.
DOES YOUR WORLD HAVE MANY SUPER HEROES?
A FEW.
THEN YOU KNOW THEY STICK THEIR NOSES WHERE THEY'RE NOT WANTED.
I'VE BEEN TRYING TO SOLVE MY GHOST-SPIDER PROBLEM FOR SOME TIME NOW.
I THINK I'VE FINALLY CRACKED IT.
I DON'T WANT TO HURT HER. I JUST WANT TO MAKE HER SEE THAT SHE BELONGS WITH ME.
SHE'S HALF OUR AGE!
PFFT. I'M HALF OUR AGE, THANKS TO THE MIRACLE OF CLONING.
WHAT?
NOTHING. WHAT DO YOU HAVE THERE?
VICTORY. IF YOU CAN CATCH HER, I CAN SUBDUE HER. TOGETHER, WE CAN DEFEAT GHOST-SPIDER.
HEH. I'VE ALWAYS WORKED BETTER AS A TEAM.

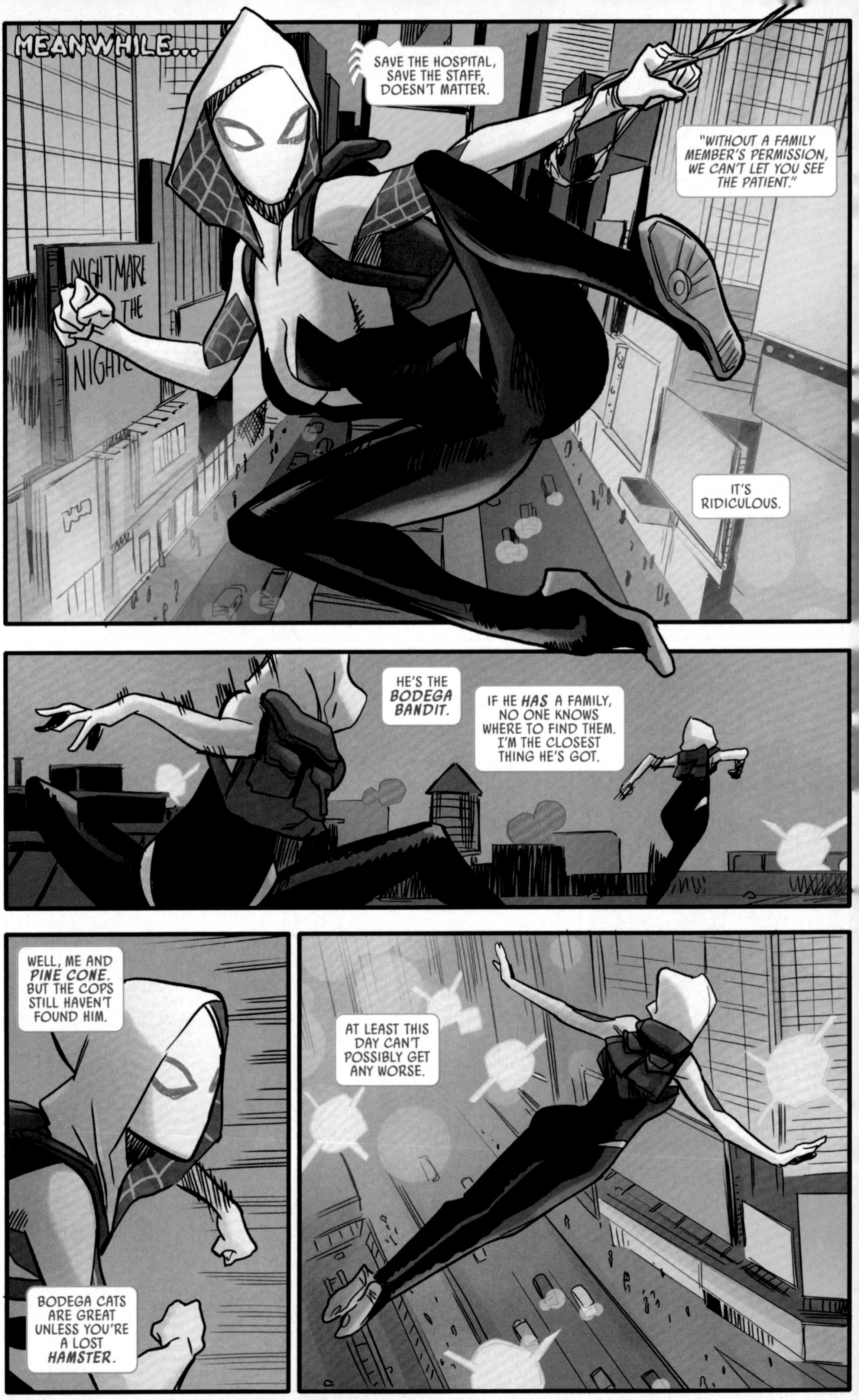
MEANWHILE...
SAVE THE HOSPITAL, SAVE THE STAFF, DOESN'T MATTER.
"WITHOUT A FAMILY MEMBER'S PERMISSION, WE CAN'T LET YOU SEE THE PATIENT."
IT'S RIDICULOUS.
NIGHTMARE THE NIGHT
HE'S THE *BODEGA BANDIT.*
IF HE *HAS* A FAMILY, NO ONE KNOWS WHERE TO FIND THEM. I'M THE CLOSEST THING HE'S GOT.
WELL, ME AND *PINE CONE.* BUT THE COPS STILL HAVEN'T FOUND HIM.
BODEGA CATS ARE GREAT UNLESS YOU'RE A LOST *HAMSTER.*
AT LEAST THIS DAY CAN'T POSSIBLY GET ANY WORSE.

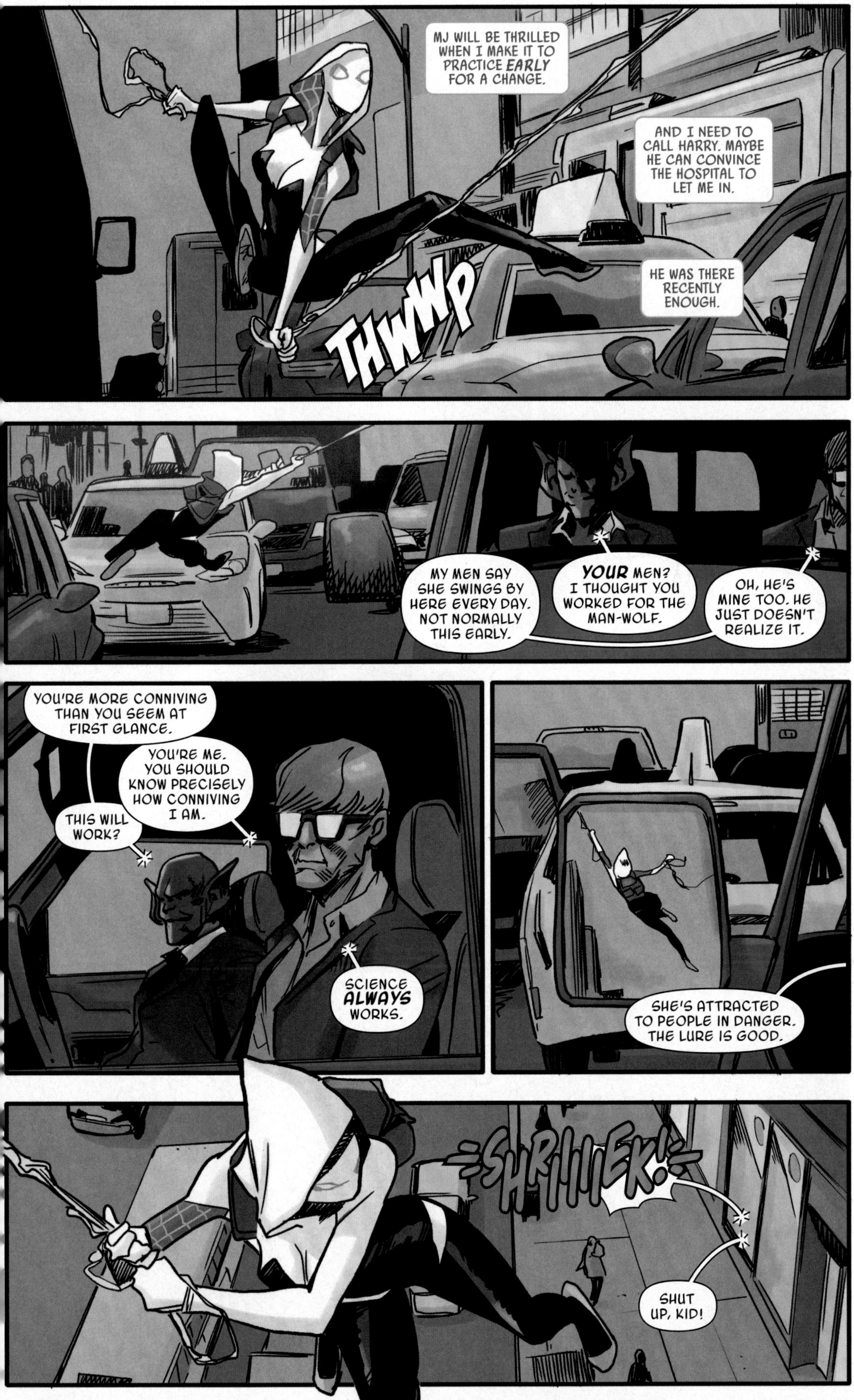
MJ WILL BE THRILLED WHEN I MAKE IT TO PRACTICE EARLY FOR A CHANGE.
AND I NEED TO CALL HARRY. MAYBE HE CAN CONVINCE THE HOSPITAL TO LET ME IN.
HE WAS THERE RECENTLY ENOUGH.
THWWP
MY MEN SAY SHE SWINGS BY HERE EVERY DAY. NOT NORMALLY THIS EARLY.
YOUR MEN? I THOUGHT YOU WORKED FOR THE MAN-WOLF.
OH, HE'S MINE TOO. HE JUST DOESN'T REALIZE IT.
YOU'RE MORE CONNIVING THAN YOU SEEM AT FIRST GLANCE.
YOU'RE ME. YOU SHOULD KNOW PRECISELY HOW CONNIVING I AM.
THIS WILL WORK?
SCIENCE ALWAYS WORKS.
SHE'S ATTRACTED TO PEOPLE IN DANGER. THE LURE IS GOOD.
SHRIIIIEK!
SHUT UP, KID!

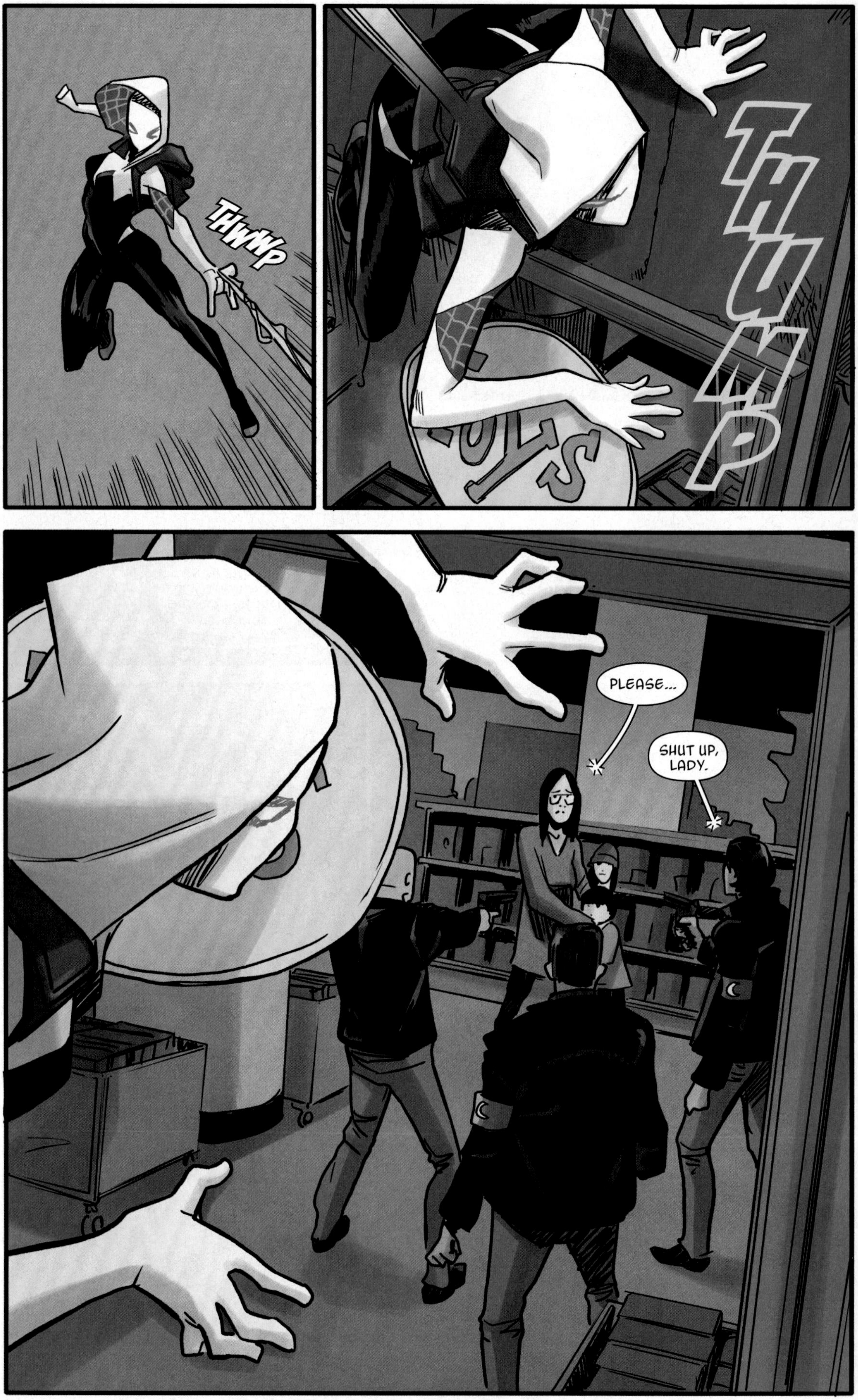
THWWP
THUMP
PLEASE...
SHUT UP, LADY.

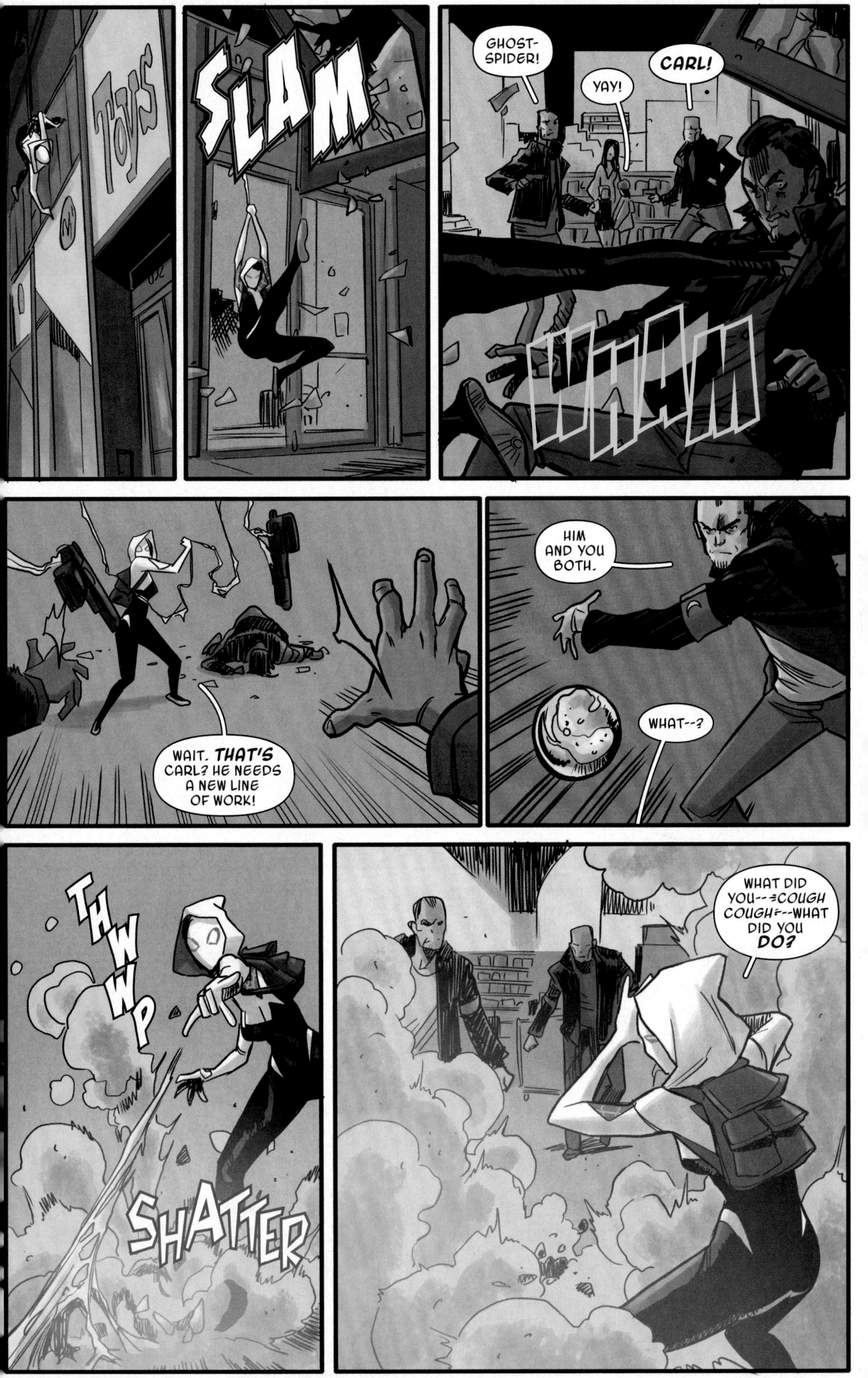

Toys
SLAM
GHOST-SPIDER!
YAY!
CARL!
WHAM
WAIT. THAT'S CARL? HE NEEDS A NEW LINE OF WORK!
HIM AND YOU BOTH.
WHAT--?
THWWP
SHATTER
WHAT DID YOU-- =COUGH COUGH= --WHAT DID YOU DO?

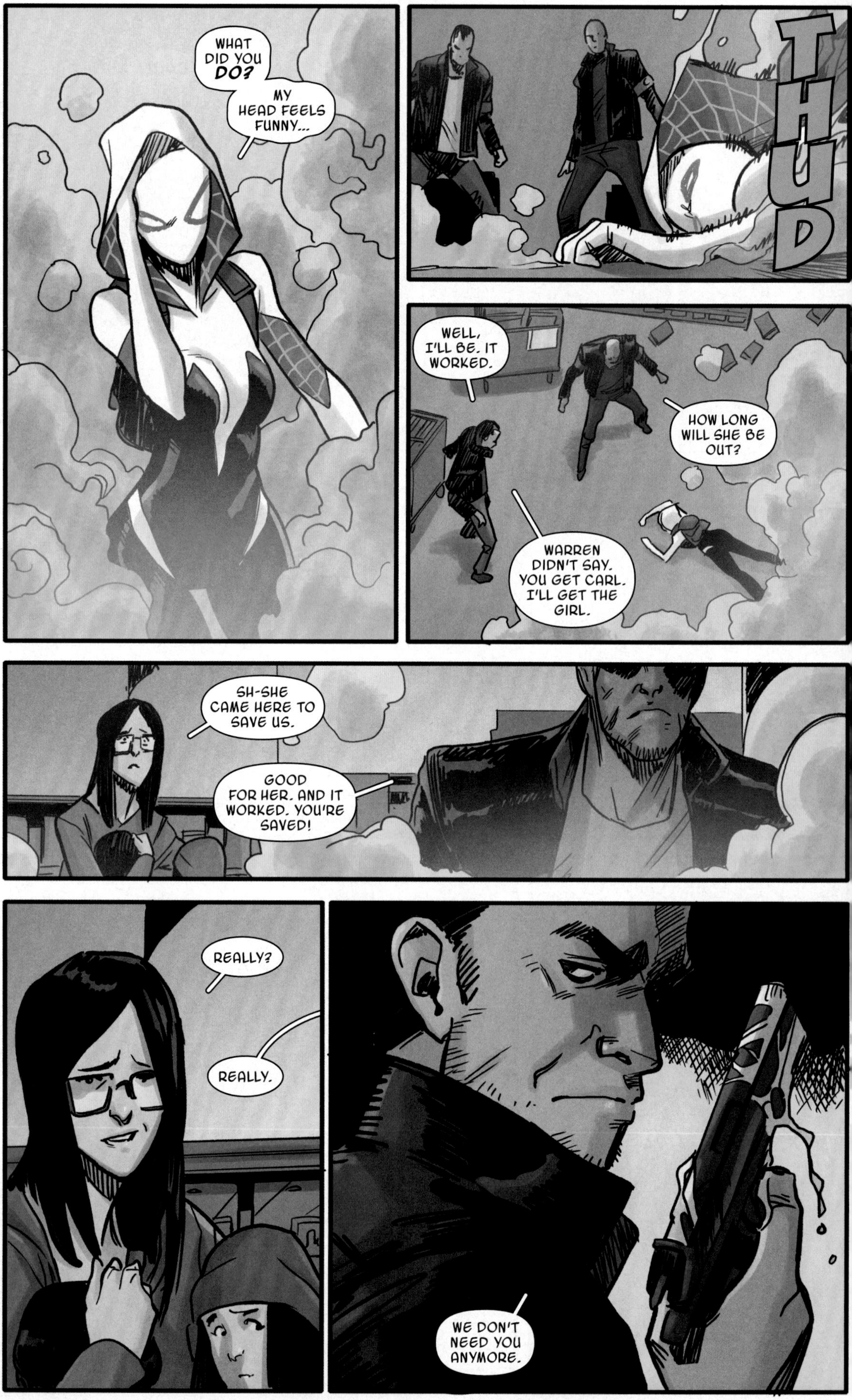
WHAT DID YOU DO?
MY HEAD FEELS FUNNY...
THUD
WELL, I'LL BE. IT WORKED.
HOW LONG WILL SHE BE OUT?
WARREN DIDN'T SAY. YOU GET CARL. I'LL GET THE GIRL.
SH-SHE CAME HERE TO SAVE US.
GOOD FOR HER. AND IT WORKED. YOU'RE SAVED!
REALLY?
REALLY.
WE DON'T NEED YOU ANYMORE.

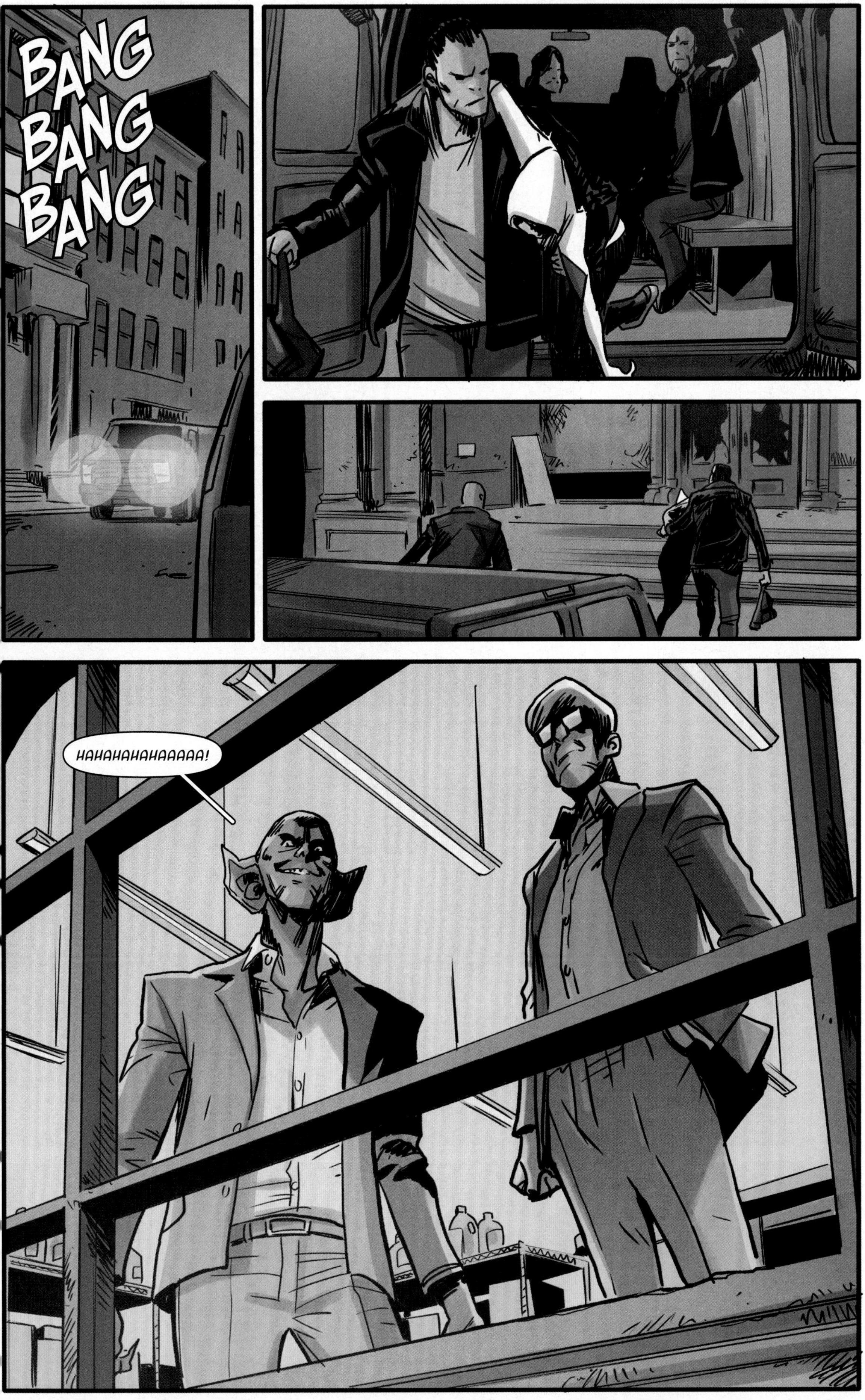
BANG
BANG
BANG
HAHAHAHAHAAAAA!

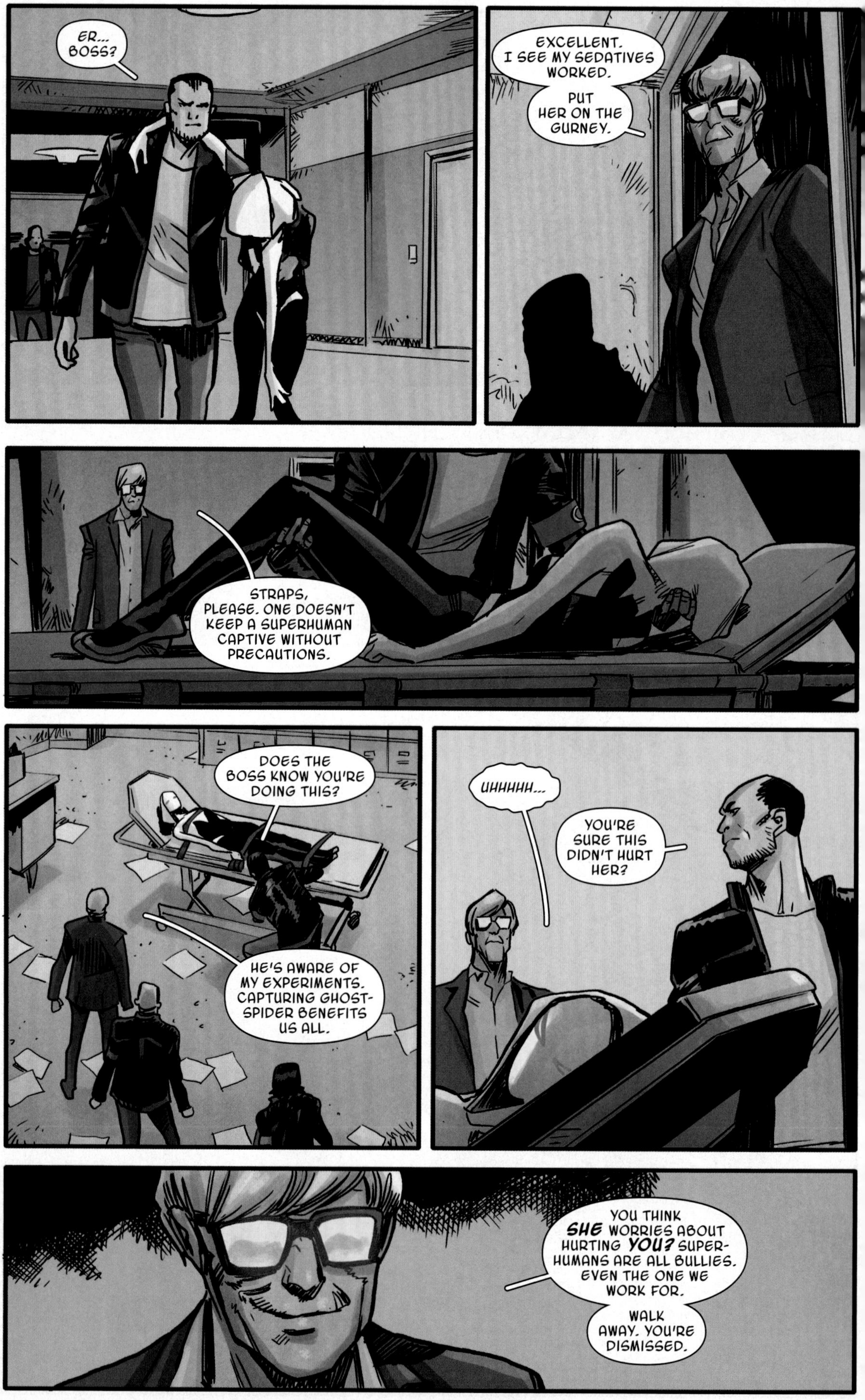
ER... BOSS?
EXCELLENT. I SEE MY SEDATIVES WORKED.
PUT HER ON THE GURNEY.
STRAPS, PLEASE. ONE DOESN'T KEEP A SUPERHUMAN CAPTIVE WITHOUT PRECAUTIONS.
DOES THE BOSS KNOW YOU'RE DOING THIS?
HE'S AWARE OF MY EXPERIMENTS. CAPTURING GHOST-SPIDER BENEFITS US ALL.
UHHHHH...
YOU'RE SURE THIS DIDN'T HURT HER?
YOU THINK SHE WORRIES ABOUT HURTING YOU? SUPER-HUMANS ARE ALL BULLIES. EVEN THE ONE WE WORK FOR.
WALK AWAY. YOU'RE DISMISSED.

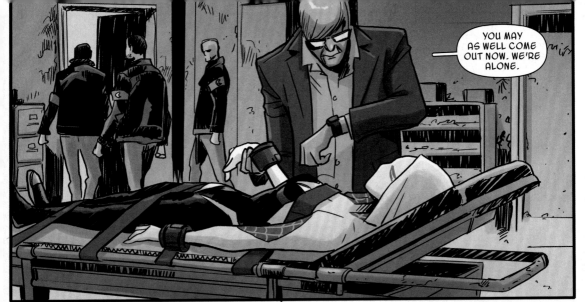

YOU MAY AS WELL COME OUT NOW. WE'RE ALONE.

NOT ENTIRELY.

MY DEAR MISS STACY IS HERE WITH US.

AND QUITE UNCONSCIOUS, THANKS TO ME.

YES, YES, WE'RE A GENIUS.

AND NOW, THANKS TO HER, THE MULTIVERSE IS OURS!

THE NECKLACE?

THE KEY TO EVERYTHING.

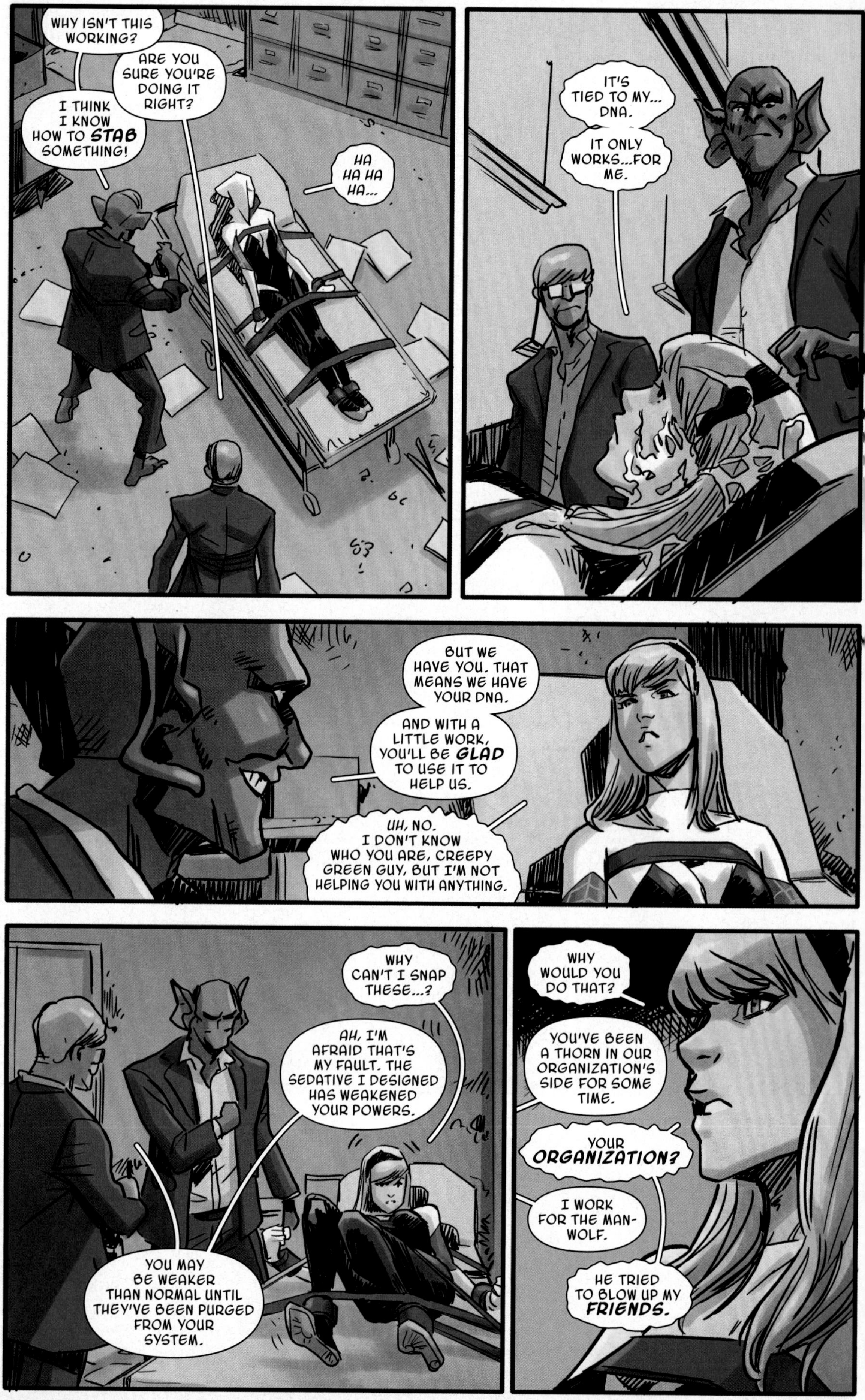
WHY ISN'T THIS WORKING?
ARE YOU SURE YOU'RE DOING IT RIGHT?
I THINK I KNOW HOW TO STAB SOMETHING!
HA HA HA HA...
IT'S TIED TO MY... DNA.
IT ONLY WORKS...FOR ME.
BUT WE HAVE YOU. THAT MEANS WE HAVE YOUR DNA.
AND WITH A LITTLE WORK, YOU'LL BE GLAD TO USE IT TO HELP US.
UH, NO. I DON'T KNOW WHO YOU ARE, CREEPY GREEN GUY, BUT I'M NOT HELPING YOU WITH ANYTHING.
WHY CAN'T I SNAP THESE...?
AH, I'M AFRAID THAT'S MY FAULT. THE SEDATIVE I DESIGNED HAS WEAKENED YOUR POWERS.
YOU MAY BE WEAKER THAN NORMAL UNTIL THEY'VE BEEN PURGED FROM YOUR SYSTEM.
WHY WOULD YOU DO THAT?
YOU'VE BEEN A THORN IN OUR ORGANIZATION'S SIDE FOR SOME TIME.
YOUR ORGANIZATION?
I WORK FOR THE MAN-WOLF.
HE TRIED TO BLOW UP MY FRIENDS.

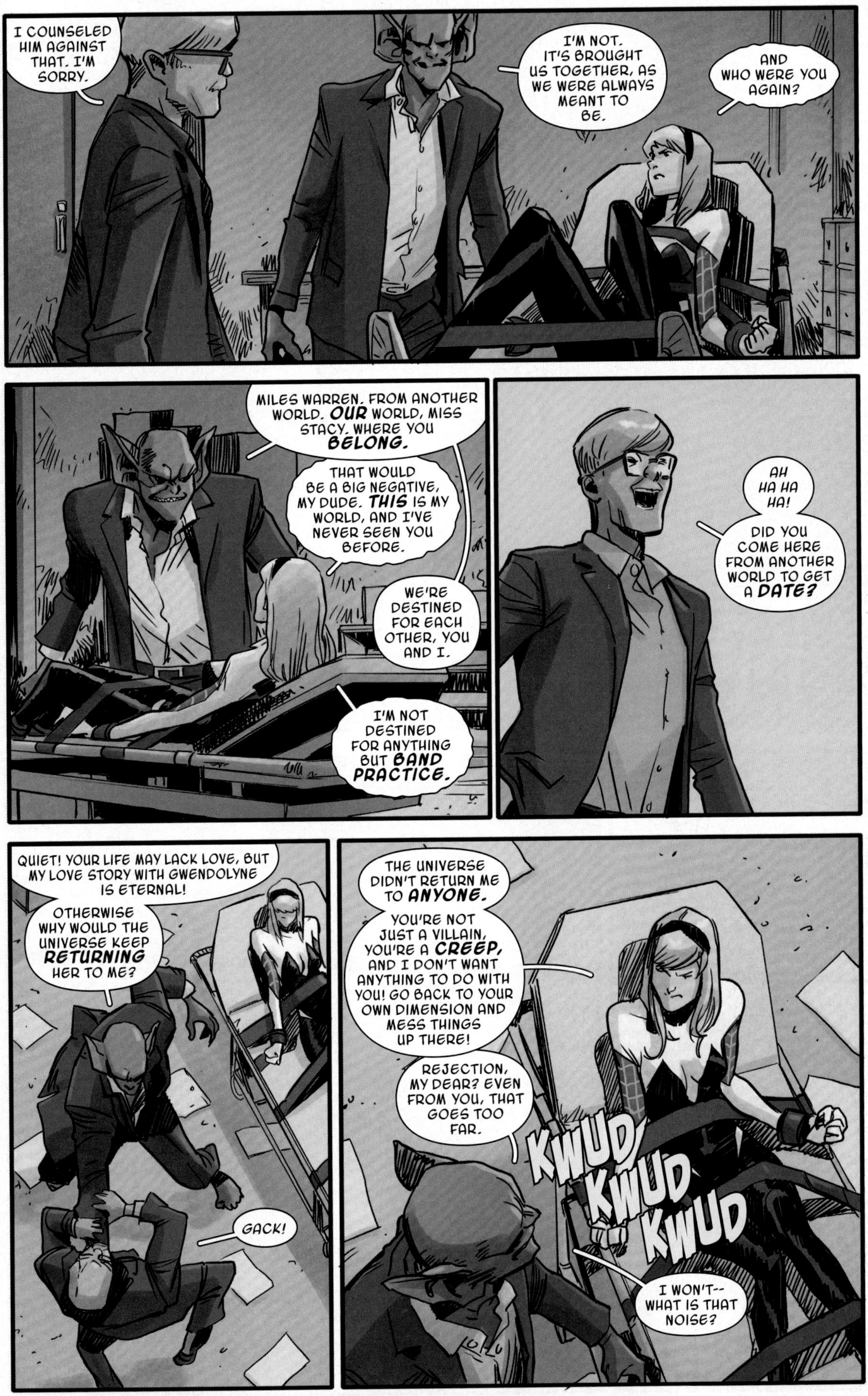
I COUNSELED HIM AGAINST THAT. I'M SORRY.
I'M NOT. IT'S BROUGHT US TOGETHER, AS WE WERE ALWAYS MEANT TO BE.
AND WHO WERE YOU AGAIN?
MILES WARREN. FROM ANOTHER WORLD. OUR WORLD, MISS STACY. WHERE YOU BELONG.
THAT WOULD BE A BIG NEGATIVE, MY DUDE. THIS IS MY WORLD, AND I'VE NEVER SEEN YOU BEFORE.
WE'RE DESTINED FOR EACH OTHER, YOU AND I.
I'M NOT DESTINED FOR ANYTHING BUT BAND PRACTICE.
AH HA HA HA!
DID YOU COME HERE FROM ANOTHER WORLD TO GET A DATE?
QUIET! YOUR LIFE MAY LACK LOVE, BUT MY LOVE STORY WITH GWENDOLYNE IS ETERNAL!
OTHERWISE WHY WOULD THE UNIVERSE KEEP RETURNING HER TO ME?
GACK!
THE UNIVERSE DIDN'T RETURN ME TO ANYONE.
YOU'RE NOT JUST A VILLAIN, YOU'RE A CREEP, AND I DON'T WANT ANYTHING TO DO WITH YOU! GO BACK TO YOUR OWN DIMENSION AND MESS THINGS UP THERE!
REJECTION, MY DEAR? EVEN FROM YOU, THAT GOES TOO FAR.
KWUD KWUD KWUD
I WON'T-- WHAT IS THAT NOISE?

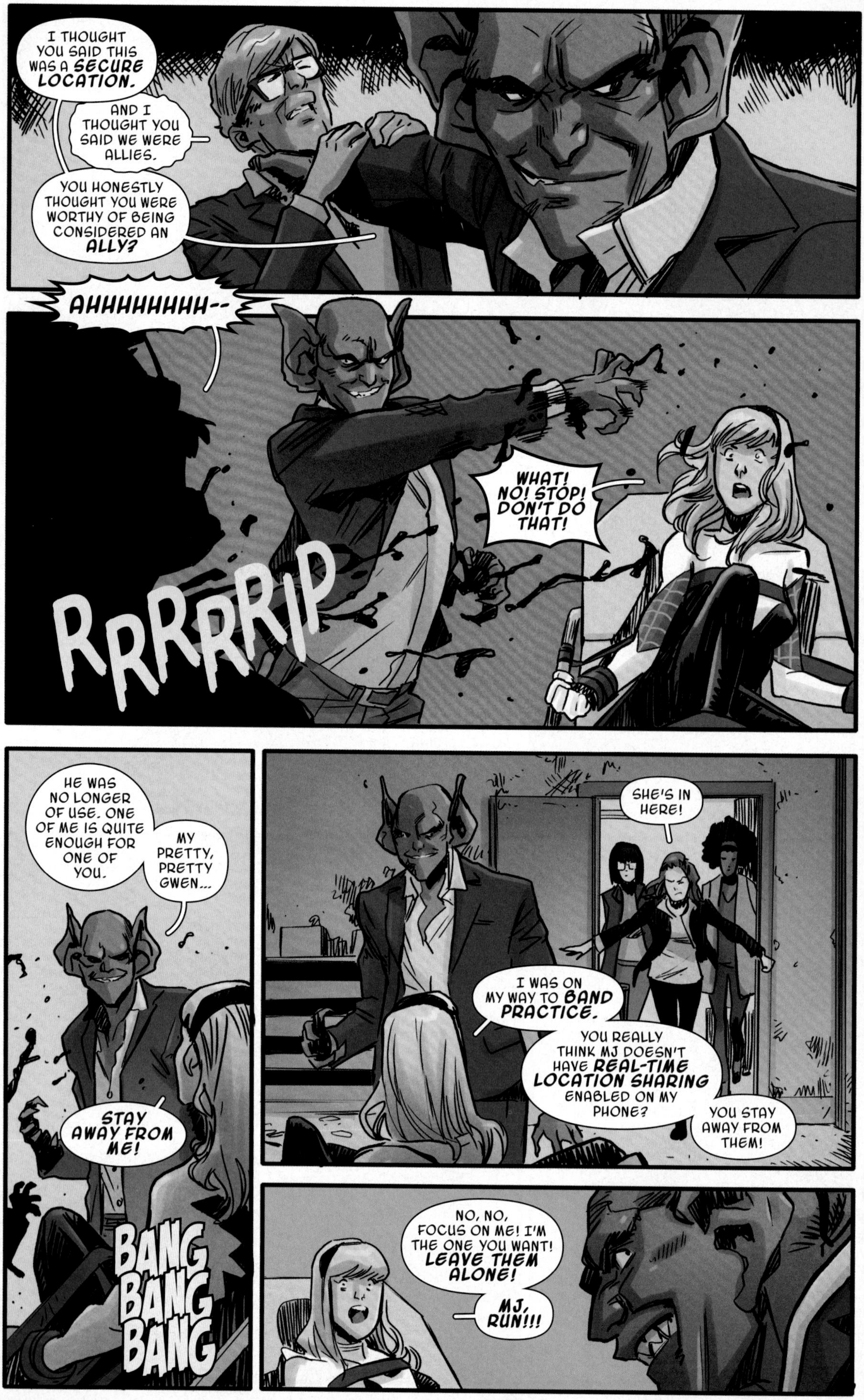
I THOUGHT YOU SAID THIS WAS A SECURE LOCATION.
AND I THOUGHT YOU SAID WE WERE ALLIES.
YOU HONESTLY THOUGHT YOU WERE WORTHY OF BEING CONSIDERED AN ALLY?
AHHHHHHHH--
RRRRRIP
WHAT! NO! STOP! DON'T DO THAT!
HE WAS NO LONGER OF USE. ONE OF ME IS QUITE ENOUGH FOR ONE OF YOU.
MY PRETTY, PRETTY GWEN...
STAY AWAY FROM ME!
BANG BANG BANG
SHE'S IN HERE!
I WAS ON MY WAY TO BAND PRACTICE.
YOU REALLY THINK MJ DOESN'T HAVE REAL-TIME LOCATION SHARING ENABLED ON MY PHONE?
YOU STAY AWAY FROM THEM!
NO, NO, FOCUS ON ME! I'M THE ONE YOU WANT! LEAVE THEM ALONE!
MJ, RUN!!!

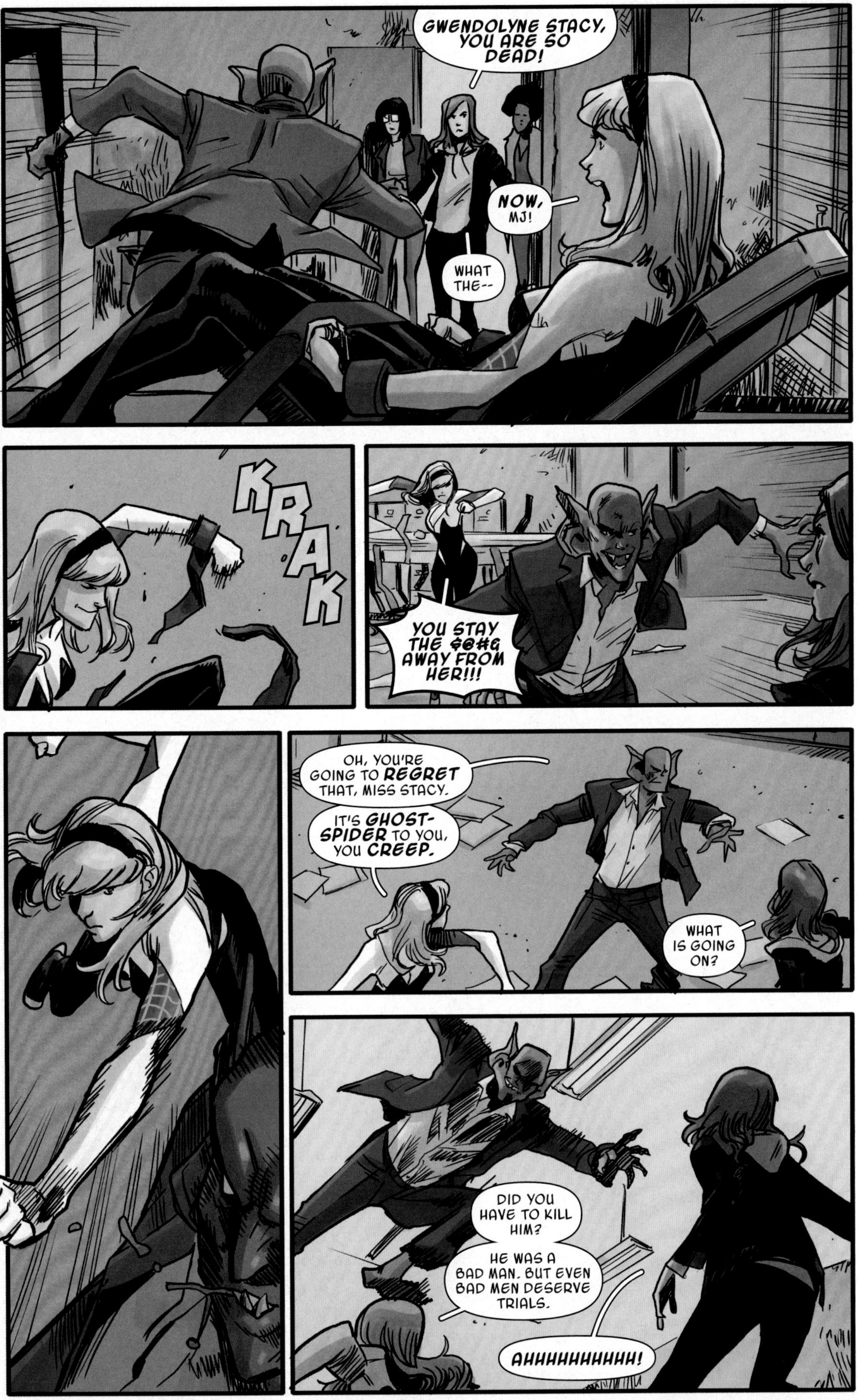
GWENDOLYNE STACY, YOU ARE SO DEAD!
NOW, MJ!
WHAT THE--
KRAK
YOU STAY THE $@#G AWAY FROM HER!!!
OH, YOU'RE GOING TO REGRET THAT, MISS STACY.
IT'S GHOST-SPIDER TO YOU, YOU CREEP.
WHAT IS GOING ON?
DID YOU HAVE TO KILL HIM?
HE WAS A BAD MAN. BUT EVEN BAD MEN DESERVE TRIALS.
AHHHHHHHHHH!

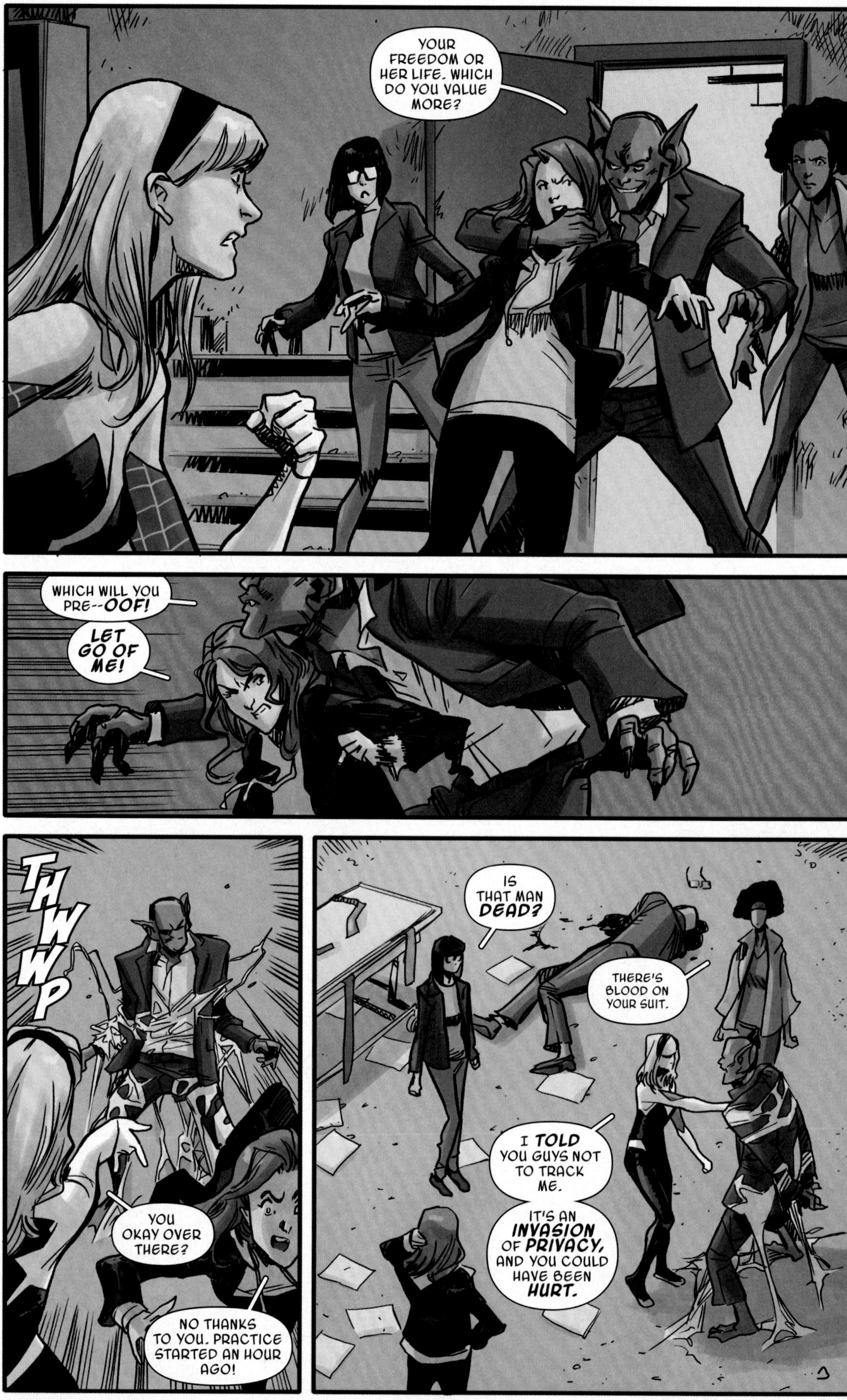
YOUR FREEDOM OR HER LIFE. WHICH DO YOU VALUE MORE?
WHICH WILL YOU PRE--OOF!
LET GO OF ME!
THWWP
YOU OKAY OVER THERE?
NO THANKS TO YOU. PRACTICE STARTED AN HOUR AGO!
IS THAT MAN DEAD?
THERE'S BLOOD ON YOUR SUIT.
I TOLD YOU GUYS NOT TO TRACK ME.
IT'S AN INVASION OF PRIVACY, AND YOU COULD HAVE BEEN HURT.

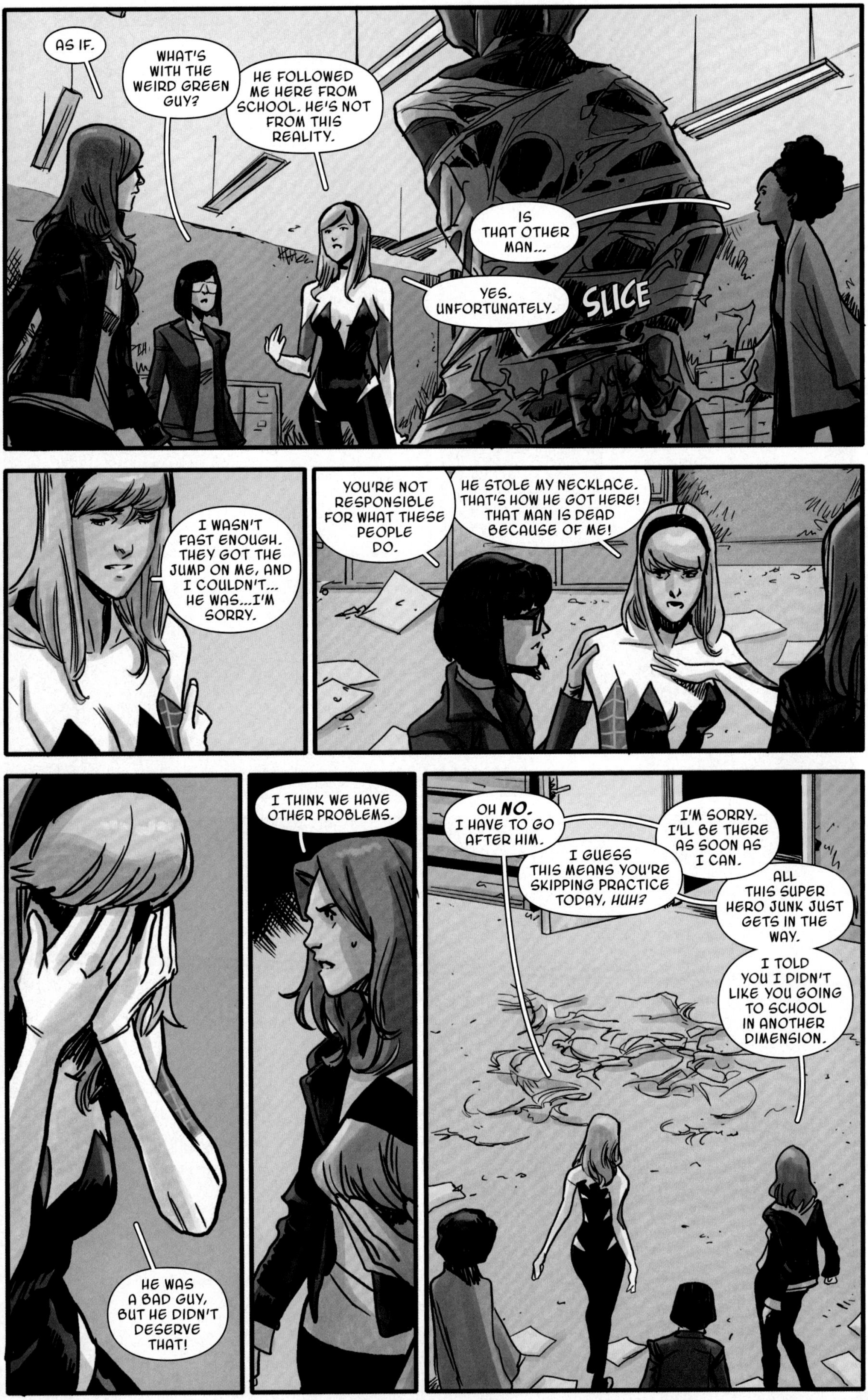
AS IF.
WHAT'S WITH THE WEIRD GREEN GUY?
HE FOLLOWED ME HERE FROM SCHOOL. HE'S NOT FROM THIS REALITY.
IS THAT OTHER MAN...
YES. UNFORTUNATELY.
SLICE
I WASN'T FAST ENOUGH. THEY GOT THE JUMP ON ME, AND I COULDN'T... HE WAS...I'M SORRY.
YOU'RE NOT RESPONSIBLE FOR WHAT THESE PEOPLE DO.
HE STOLE MY NECKLACE. THAT'S HOW HE GOT HERE! THAT MAN IS DEAD BECAUSE OF ME!
HE WAS A BAD GUY, BUT HE DIDN'T DESERVE THAT!
I THINK WE HAVE OTHER PROBLEMS.
OH NO. I HAVE TO GO AFTER HIM.
I'M SORRY. I'LL BE THERE AS SOON AS I CAN.
I GUESS THIS MEANS YOU'RE SKIPPING PRACTICE TODAY, HUH?
ALL THIS SUPER HERO JUNK JUST GETS IN THE WAY.
I TOLD YOU I DIDN'T LIKE YOU GOING TO SCHOOL IN ANOTHER DIMENSION.

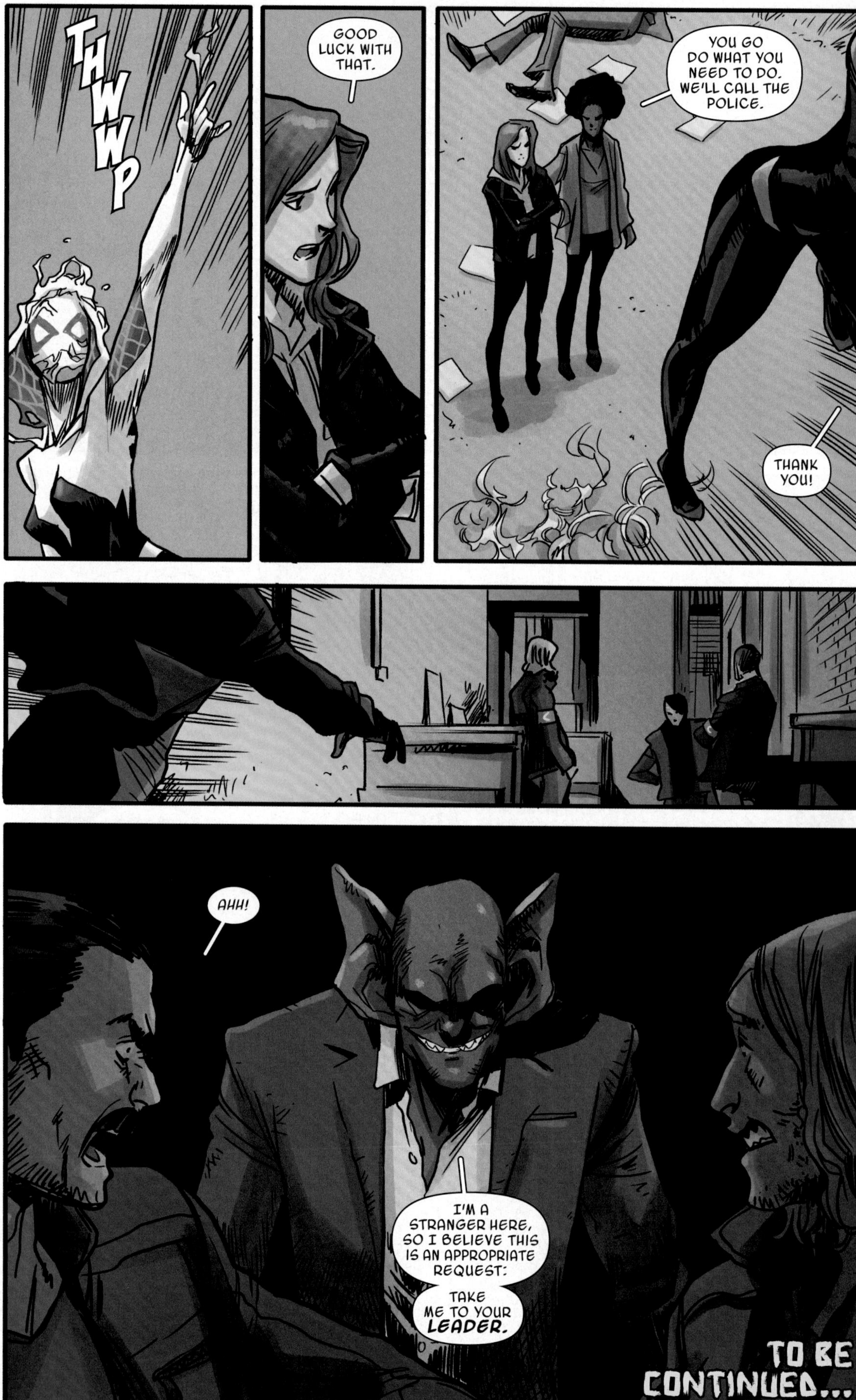
THWWP
GOOD LUCK WITH THAT.
YOU GO DO WHAT YOU NEED TO DO. WE'LL CALL THE POLICE.
THANK YOU!
AHH!
I'M A STRANGER HERE, SO I BELIEVE THIS IS AN APPROPRIATE REQUEST:
TAKE ME TO YOUR LEADER.
TO BE CONTINUED...

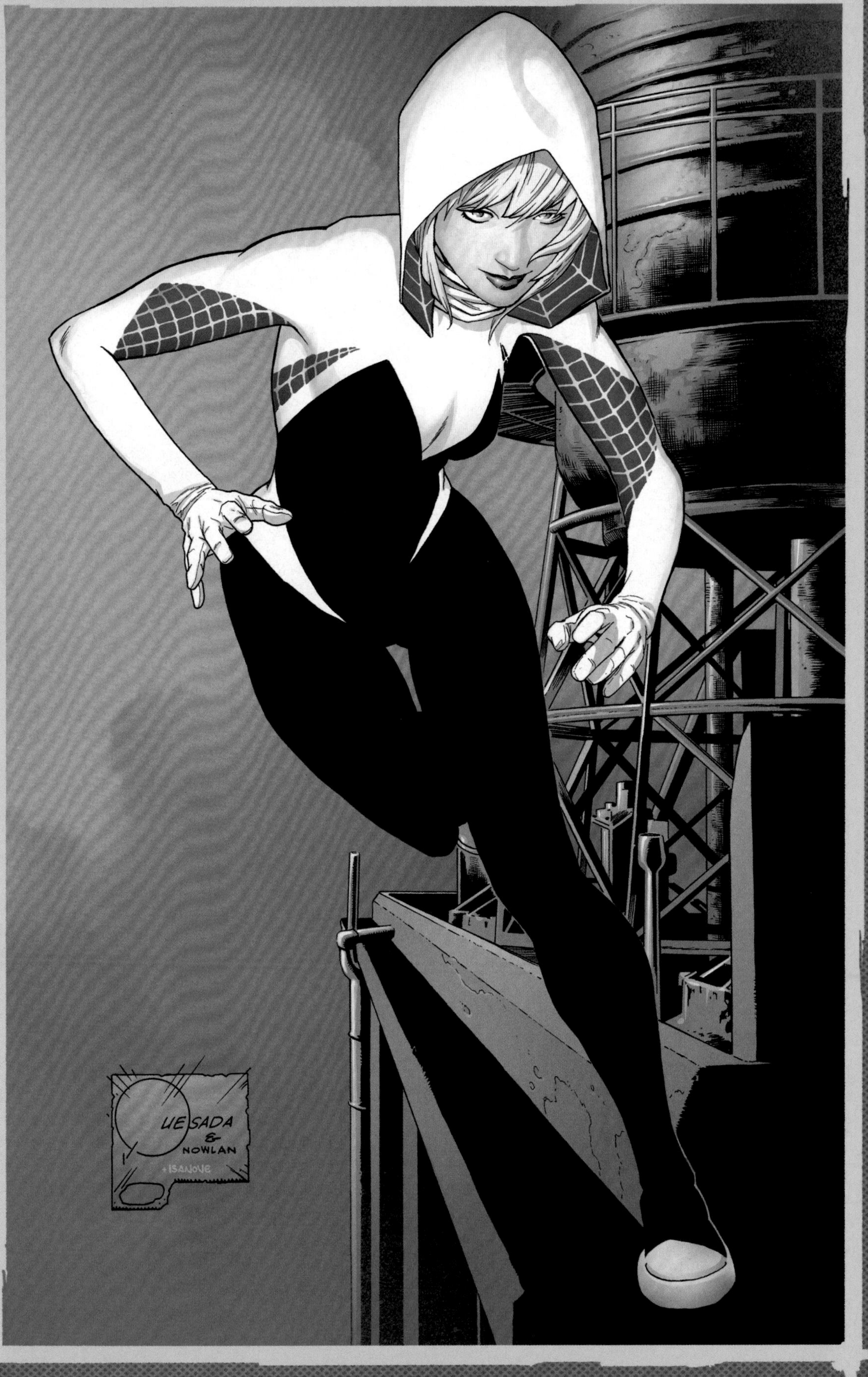
UESADA
&
NOWLAN
+ISANOVE
#1 Variant by Joe Quesada, Kevin Nowlan & Richard Isanove

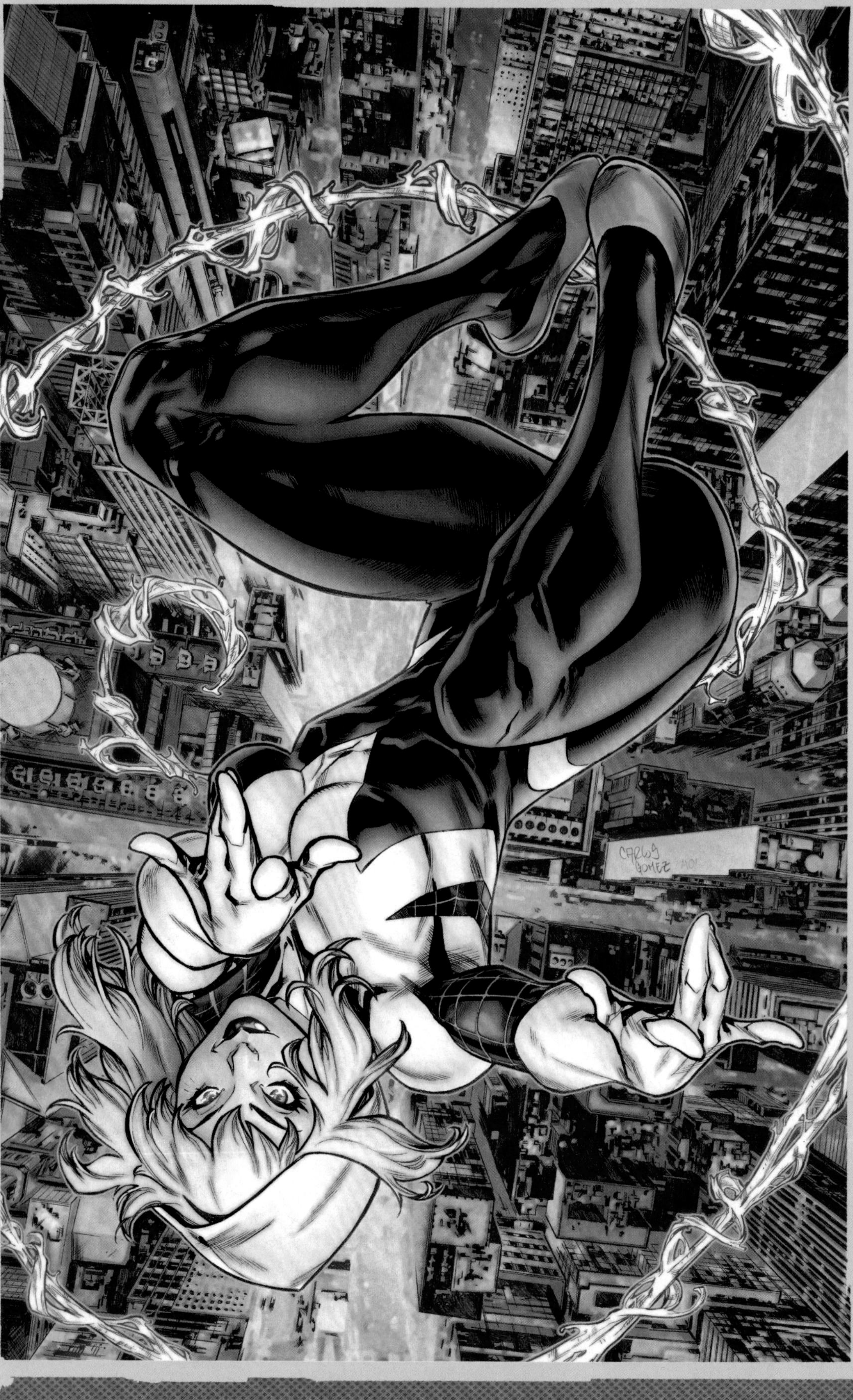

#1 Variant by **Carlos Gómez** & **Morry Hollowell**

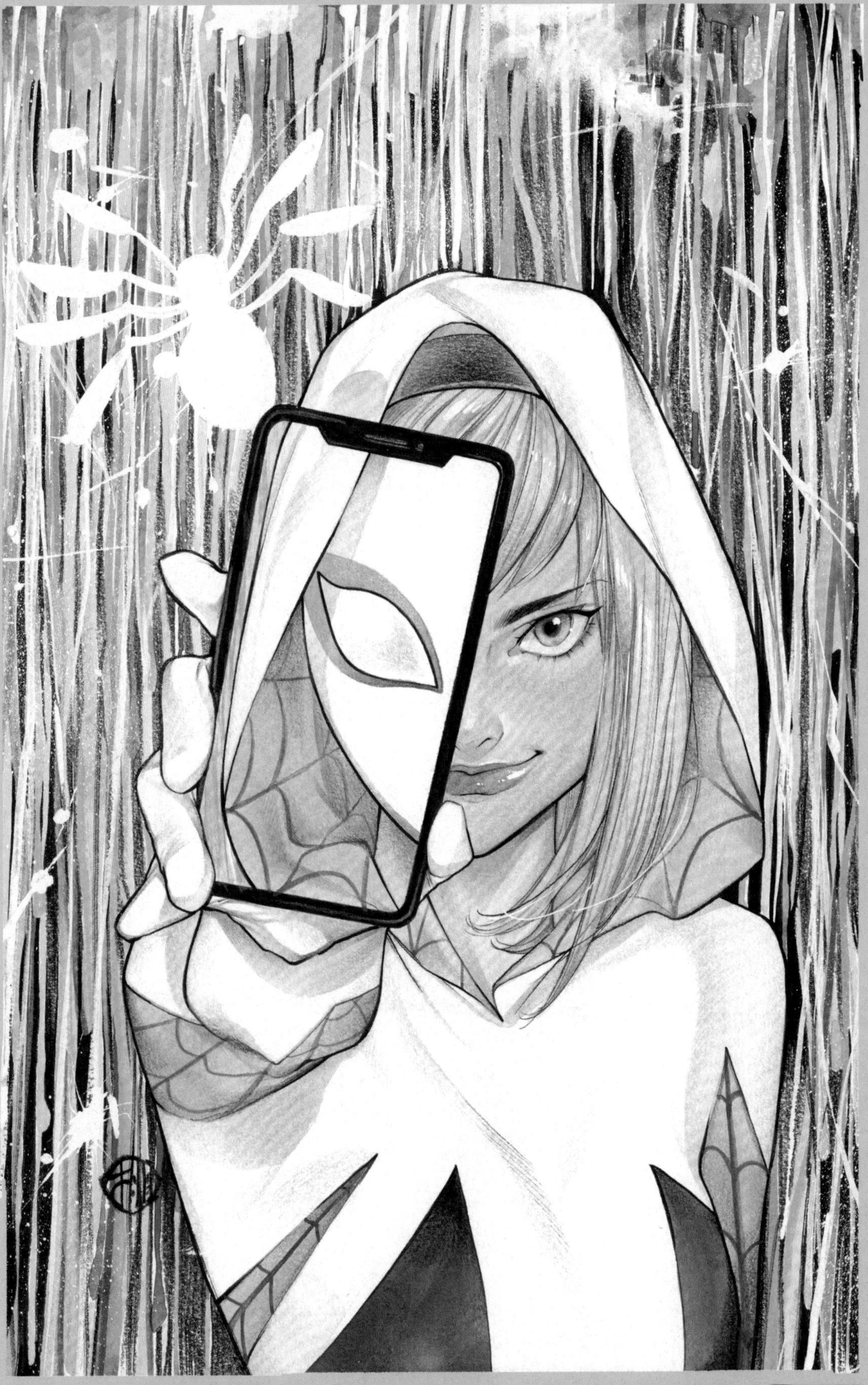

#2 Variant by Peach Momoko

#3 Mary Jane Variant by **Russell Dauterman**

#4 2099 Variant by **Bengal**

#5 2020 Variant by
Mahmud Asrar & **Matthew Wilson**